PIPE FITTINGS

Here are the common steel pipe fittings. Nipples are simply short lengths of pipe threaded on both ends. Reducing fittings join two different sizes of pipe.

Compression fittings of the flared-tube type are the easiest for the novice to handle when working with copper tubing.

STANDARD STEEL PIPE (All Dimensions in Inches)					
Nominal Size	Outside Diameter	Inside Diameter	Nominal Size	Outside Diameter	Inside Diameter
1/8	0.405	0.269	1	1.315	1.049
1/4	0.540	0.364	1 1/4	1.660	1.380
3/8	0.675	0.493	1 1/2	1.900	1.610
1/2	0.840	0.622	2	2.375	2.067
3/4	1.050	0.824	2 1/2	2.875	2.469

SQUARE MEASURE

144 sq in = 1 sq ft
9 sq ft = 1 sq yd
272.25 sq ft = 1 sq rod
160 sq rods = 1 acre

VOLUME MEASURE

1728 cu in = 1 cu ft
27 cu ft = 1 cu yd

MEASURES OF CAPACITY

1 cup = 8 fl oz
2 cups = 1 pint
2 pints = 1 quart
4 quarts = 1 gallon
2 gallons = 1 peck
4 pecks = 1 bushel

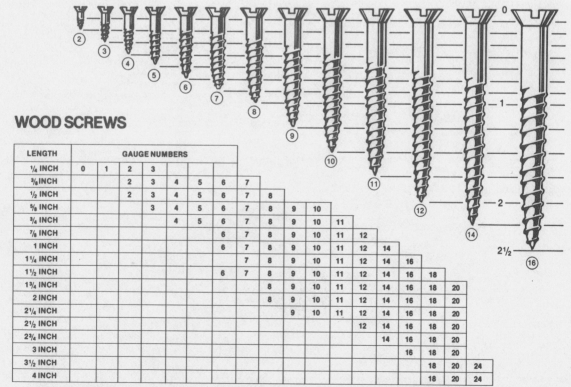

WOOD SCREWS

LENGTH	GAUGE NUMBERS													
1/4 INCH	0	1	2	3										
3/8 INCH			2	3	4	5	6	7						
1/2 INCH			2	3	4	5	6	7	8					
5/8 INCH				3	4	5	6	7	8	9	10			
3/4 INCH					4	5	6	7	8	9	10	11		
7/8 INCH							6	7	8	9	10	11	12	
1 INCH							6	7	8	9	10	11	12	14
1 1/4 INCH								7	8	9	10	11	12	14	16
1 1/2 INCH							6	7	8	9	10	11	12	14	16	18
1 3/4 INCH									8	9	10	11	12	14	16	18	20
2 INCH								8	9	10	11	12	14	16	18	20
2 1/4 INCH									9	10	11	12	14	16	18	20
2 1/2 INCH											12	14	16	18	20
2 3/4 INCH											14	16	18	20
3 INCH												16	18	20
3 1/2 INCH													18	20	24
4 INCH													18	20	24

WHEN YOU BUY SCREWS, SPECIFY (1) LENGTH, (2) GAUGE NUMBER, (3) TYPE OF HEAD—FLAT, ROUND, OR OVAL, (4) MATERIAL—STEEL, BRASS, BRONZE, ETC., (5) FINISH—BRIGHT, STEEL BLUED, CADMIUM, NICKEL, OR CHROMIUM PLATED.

Popular Mechanics
do-it-yourself yearbook
1984

For your home

- Exciting products for better living
- Projects to improve your home

For the craftsman

- Great craft projects of the year
- Shop projects and expert know-how
- The best of the new tools

For the outdoorsman

- New survival and outdoor gear
- Know-how tips from the experts

For the gardener

- Greenhouse and cold frame projects
- Garden carts you can build

PLUS:

- Home energy guide
- Special projects for the home garage
- Great projects just for fun

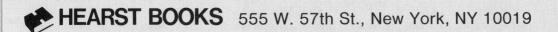 **HEARST BOOKS** 555 W. 57th St., New York, NY 10019

EDITOR	Clifford B. Hicks
ASSOCIATE EDITOR	Nancy Dills
ART DIRECTOR	Ralph Leory Linnenburger
ASSISTANT EDITOR	Tom Balow
PHOTOGRAPHY	Joe Fletcher
ART ASSISTANT	Marian C. Linnenburger
CONTRIBUTING EDITORS	David Paulsen
	Benjamin Lee

Published by Hearst Books
A Division of The Hearst Corporation
555 West 57th Street
New York, N.Y. 10019

ISBN 0-87851-087-7
Library of Congress 75-648427

CONTENTS

BUILD A BEAUTIFUL colonial pie safe, and use it to store your finest china or glassware. Plans for this well-crafted reproduction start on page 24.

On the following pages

Exciting new products and handsome do-it-yourself projects

NEW UNDERWATER GEAR now is appearing topside in novel uses. Check out the latest in wet suits, cameras, lights and depth finders on page 164.

HERE'S A TOPNOTCH project for the avid gardener that will extend the growing season indefinitely. It's a greenhouse you attach to your home, along with a cold frame you attach to the greenhouse. The structure is made from readily available parts. Plans start on page 78.

HERE'S SEA GYPSY, one of a new crop of boats that gives you a choice of power. If the wind is down you can cruise on diesel. Wind up? Sail with the gaff rig. See page 162.

RUGGED WORKBENCH is designed to withstand heavy-duty work on your car. Plans start on page 186.

WHAT DO YOU get when you cross a dulcimer with a banjo? A banjimer. We show you how to make it, then play it. See page 182.

KEEP YOUR INDOOR firewood neatly stacked in one of our distinctive and easily built log holders. See page 28.

THIS ELEGANT contemporary table does triple duty. Besides serving as a dining table, you can put down the leaf and convert it for use as a roomy desk or an attractive sideboard. See the plans on page 33.

VERSATILE AND practically indestructible, these hanging wall bins will do jobs that shelves can't match. They are one of three ways to find extra space in your garage. See the article on page 189.

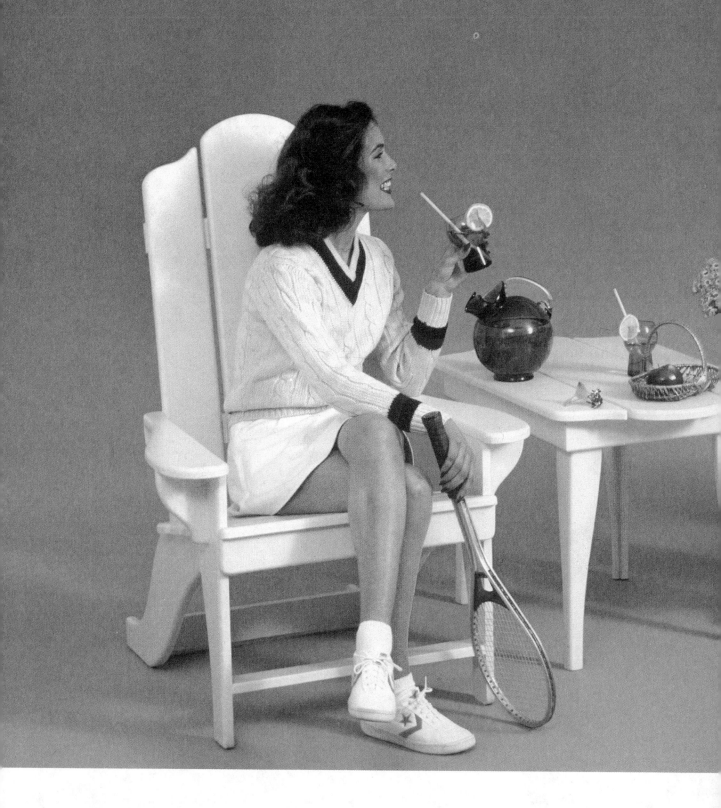

Build this classic
Adirondack lawn furniture

■ THE VERY LOOK of this classic wooden lawn furniture conjures up images of more serene times. Though simple in design, this furniture from years past boasts an elegance all its own.

You can use practically any kind of lumber to construct this Adirondack-style furniture. If you apply wood preservative—an undercoat and two top coats of high-quality exterior paint—any species should weather quite well.

We chose a hardwood, poplar, for its added strength.

The chair and table are made from 4/4 stock

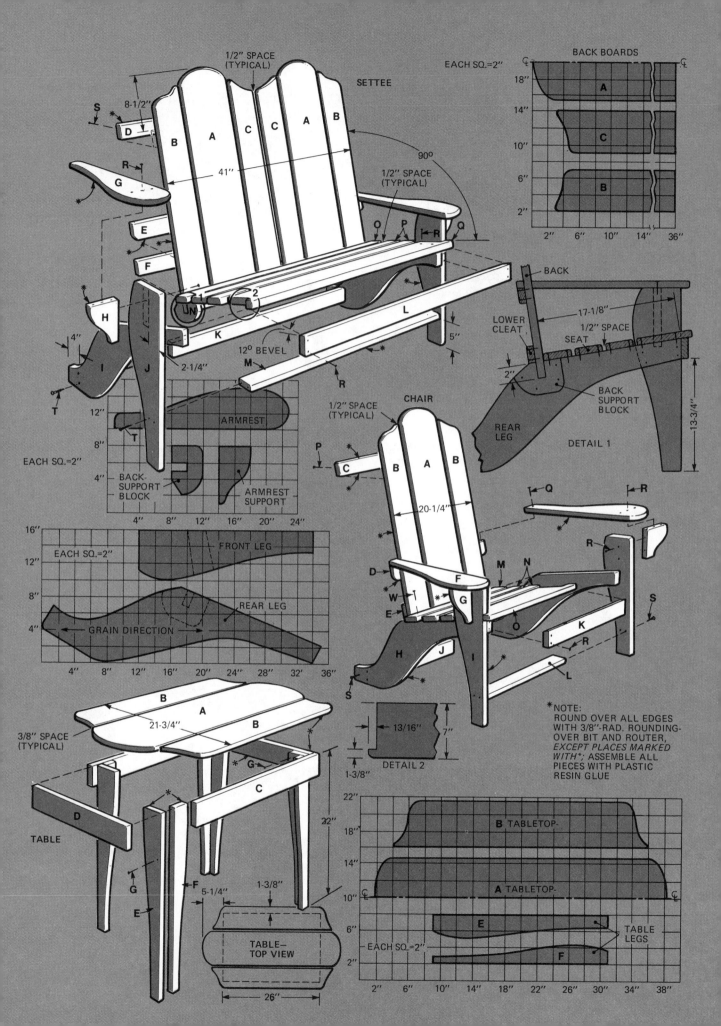

SETTEE

1/2" SPACE (TYPICAL)

8-1/2"

S

D

R

G

B   A   C   C   A   B

41"

90°

1/2" SPACE (TYPICAL)

E

F

O P   R Q

H

N

K

L

I

J

2-1/4"

12° BEVEL

M

5"

R

BACK BOARDS

EACH SQ.=2"

18"

14"

10"

6"

2"

A

C

B

2"   6"   10"   14"   36"

BACK

LOWER CLEAT

17-1/8"

1/2" SPACE

SEAT

2"

BACK SUPPORT BLOCK

REAR LEG

13-3/4"

DETAIL 1

12"

8"

4"

EACH SQ.=2"

ARMREST

BACK-SUPPORT BLOCK

ARMREST SUPPORT

T

T

4"   8"   12"   16"   20"   24"

16"

12"

8"

4"

EACH SQ.=2"

FRONT LEG

REAR LEG

GRAIN DIRECTION

4"   8"   12"   16"   20"   24"   28"   32"   36"

CHAIR

1/2" SPACE (TYPICAL)

P

C

B   A   B

20-1/4"

D

W

E

F

G

M   N

H   J   I

O

K

R

S

Q

R

R

S

L

*NOTE: ROUND OVER ALL EDGES WITH 3/8"-RAD. ROUNDING-OVER BIT AND ROUTER, *EXCEPT PLACES MARKED WITH*; ASSEMBLE ALL PIECES WITH PLASTIC RESIN GLUE

TABLE

B   A   B

21-3/4"

3/8" SPACE (TYPICAL)

G

C

D

G

F

E

TABLE

22"

13/16"

7"

1-3/8"

DETAIL 2

5-1/4"

1-3/8"

TABLE—TOP VIEW

26"

22"

18"

14"

10"

6"

2"

EACH SQ.=2"

B TABLETOP-

A TABLETOP-

E

F

TABLE LEGS

2"   6"   10"   14"   18"   22"   26"   30"   34"   38"

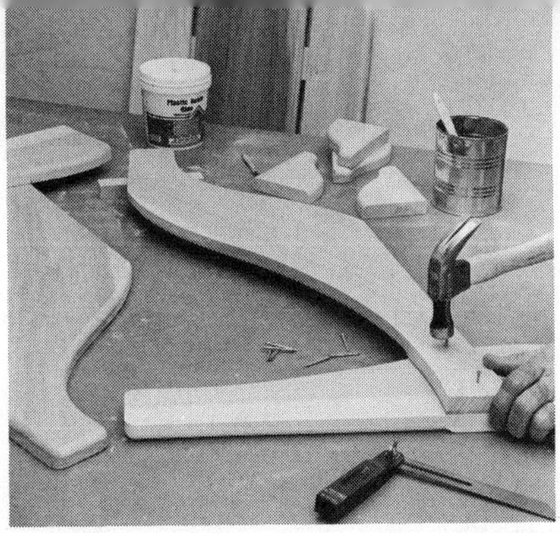

1 START EACH assembly with legs. Use plastic resin glue throughout.

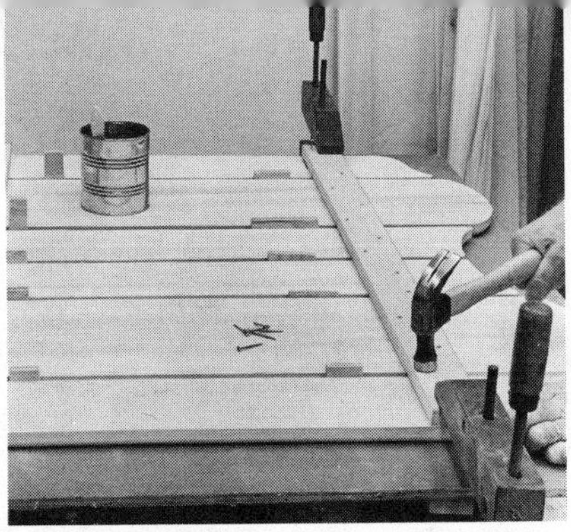

2 CLAMP CLEATS to back boards, then nail. Use spacers for accuracy.

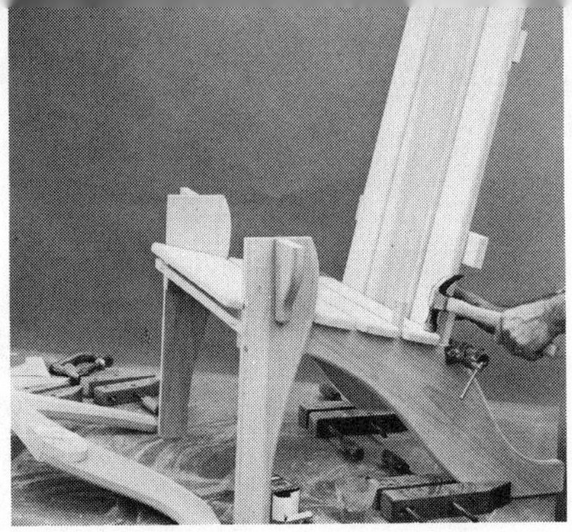

3 BAR CLAMP at back and spacing strip on front keep legs aligned.

(13/16 in. thick), while the settee uses both 4/4 and 5/4 stock (1 1/16 in. thick).

Using the drawing grids for reference, make paper patterns for all contoured parts and trace them onto the appropriate-sized stock. The rear legs should be positioned so that the long part of the leg is in line with the grain direction of the board. When assembled, this will make the leg as strong as possible.

Next, cut the contours with either a band saw or a sabre saw. Then sand out the saw marks from the edge with a drum sander mounted in your drill press or portable drill. Or, use a spoke shave.

Next, round over all edges except those indicated with an asterisk (*) on the drawing, using a ⅜-in. rounding-over bit in a router. This will give all the pieces a soft, comfortable look, while also reducing the possibility of wood splinters. All edges that have not been removed by the router should be eased with sandpaper before the parts are assembled.

Use highly water-resistant plastic resin glue for all assemblies. It is far less expensive than waterproof resorcinol glue and will serve quite well for this application. Also, hot-dipped galvanized nails are used throughout.

Because hardwood is being used, the nailing will be more difficult—a difficulty compounded by using the generally rough and nubby hot-dipped galvanized nails. For this reason, you may want to drill pilot holes for the nails.

In any case, do not nail closer than ¼ in. to the edge of the board and ⅜ in. to the end of a board without using a pilot hole.

Assemble the chair and settee in the following order: Glue and nail the back support blocks to the rear legs, then attach the rear legs to the front legs. Join the armrest support to the front legs, then assemble the backs as separate units. Use ½-in.-thick spacers to keep the back boards aligned properly.

Apply glue, then clamp and nail the cleats to the back boards, as shown in the photo.

Keep in mind that the middle cleat is 3¾ in. longer than the backboard assembly is wide to accommodate the armrests. Just center it on the back. When the armrests are finally attached, the cleat ends can be cut to exactly the size and shape needed for a professional-looking fit.

Next, support the leg assembly in the upright position as shown in photo No. 3, and slide the back assembly into the notched supports. Then attach the aprons, stretchers and armrests and you are finished.

Assemble the table by first joining the aprons, then nailing the top boards in place. Nail the leg parts together. Then glue and nail the completed legs to the aprons from the inside.

To complete the job, sand all surfaces thoroughly and apply a high-quality wood preservative following the manufacturer's directions on the can. Then give all the pieces three coats of paint.

MATERIALS LIST—SETTEE

Key	No.	Size and description (use)
A	2	13/16 × 9¼ × 36″ poplar (back)
B	2	13/16 × 5 × 33½″ poplar (back)
C	2	13/16 × 5 × 33½″ poplar (back)
D	1	13/16 × 2½ × 41″ poplar (upper cleat)
E	1	13/16 × 2½ × 44½″ poplar (middle cleat)
F	1	13/16 × 2½ × 41″ poplar (lowei cleat)
G	2	13/16 × 5 × 22″ poplar (armrest)
H	2	13/16 × 4 × 6½″ poplar (arm support)
I	2	13/16 × 10 × 35″ poplar (rear leg)
J	2	13/16 × 6 × 22″ poplar (front leg)
K	1	13/16 × 2¾ × 41″ poplar (rear stretcher)
L	1	1 1/16 × 3 × 44¼″ poplar (apron)
M	1	1 1/16 × 3 × 42⅝″ poplar (front stretcher)
N	2	13/16 × 4 × 6″ poplar (back support block)
O	1	1 1/16 × 3¼ × 44¼″ poplar (seat)
P	2	1 1/16 × 3½ × 44¼″ poplar (seat)
Q	1	1 1/16 × 7 × 44¼″ poplar (seat)
R	*	6d hot-dipped galvanized finishing nails
S	*	4d hot-dipped galvanized nails
T	8	2½″ No. 10 fh screws

*As reqd.

MATERIALS LIST—TABLE

Key	No.	Size and description (use)
A	1	13/16 × 9¼ × 36¼″ poplar (top)
B	2	13/16 × 5⅞ × 32″ poplar (top)
C	2	13/16 × 3 × 26″ poplar (apron)
D	2	13/16 × 3 × 17⅜″ poplar (apron)
E	4	13/16 × 3 × 22″ poplar (leg)
F	4	13/16 × 2¼ × 22″ poplar (leg)
G	*	4d hot-dipped galvanized finishing nails

*As reqd.

MATERIALS LIST—CHAIR

Key	No.	Size and description (use)
A	1	13/16 × 9¼ × 36″ poplar (:·ack)
B	2	13/16 × 5 × 33½″ poplar (back)
C	1	13/16 × 2½ × 20¼″ poplar (upper cleat)
D	1	13/16 × 2½ × 23¾″ poplar (middle cleat)
E	1	13/16 × 2½ × 20¼″ poplar (lower cleat)
F	2	13/16 × 5 × 22″ poplar (armrest)
G	2	13/16 × 4 × 6½″ poplar (arm support)
H	2	13/16 × 10 × 35″ poplar (rear leg)
I	2	13/16 × 6 × 22″ poplar (front leg)
J	1	13/16 × 2¾ × 20¼″ poplar (rear stretcher)
K	1	13/16 × 3 × 23½″ poplar (apron)
L	1	13/16 × 3 × 21⅞″ poplar (front stretcher)
M	1	13/16 × 3¼ × 23½″ poplar (seat)
N	2	13/16 × 3½ × 23½″ poplar (seat)
O	1	13/16 × 7 × 23½″ poplar (seat)
P	*	4d hot-dipped galvanized nails
Q	*	2″ No. 10 fh screws
R	*	6d hot-dipped galvanized finishing nails
S	8	2½″ No. 10 fh screws

*As reqd.

1 OUR OAK RACK interlocks and joins together without hardware; each box holds six bottles of your favorite wine. Reproduction bin pulls add a hint of mission furniture to the handsome rack.

Three handsome wine racks

■ IT'S SAFE TO SAY that many people who buy wine by the case like to display their stock as part of their home decor. On these pages, we show three wine racks created in our workshop. Plans and instructions for making all three are on the following pages.

The racks shown on these pages satisfy various needs: No. 1 is a clever box-type arrangement

that can be used one atop the other, as shown, or individually, if preferred. The sides, top and bottom interlock in an ingenious system. No. 2 is for those who stock considerable amounts of wine. You might never guess it with a quick glance, but there are more than four cases of wine bottles in the pair of large racks shown in the photograph. No. 3 is a traditional Mediterranean-style iron

2 THIS WINE RACK has the capacity to hold all of your prize stock—about 10 cases. Crafted in plywood, the rack gets its strength from interlocking diagonals. The natural finish gives it a clean look.

3 Spanish-style ornamental iron rack is an excellent project for those who prefer to work in metal. The rack shown holds 18 bottles.

wine rack. Each circular bay is used to contain one bottle; the rack holds 18 bottles in all.

THE OAK RACK

This countertop beauty is designed using the modular system. Each module holds six wine bottles; thus, you will need a pair if you buy your wine by the case. The tops and bottoms of the module sides are routed to a specific rabbet conformation, and the top and bottom pieces are dadoed to receive the sides.

The result is a rack that stacks securely without any hardware. If you desire, the top can be removed by lifting off.

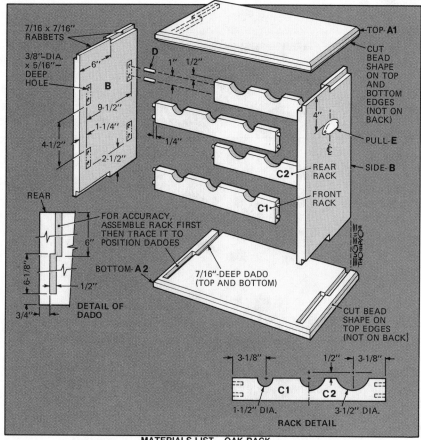

THE INTERLOCK FEATURE

1 To create the interlocking joint, use the router freehand or to a stop.

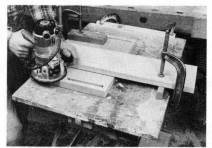

5 To prevent chance of router drift, clamp on a guide for the shoe.

9 Use dowel centers to transfer marks from racks to sides. Note the marks.

RACK DETAIL

Key	No.	Size and description (use)
A	2	7/8 x 12¾ x 18½" oak (top and bottom)
B	2	7/8 x 12 x 14⅝" oak (sides)
C	4	7/8 x 2 x 15¼" oak (front and rear racks)

D	16	⅜"-dia. x 1¼" hardwood dowels
E	2	Brass pulls (see note below for source)

MATERIALS LIST—OAK RACK

Misc.: 100-, 150-, and 180-grit sandpaper; Carver Tripp Spanish Oak stain; tack cloth; McCloskey Heirloom semigloss varnish; turpentine.

Start by cutting the parts to size. Since you are working with oak, make certain you work only with sharp blades and cutting tools. After cutting all the parts, sand them smooth, starting with 100-grit paper and finishing with 120.

Cut the rabbets in the side pieces before assembly. Lay them out as shown in the drawing and use your router and a ⅜-in. rabbet cutter. Because you are shaping oak, you should make the cuts in two passes. Do the first pass at half-depth and the final one at full depth. The rabbet width must be at least half the thickness of the wood stock.

When the cuts are completed, sand the sides, using 150-grit paper to remove any "whiskers" that have been made by the router cutter.

assembling the modules

Next, assemble the modules. You install the bottle racks using blind dowels and white glue. Use a minimum amount of glue to avoid squeeze-out. If any glue should squeeze out of a joint, allow it to dry and harden overnight. The next day, you can remove it cleanly and easily, using a razor-sharp chisel.

The easiest method for assembly is to use the techniques shown in the photos on page 15. Make sure you use match marks on the rack ends and mating surfaces of the sides so the module will go together without aggravation.

When it is assembled, clamp the module and allow it to stand overnight; use protective scraps of wood or cardboard between the clamp jaws and the wood to protect the latter from tool marks.

Cut the top and bottom pieces to size and shape the edges using your router. Next, align the module on the base piece.

The rack should be flush at the back and the space at the ends should be equal. Check these dimensions and move the module about until they are correct.

2 Avoid damage to wood by making the first pass at half-depth.

3 Clean out the rounded corners left by the bit, using a sharp, ¼-in.-wide chisel.

4 After box is assembled, position it on base, mark for dadoes. Repeat for top.

6 Carefully clean out dadoes using a chisel.

7 To avoid drill-bit drift in end grain, center-punch holes.

8 Bore dowel holes to desired depth; note masking-tape depth stop on bit.

10 Bore blind dowel holes on marked sides. Check the drill stop often.

11 Cut dowels to length, apply glue and insert them into the rack.

12 Align match marks, assemble rack. Use at least four clamps overnight.

using the router

When you're satisfied with the rack position, trace around both rabbeted ends, using a pencil. Remove the rack and set up the base piece for routing with a straight cutter. Make a test cut in scrap to check the dado for width and depth. Also, stop the router in the scrap and mark the outermost edge of the shoe on the scrap. Remove the router and measure the distance from the mark to the cutter edge.

Use this dimension to locate the fence (guide) for your router to ride against when routing the dadoes in the bottom (and top). Remember that you will only cut halfway across, and then the guide must be moved ⅜ in. to finish the other half of the dado. Clean out the rounded corners, using a sharp narrow chisel. Make certain you test-fit the mating members frequently as you do this dado-shaping step.

Repeat the procedure to create the top piece. Make certain that you mark the top, using the *top*

ends of the module. Remember that there is almost always some warp or cup in a piece of hardwood; thus, it is very likely that your rack top and bottom pieces will only stack one way—the way they were laid out originally.

finishing the rack

When all carpentry is completed, you can proceed with the finish. *Note:* You can rout the rabbets in the sides freehand if you are experienced with a router. If you have reason to doubt your control of the tool, clamp a stop block to keep you from routing beyond the rabbet center point.

Sand the entire rack with 150-grit paper, dust or vacuum off the sawdust and apply the oil stain of your choice. The rack shown was stained with Carver Tripp's Spanish Oak oil stain. Apply the stain, following label instructions. After wiping the piece, let it dry for 24 hours.

The rack shown is sealed with 3-lb.-cut, water-white shellac thinned 50 percent with denatured

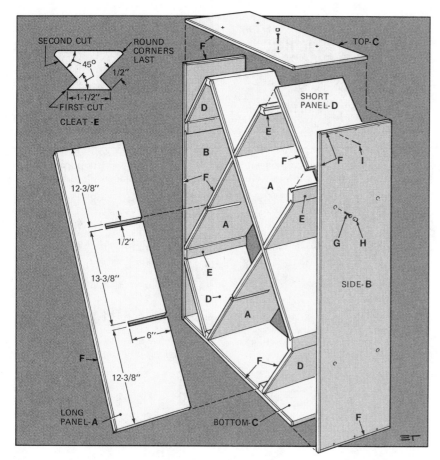

SECOND CUT — ROUND CORNERS LAST

45°

1/2"

1-1/2"

FIRST CUT

CLEAT -E

12-3/8"

1/2"

13-3/8"

6"

12-3/8"

LONG PANEL-A

F

TOP-C

F

SHORT PANEL-D

D

E

B

F

F

A

A

E

E

D

A

F

I

I

G   H

SIDE-B

D

F

BOTTOM-C

F

1 Use a block plane to trim edge banding flush with panel surface, then sand.

5 Masking tape must be used to hold glued joint together; clamps won't hold.

alcohol. Use a quality bristle brush to apply it and allow the shellac to dry for at least four hours.

To finish, lightly rub the shellac with 180-grit paper wrapped around a felt block. Rub lightly, and with the grain only. Dust off the piece and wipe thoroughly with a tack cloth. Apply one coat of varnish, as it comes from the can. The rack shown on page 12 was finished with McCloskey's Heirloom semigloss varnish, which dries to a "hand-rubbed waxed" look.

EGG-CRATE RACK

Intended for serious wine buffs, this pair of racks holds about five cases each, for a total storage space of 10 cases. Like the oak rack, it is built using the modular system. In the photo on page 13 we have two racks arranged to display a modest wine collection.

This rack is made with ½-in. birch veneer plywood. All exposed plywood edges are faced with ⅛-in.-thick strips of solid birch. The angled joining blocks are cut from ¾ stock. If you can't obtain solid birch in this size, you can substitute maple because it has a fairly similar appearance.

Start by sawing the panels to size, making sure to allow for the add-on ⅛-in. strips. You won't

need clamps to glue on the strips; use masking tape instead to apply the necessary gluing pressure. Cut the strips ⅝-in. wide to permit some leeway in gluing. They are trimmed flush to the panel surfaces with a block plane after the glue has set. Don't skimp with the tape; use 6-in.-long strips at 3-in. intervals to obtain good contact throughout. A word of caution about masking tape: Some brands of tape leave a sticky residue when removed; this type must be avoided. Test the tape on scrap to make sure yours comes away clean.

notching the cross panels

The diagonal cross panels are assembled with edge half-lap joints: ½-in.-wide notches are cut halfway through the mating pieces. You can make these notches in one pass on the radial-arm (or table) saw, using a dado head. If you don't have a dado head, simply make two kerf cuts with a smooth-cutting, regular saw blade.

Here's how to obtain uniformly spaced cuts: Clamp a stop on the radial-arm fence 12⅜ in. from the blade. Cut 6 in. into the panel to make the first cut for a notch, then flip the panel over, *end-to-end,* and make the first cut for the second notch. Do this with the eight panels, then shift the stop block so the second kerf cut will be ½ in.

2 Make double kerf cuts to form notches. Do all first cuts, then shift.

3 Two 45° bevel cuts are first made on lower part of the joining blocks.

4 Fence is repositioned and the blade is elevated for the second cuts.

6 Test-fit panels together; do this work on a flat surface for accuracy.

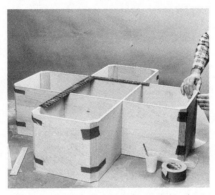

7 To obtain tight joints when gluing in end panels, hold them with duct tape.

MATERIALS LIST—EGG-CRATE RACK

Key	No.	Size and description (use)
A	4	½ x 11⅝ x 39⅛″ birch plywood (long panel)
B	2	½ x 11⅝ x 38¾″ birch plywood (side)
C	2	½ x 11⅝ x 38″ birch plywood (top, bottom)
D	4	½ x 11⅝ x 12⅛″ birch plywood (short panel)
E	8	1⁵⁄₁₆ x 2½ x 11¾″ birch (cleat)
F	36 ft.	⅛ x ½″ birch (edging)
G	16	1½″ No. 8 fh screw
H	16	⅜″-dia. dowel plug
I		6d finishing nails (as reqd.)

from the first one, measured outside to outside.

Don't automatically shift the block ½ in. from the first position, or you will have an error equal to the saw blade thickness! Repeat the sawing on the eight panels, alternately flipping them over for the second notch cut.

A quick way to drop out the notch waste is to bore a ½-in.-dia. hole at the inside juncture. Otherwise, use a sabre saw with a narrow blade and work it across the corner. Sand the faces of all the panels. This tends to loosen the fit of the panels in the notches, but the slight looseness is okay. In fact, a tight fit will cause assembly problems.

making the joining blocks

Now, you make the angled joining blocks. These can be made on either a table or a radial-arm saw. Here's how it's done on the table saw: Tilt the blade for a 45° bevel cut. Make two passes in each block to cut the shallower bottom kerfs first. Then raise the blade and reposition the fence to make the second series of cuts, which will drop out the waste. These deeper cuts are made last so *a nontippable wide surface is always on the table.*

If you should have a molding cutter head for the saw, with a suitable small-radius shape, use it

to cut the small corner-round on the blocks. Otherwise, do the rounding over with a block plane and sander. Sand all of the exposed surfaces of the blocks before assembly.

The blocks are glued to the panel ends for the first stage of assembly. Here, masking tape is an absolute necessity because ordinary clamps simply can't get a proper hold. Two strips of tape pulled taut will suffice. To make sure you join the blocks to the correct faces of the panels, join the panels in advance and mark the block locations. One slip-up will mess you up.

how to interlock panels

After the glue has set, interlock the panels (they won't need glue), then cut the smaller end panels to length. Working on a flat work surface, glue them in place. Since many plywood panels have some degree of warp, it is advisable to use a stronger tape for this gluing operation to ensure against the parts popping apart. Duct tape is a good choice. Again, check the product first for clean sticking and removal.

Wood screws and glue are used to attach the side members. The heads are then concealed with wood plugs. Clamp the top and bottom members in place and bore ¹⁄₁₆-in. pilot holes for the screws.

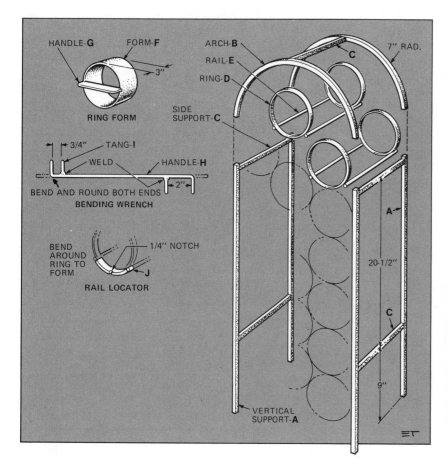

1 Form the rings around the ring form. Hold form in a vise.

5 To bend the main arch, insert the steel between tangs of the wrench.

Remove the clamps, bore the shallow larger hole for the plug, then rebore for the screw body and shank diameters, respectively. Glue and screw the top and bottom panels in, repeat the steps and attach the left and right side members. The abutted corners are secured with glue and 1½-in. (4d) finishing nails. When both sections are completed, stack them one atop the other and drill the screw holes for the mending plates. These plates will serve to keep the sections from shifting.

finishing the rack

If you have paint spray equipment and a suitable place to work, you can apply practically any kind of finish. But brush application of a regular top-coat finish will be particularly difficult in those angled corners.

A good solution is to use a penetrating Danish oil finish such as Deftco (made by Deft Inc.). This provides a tough satin finish and is easy to apply. It is available in Natural, Medium, Dark and Black Walnut. We used the clear Natural finish.

MEDITERRANEAN WINE RACK

A solid furniture accessory, this metal wine rack is 36 in. high, weighs 35 pounds and holds 18 bottles of wine. Each bottle is held within two rings, one at the neck and one at its base. A number of blacksmithing and welding techniques are utilized in its construction.

Begin by shaping the rings. If you have a power hacksaw, you can slice ½-in.-thick sections of a 5- or 6-in.-dia., thick-wall pipe.

An alternative method, shown here, is to make a form around which to bend the rings (see the ring-form detail in the drawing). A section of 5-in.-dia., thick-wall pipe can serve as the form. Weld a strip of steel across the bottom of the form to secure it in a vise.

using the bending wrench

A bending wrench shown in the drawing helps shape the rings. One other shopmade tool, a rail locator (see detail J), is used later to locate the rails supporting the wine bottles. Since it has the same contour as the rings, shape it when you bend them.

2 The C-clamp keeps the ends of the ring together while they are welded.

3 Clean the outside of the ring weld on a bench grinder. Hold ring vertically.

4 Clean hard-to-reach spots with a small portable grinder.

6 Clamp first three rings to arch and to each other. Weld parts together.

7 Clamp rails to 2x4s to hold securely while they are being welded.

MATERIALS LIST—METAL RACK		
Key	No.	Size and description (use)
A	4	½ x ½ x 30″ mild steel (vertical support)
B	2	½ x ½ x 22″ mild steel (arch)
C	5	½ x ½ x 12″ mild steel (side support)
D	36	$^3/_{16}$ x ½ x 15¾″ mild steel (ring)
E	36	¼″-dia. x 12½″ mild steel (rail)
F	1	3″ x 5″-dia. thick-wall steel pipe (ring form)
G	1	$^3/_{16}$ x 1½ x 5″ boiler plate (ring-form handle)
H	1	⅝ x ⅝ x 15″ mild steel (wrench handle)
I	2	⅝ x ⅝ x 1½″ mild steel (wrench tang)
J	1	$^3/_{16}$ x ½ x 2½″ mild steel (rail locator)

Use a hacksaw to cut the strips for the 36 rings to length. Grind all ends smooth if needed. Secure the form in a vise. Lock one end to the form with lever-jaw pliers and bend the ring by pulling and bending with the bending wrench. Close the rings with a C-clamp and weld the inner and outer surfaces together. Grind the weld clean. True up the ring in a vise with a hammer. The main arches of the wine rack are 14 in. in diameter. One way to shape them is to use an automobile wheel as a form. Heat the length of ½-in. square steel in a forge or with an oxyacetylene torch to cherry red.

To avoid heating the steel, you can also bend the arches, using a vise and the bending wrench. First lay out the arch shape on cardboard. Then secure the bending wrench in the vise, tangs upward. Place one end of the steel between the tangs and begin to bend; continue bending the length of the steel, occasionally removing the work and checking the shape against the arch.

After bending both arches, check to see that they are identical. Cut the vertical supports and grind smooth the ends that will rest on the floor. Weld supports to the arches.

Next, position the three top rings within one of the arches; test-position the rest of the rings, then remove them. Clamp the first three rings to the arch and to each other and weld them in place. Clamp and weld the remaining rings. Attach rings on the second arch to line up with their mates; clean welds. Join arches by welding the side supports. To keep arches plumb and square, clamp several flat pieces of steel bridging the 12-in. gap between arches.

To find the position of the rails that hold the bottles, first find the exact bottom of each ring. You can do this by placing a piece of shot, a dried pea or a pencil inside each ring and marking the spot where it settles. Line up the notch of the rail locator with this mark; mark the ring at each end of the locator. Turn the rack upside down and weld a rail onto the bottom of the ring directly above these two outer marks.

Finish by spray painting black with a rust-resistant metal paint.

A hutch table of solid pine

By JAMES R. BERRY

LARGE STORAGE space, ideal for bedding (above), is nearly undetectable with the lid closed (above right).

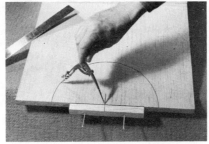

1 LAY OUT arc on bottom of each side. Because circle's centerpoint falls on edge, add a block.

■ THE HUTCH table has so many attractive design features that if it hadn't been developed in Europe in the 1600s (and brought to the United States in the early 1700s) it would have been invented here. No other piece of furniture is quite as versatile.

Begin building the table by edge-joining enough stock for both table sides. Use glue and ⅜-in.-diameter dowels, and clamp both assemblies overnight.

Next, lay out the arcs on each side by drawing a series of circles with a compass and pencil, starting with a 5-in.-radius circle along the bottom edge.

Move to the top side corners and draw the 2-in.-radius circles shown on the drawing. (This is also a good

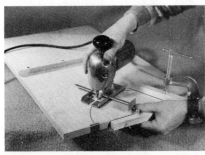

2 MAKE CUT with sabre saw and pivot guide. Apply tape to cut line and support waste with clamp.

3 TOP OF SIDE has three arcs. Draw outside ones first, then middle one. Connect them with tangent lines.

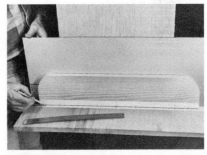

4 TO AVOID sanding out pencil marks, apply tape to stringer and top, mark screw locations on tape.

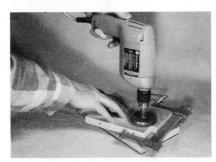

5 PREBORE holes in leg wing, then cut arc with hole saw. Block clamped to wing provides center.

6 AFTER BOTH panels are joined to sides, bore hinge-peg holes. Use a drill guide to ensure accuracy.

7 TO MAKE hinge pegs, bore dowel holes in larger dowel and wooden door pull, then join with small dowel.

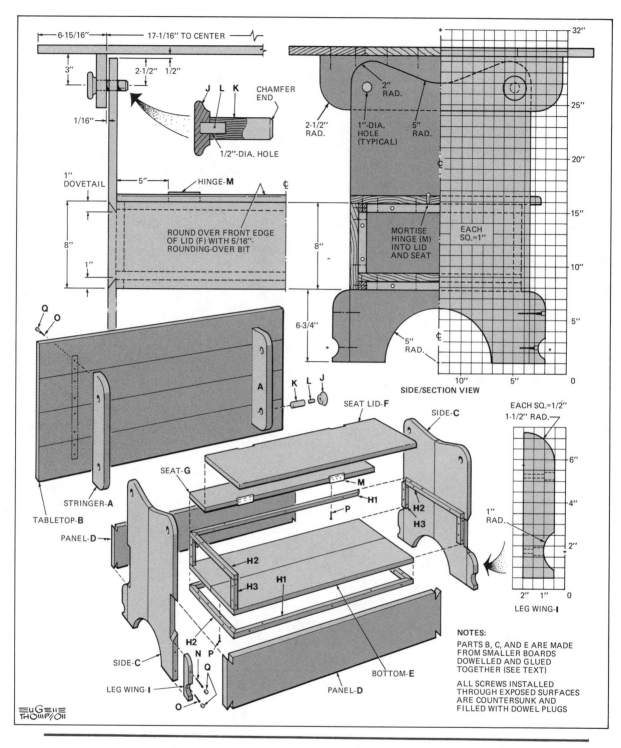

NOTES:

PARTS B, C, AND E ARE MADE
FROM SMALLER BOARDS
DOWELLED AND GLUED
TOGETHER (SEE TEXT)

ALL SCREWS INSTALLED
THROUGH EXPOSED SURFACES
ARE COUNTERSUNK AND
FILLED WITH DOWEL PLUGS

MATERIALS LIST—HUTCH TABLE

Key	No.	Size and description (use)
A	2	1 1/16 × 5 × 23″ pine (stringer)
B	1*	3/4 × 29 × 48″ pine (tabletop)
C	2	3/4 × 17 × 28″ pine (side)
D	2	3/4 × 8 × 34″ pine (panel)
E	1	3/4 × 15 1/2 × 32 1/2″ pine (bottom)
F	1	3/4 × 10 3/4 × 32 3/8″ pine (seat lid)

Key	No.	Size and description (use)
G	1	3/4 × 7 1/4 × 32 1/2″ pine (seat)
H1	3	3/4 × 3/4 × 32 1/2″ pine (cleat)
H2	4	3/4 × 3/4 × 15 1/2″ pine (cleat)
H3	4	3/4 × 3/4 × 5 3/4″ pine (cleat)
I	4	3/4 × 1 1/2 × 6 3/4″ pine (leg wing)
J	4	1 1/2″-dia. wood door pull
K	4	1″-dia. × 3″ dowel

Key	No.	Size and description (use)
L	4	1/2″-dia. × 1 1/4″ dowel
M	2	3/4 × 3″ hinge
N	4	2″ No. 10 fh screw
O	20	1 1/2″ No. 10 fh screw
P	51	1 1/4″ No. 10 fh screw
Q	24	Dowel plugs
		*Constructed from four 1×8s, each 48″ long

time to locate the center points for the hinge peg holes. Measure down 2½-in. from the side's top edge and 1½-in. in from the side edge and mark the intersection. Do this for both corners, then bore ¹⁄₁₆-in.-diameter holes through these points. Do not enlarge the holes yet.)

Next, draw the 5-in.-radius arc between the two circles as shown. Because the arc's center point falls 3 in. off the board's surface, you'll need to make the simple jig shown in photo No. 3. Just nail a ¾x5x28-in. board to two ¾x¾x18-in. "legs," then simply clamp the legs in place.

Join the three arcs with tangent lines, then bore a blade entry hole and a sabre-saw pivot guide hole in the jig.

Cutting these curves with a pivot guide will assure the best cut and the least sanding later.

Also, bore a pivot guide hole in the bottom support block and cut out that arc similarly. Finish-sand all curves with a drum sander.

front and rear panels

Cut the front and rear panels to size, then lay out the pins of the large dovetail joints on the panel ends. Cut the panel ends, then carefully trace the resulting shape onto the table side edges.

Cut the socket of all four joints and then carefully fit the panels to the sides, using fine-grit sandpaper.

Dry-assemble the four parts and clamp them in a square position. Tack-nail a temporary diagonal brace across the top edge of the front and rear panels. Now measure the exact dimension between the sides and the panels, and cut the cleats (parts H1, H2, H3) to matching sizes.

Next, bore and countersink screw clearance holes in all the cleats as shown on the drawing. Note that cleats H2 only have two holes bored in their top edges. These will be used to fasten the stationary rear portion of the seat. The front lid is movable.

Disassemble the table, then reassemble it with glue. Check for square, then reinstall the diagonal brace across the top edge of the panels and add one across the bottom edges, in the opposite direction.

When the glue is dry, remove the clamps and braces and install the upper cleat on both sides of the table and the rear panel. The front panel does not need an upper cleat.

Next, cut both portions of the seat to size and

check for fit. The rear portion should abut the sides tightly; the front board should have ¹⁄₁₆-in. clearance on each end (⅛ in. overall). Once you're satisfied, mark the hinge positions and remove both boards.

Mortise the edges to accept the hinges, then install the hinges on both boards and carefully slide this assembly into place. If both still fit properly, unscrew the front board and set it aside. Install the back portion permanently by turning screws through the cleats into the underside of the board.

Install the vertical cleats in similar fashion, then glue up stock for the compartment bottom. When it is dry, cut it and fit it into place. Install the lower cleats around the bottom and attach.

tabletop and stringers

Begin making the tabletop by doweling and gluing up stock to the size given in the materials list.

When the top is dry, place the poorer side down on the bench and invert the rest of the table assembly on top of the better side. Center the assembly, then place a stringer against each side with a ¹⁄₁₆-in. spacer between. Apply masking tape to the outside face of both stringers and to the tabletop underneath the stringers. Then mark the position of the attaching screws. (See photo No. 4.) Allow two screws per board of stock that was glued up to make the top.

Next, counterbore the clearance holes in the tabletop and the pilot holes in the stringers. Install the screws and conceal the heads with dowel plugs.

Invert the top once more, slide the table assembly between the stringers and mark the position of the hinge peg holes. To do this, slide ½-in.-thick shims between the tabletop and the top of the sides. Then insert a finishing nail into the ¹⁄₁₆-in.-diameter holes that were bored earlier in the table sides. Tap the nail with a hammer so it leaves an impression on the inside of the stringers. Remove the assembly and bore the hinge peg holes in the sides and the stringers.

Next, assemble the hinge pegs as shown in photo No. 7 and make sure that when installed, the top works well.

Cut the leg wings to size and shape and install them, then reinstall the movable lid and the assembly is complete.

Finish-sand the whole piece and apply the finish of your choice.

COLONIAL PIE SAFES no longer cool pies made by the dozen. Modern methods let you bake one pie at a time, so you can use this reproduction of a pie safe as a kitchen cupboard.

Build a colonial pie safe

By RALPH S. WILKES

■ THE PIE SAFE, variously called the pie cupboard, kitchen safe, tin safe, and even the meat safe, came into use in the 1700s and was made until about 1880. A large cabinet, made to hold pies, bread, and sometimes meat, it had pierced tin panels in the doors and usually on the ends. The tin panels were for ventilation and to keep out insects, but they also served a decorative purpose. Usually, the cabinets had one or two drawers, most often above, but sometimes below, the tin-paneled doors. The wood was often pine or poplar.

Pie safes are classified as American country furniture and are popular today, particularly among young people. Antique shop and auction prices begin at about $200. You can buy everything needed to build a reproduction of this popular item at a cost of less than half that figure.

I chose No. 2 white pine for the cabinet shown because it is easy to work, attractive when finished, and materials can be found in nearly any lumberyard. No. 2 white pine is much less costly than clear pine and a few small knots enhance the appearance of authenticity. By planning saw cuts in advance, I was able to avoid using stock with large knots or other blemishes.

Start constructing the pie safe by making the doors and side panels. Cut frames from 1-in. stock (actually measuring ¾-in.) Note that door stile K is ¼ in. wider than the other door stiles because the right door overlaps the left. The short horizontal side frame pieces are 4, 5, and 10 in. wide. All other frame parts are 2 in. wide. You can save time by ripping, planing the edges, and sanding all framing stock before assembly.

Cut pieces to the proper length and prepare the joints for mortise and tenons. Cut the ¼-in. rabbet on the door stiles. Test-assemble frames and mark the edges for the tin-panel slots.

cutting the tin-panel slots

To make this slot, use a fine-tooth plywood blade on your table or radial-arm saw. Set the saw for a cut just over ½ in. deep.

You are now ready to make the pierced tin panels. You may find a brown protective coating on both sides of the tin when you buy it. This coating can be readily removed with paint thinner (mineral spirits) and No. 00 steel wool. Use the steel wool with lengthwise strokes in the final stages.

With standard 20-in.-width flashing tin available in hardware and building material stores, there is no waste, as 6 linear feet provide material for the 10x14-in. panels, leaving 2 in. for a practice strip.

To pierce the panels, you need a round punch, a tool for slotting, and a suitable backing. See the drawing at the end of the story for the shapes of punches you need. A chunk of hardwood, preferably 12 in. or more in diameter and sanded reasonably smooth on one end, makes an ideal backing.

BEGIN construction with doors and sides that contain the tin panels. Test-assemble first for a good fit, then again to center the pattern of each panel.

START construction by attaching the cabinet frame to side panels with ¾-in., No. 10 flathead screws. Screws are countersunk in vertical cleats.

AFTER side panels, doors, shelves and bottom are installed, assemble drawer runners. You will find it easier to work from back and through top.

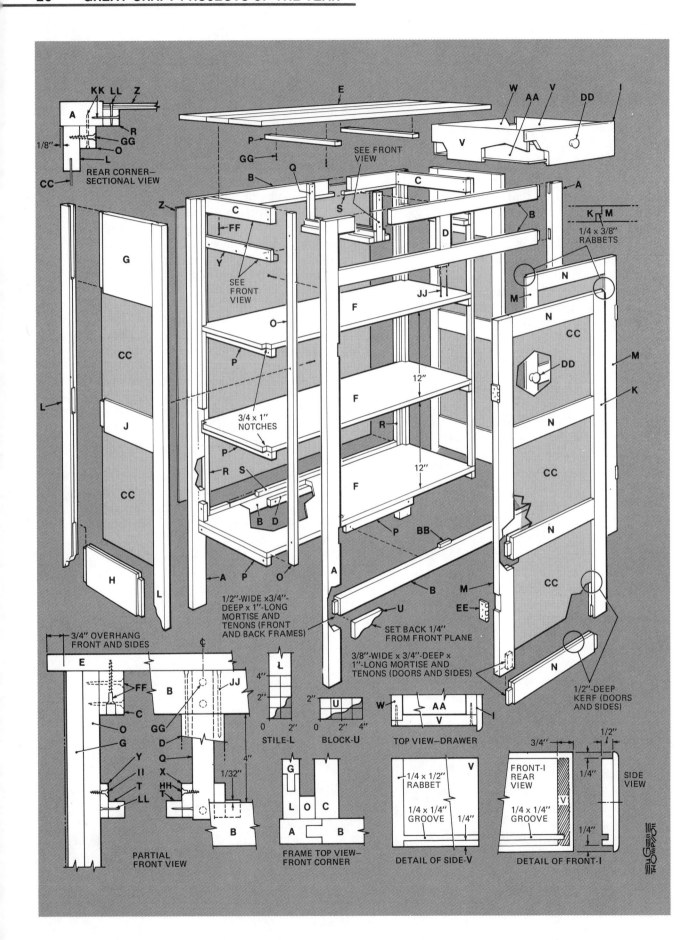

KK LL Z
A
1/8″
R
GG
O
L
CC
**REAR CORNER—
SECTIONAL VIEW**

E

P
GG
B
Z
Q
SEE FRONT
VIEW
C
S
C
A
W
V
AA
DD
I
V
K M
1/4 x 3/8″
RABBETS

FF
Y
SEE
FRONT
VIEW
D
B
N
M
N
CC
M

G
O
P
F
JJ

CC
12″
DD
K

J
3/4 x 1″
NOTCHES
P
F
R
N

CC
R S
F
12″
CC
B D
N

H
P
BB
M
EE
B
A
P
O
A
P
B

L
1/2″-WIDE x3/4″-
DEEP x 1″-LONG
MORTISE AND
TENONS (FRONT
AND BACK FRAMES)
U
SET BACK 1/4″
FROM FRONT PLANE
N
1/2″-DEEP
KERF (DOORS
AND SIDES)

3/8″-WIDE x 3/4″-DEEP x
1″-LONG MORTISE AND
TENONS (DOORS AND SIDES)

3/4″ OVERHANG
FRONT AND SIDES
E
FF
B
JJ
C
4″
2″
L
2″
U
W
AA
V
I
V
3/4″
1/2″
O
GG
G
D
Y
Q
II
X
HH
T
T
LL
Q
1/32″
4″
0   2″
STILE-L
0   2″   4″
BLOCK-U
TOP VIEW—DRAWER
FRONT-I
REAR
VIEW
V
1/4″
SIDE
VIEW
1/4″

B
**PARTIAL
FRONT VIEW**
G
L O C
A   B
**FRAME TOP VIEW—
FRONT CORNER**
1/4 x 1/2″
RABBET
1/4 x 1/4″
GROOVE   1/4″
V
DETAIL OF SIDE-V
1/4 x 1/4″
GROOVE
DETAIL OF FRONT-I

Before you begin piercing the panels, make a few practice holes and slots in a piece of scrap in order to determine the force needed to make the perforations. A lightweight ball-peen hammer does a good job.

The pattern shown was one of the most common in the 19th century. After enlarging the pattern to the 10x14-in. panel size, make two or three extra copies in case you damage one while using it. Secure the pattern to the tin at the corners with masking tape and you are ready to begin the job of piercing.

The panel may tend to curl upward as you work. You can prevent this by tacking it down loosely with a couple of upholstery tacks through perforations already made. Break this job up into several sessions because it can become tedious.

Test-assemble frames again with tin panels before the final assembly with glue. Be sure the panel designs are centered.

Build the front and back frames for the cabinet from 5/4 stock (which actually measures about 1⅛ in. thick). Glue the joints and check carefully to be sure the corners remain square when tightening the bar clamps.

Attach the two end panels with flathead wood screws from the inside of the vertical frame cleats. Cut and install the floor of the cabinet by inverting the entire assembly, holding the bottom in place with cleats. Then install the shelves.

Mark the hinge locations on the doors and front frames, mortise, and mount the doors.

Make the runners for the two drawers of maple, cherry, or other close-grained hardwood. Construct the drawers and try them for proper fit before gluing. Turn knobs for the drawers and right door on the lathe or, if you wish, purchase them at a hardware or building supply store.

Make the top of the pie safe by edge-gluing two or more pieces. The plywood back is a piece of plain ¼-in. mahogany wall paneling. Use a piece of the same 4x8-ft. panel for the drawer bottoms.

Now that you have it all together, go around the panel edges with masking tape. Then go over all edges once, not to round them, but to knock off sharpness with No. 180-grit abrasive paper on a sanding block. Dust and tack off.

Select a stain which is appropriate for the wood, such as Minwax No. 230 Early American stain/sealer. After allowing a day for drying, sand lightly with the same grade of paper, clean, apply white shellac to the end grain, and apply polyurethane.

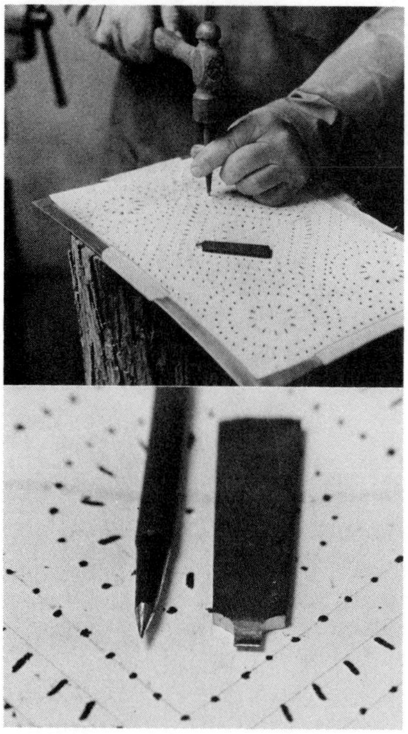

MAKE YOUR piercing tools from a nailset and an 8-in. file. An upright log makes a good work block. The piercing job takes about five hours.

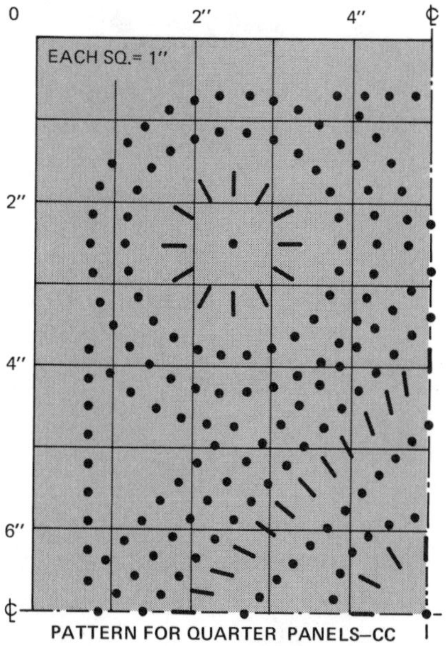
0
2″
4″
¢
EACH SQ.= 1″
2″
4″
6″
¢

PATTERN FOR QUARTER PANELS—CC

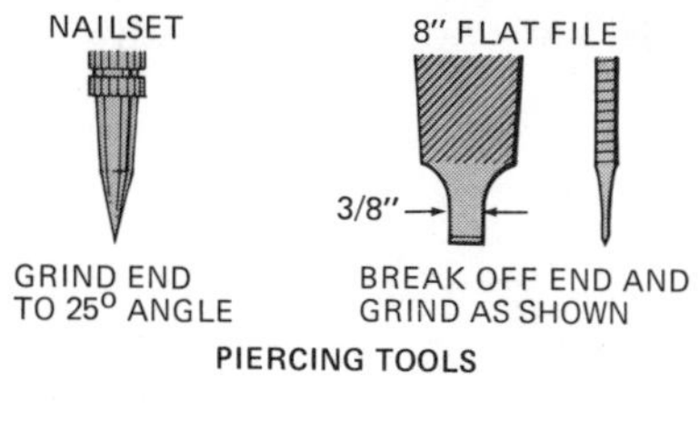
NAILSET
8″ FLAT FILE
3/8″
GRIND END TO 25° ANGLE
BREAK OFF END AND GRIND AS SHOWN

PIERCING TOOLS

MATERIALS LIST—PIE SAFE

Key	No.	Size and description (use)
A	4	1⅛ × 2 × 55″ (frame legs)
B	5	1⅛ × 2 × 35½″ (frame rails)
C	2	1⅛ × 2 × 13″ (top cleat)
D	1	1⅛ × 2 × 4″ (frame stile)
E	1	¾ × 16 × 39½″ (top)
F	3	¾ × 13 × 36″ (bottom shelf)
G	2	¾ × 10 × 10½″ (top side rail)
H	2	¾ × 5 × 10½″ (bottom side rail)
I	2	¾ × 4½ × 16½″ (drawer front)
J	2	¾ × 4 × 10½″ (center side rail)
K	1	¾ × 2¼ × 35″ (left door stile)
L	4	¾ × 2 × 47″ (side stile)
M	3	¾ × 2 × 35″ (door stile)
N	8	¾ × 2 × 14½″ (door rails)
O	4	¾ × 1 × 43″ (corner cleats)
P	10	¾ × 1 × 13″ (cleats)
Q	2	¾ × 1 × 6¾″ (runner support)
R	2	¾ × ¾ × 41″ (vertical back cleat)
S	2	¾ × ¾ × 32½″ (horizontal back cleat)
T	4	¾ × ¾ × 13″ (runners)
U	2	¾ × 2 × 4″ (corner block)
V	4	½ × 4 × 13½″ (drawer side)
W	2	½ × 3½ × 15½″ (drawer back)
X	2	½ × 1½ × 13″ (inner runner guide)
Y	2	⅜ × 1½ × 13″ (outer runner guide)
Z	2	¼ × 34 × 41″ (back)
AA	2	¼ × 13¼ × 15½″ (drawer bottom)
BB	2	¼ × ¼ × 2″ (door stop)
CC	10	10 × 14″ No. 28 gauge flashing (tin panel)
DD	3	1½″-dia. wood knob
EE	4	1½″ butt hinge
FF	12	2″ No. 10 fh screw
GG	*	1¼″ No. 10 fh screw
HH	*	¾ No. 10 fh screw
II	*	⅝″ No. 5 fh screw
JJ	4	10d finishing nail
KK	*	6d finishing nail
LL	*	1″ wire brads

Misc.: Finish, paint thinner, steel wool, carpenter's glue, masking tape. *As required.

FIREWOOD HOLDER (above) easily supports heavy-duty canvas tote used to transport a healthy supply of logs (right). Simply hang loaded carrier onto protruding dowels and remove wood as needed.

Three log holders for your hearth

Bring your firewood indoors and keep it neatly stacked with one of these distinctive and easy-to-build log holders. Each serves the same purpose but is unique in styling, requiring different construction skills

■ HAVING A SUPPLY of firewood next to your wood stove or fireplace is handy, but it can be unsightly. Here are three log holders designed to spruce up your hearth. Each is a different style and each involves different shop skills. The oak holder was designed by Van R. Hutchinson, while the other two were inspired by PM staff members.

CANVAS TOTE HOLDER

■ THE SUPPORT FRAME for this holder was made from relatively inexpensive 2x4 lumber. Because the good-sized dadoes and lap joints provide ample gluing surfaces for a sound assembly, nails and screws are not needed. (There is one minor exception: 3d finishing nails are used when gluing and clamping the bottom cross members to the uprights to keep them from sliding out of alignment.)

Begin by selecting straight, kiln-dried 2x4s with small, tight knots. Cut them to length, then rip ¼ in. from each edge to obtain a finished 3-in. width. This removes the factory rounded corners, making for flush joints later.

Then cut the ¾-in.-deep dadoes and lap joints in the uprights and bottom cross members, using a dado head or saw blade and overlapping saw cuts. Next, bore the two angled dowel holes in the upper-side cross members as shown. A drill press with an adjustable angle vise is ideal for this job, but a portable drill can work if a sliding T-bevel is clamped to the board as a guide. A Portalign drill guide will also help do the job.

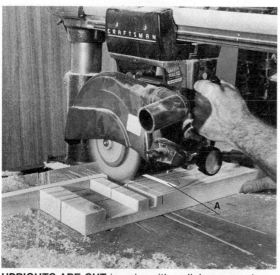

UPRIGHTS ARE CUT in pairs with radial-arm saw to assure aligned dadoes. Masking tape (A) helps alignment.

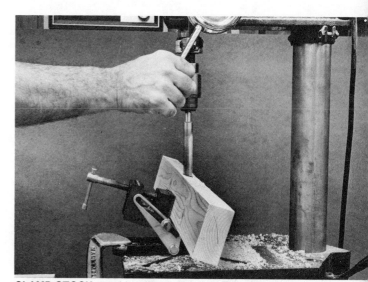

CLAMP STOCK to table with angled vise. Then bore dowel holes. Brad-point bit is best, but spade point will do.

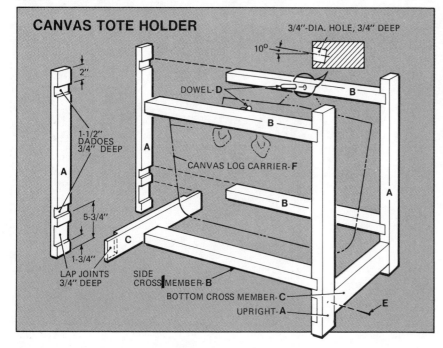

CANVAS TOTE HOLDER

3/4"-DIA. HOLE, 3/4" DEEP

10°

2"

DOWEL-D

B

B

1-1/2" DADOES 3/4" DEEP

A

CANVAS LOG CARRIER-F

A

B

5-3/4"

C

1-3/4"

LAP JOINTS 3/4" DEEP

SIDE CROSS MEMBER-B

BOTTOM CROSS MEMBER-C

UPRIGHT-A

E

ASSEMBLE AND sand pieces, then join them by adding the cross members.

MATERIALS LIST—CANVAS-TOTE HOLDER

Key	No.	Size and description (use)
A	4	1-½ × 3 × 27" fir (upright)
B	4	1-½ × 3 × 25" fir (side cross member)
C	2	1-½ × 3 × 22" fir (bottom cross member)
D	2	¾"-dia. × 3" dowel
E	8	3d finishing nails
F	1	Canvas tote

Misc.: Glue, stain, tung oil.

After a satisfactory test assembly, glue and clamp the side-section parts together. When they're dry, and these units with a pad sander and 120-grit paper.

Next, glue, nail and clamp the bottom cross members in place; when dry, ease all sharp corners by sanding as desired. Finally, apply the stain and finish of your choice. We used ZAR Teak Stain and ZAR Wipe-On clear Tung Oil Finish.

One source for the tote is L.L.Bean Inc., Freeport, ME 04032. It's model No. 8731M.

THE OPEN DESIGN of this solid oak holder conveniently accommodates logs of any size or shape.

OAK HOLDER

■ BEGIN MAKING this sturdy and decorative log holder by cutting the legs and slats to approximate length from 1-in. nominal stock. (The actual thickness of such material is 13/16 in.) Using the grid supplied in the drawing below, sketch the leg outline on one board. Then tack-nail this pattern to the other leg board, driving the nails on the waste side of the line as shown.

Use a band saw to cut the outline, leaving the top nailed sections uncut.

A sabre saw can also be used, but the legs would have to be cut separately; the doubled-up oak would be thicker than a sabre saw's cutting capacity.

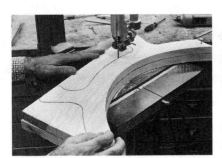

GANG-SAW the legs. Nails driven on the waste side of the outline are used to hold pieces together.

BORE HOLE at each notch corner and cut out waste. Holes simplify cutting and give notches a finished look.

MATERIALS LIST—OAK HOLDER

Key	No.	Size and description (use)
A	2	13/16 × 10 × 24" oak (leg)
B	9	13/16 × 1½ × 20½" oak (slats)
C	18	1½" No. 8 fh screws
Misc.:		Glue, stain, clear finish of choice.

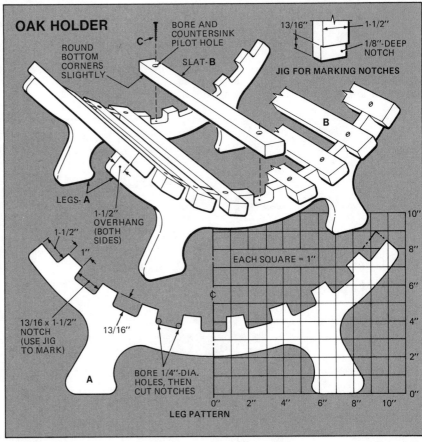

Next, cut a block of wood the same width as the slats and make a "step" in one end, as shown in the drawing. This simple jig is the most effective way to mark the notches along the curved edge.

Once the layout is complete, bore a hole in each notch corner, then cut out the waste. The small radii in the corners give the blade room to maneuver and, at the same time, impart a finished look to the notch corners.

With the legs still nailed together, sand the scrolls with a 3-in. drum sander. Then cut off the waste areas, separate the pieces and finish-sand each of them individually.

Next, rip the slats to the required width and sand off the sharp corners—especially on the bottom edges—so the slats will sit flush in the slightly rounded notch corners. Cut the slats to length, being careful that they all are exactly the same. Now carefully finish sand each slat starting with 80-grit abrasive paper and finishing with 120-grit.

Bore and countersink pilot holes for the flathead screws, then glue and screw the slats to the legs.

Finally, apply a stain and the clear finish of your choice. We used McCloskey's Tungseal with a satin finish. It has proved to be a durable finish for the constant abuse that comes from dropping logs.

WROUGHT-IRON HOLDER

■ THIS VERSATILE UNIT is made from ⅛x1-in. hot-rolled mild steel. Such flat stock is available at welding or iron-work shops, but be sure to specify hot-rolled steel. Cold rolled is too tough for the bending procedure outlined here.

Begin by making the simple bending jig shown in the drawing. The first part is made of ¾-in.-thick plywood and two pieces of ⅛-in.-thick aluminum stock. Before nailing it to the platform, bore clearance holes through it so the small piece of plywood won't split. Once the nails are driven, grip the projecting nail ends in a bench-mounted vise.

Next, cut the stock for the uprights and feet, and mark all bend lines indicated on the drawing.

One by one, insert each end of the uprights and feet into the jig slot and make the scroll bends. Then, tack-nail the second part of the jig onto the platform and make the reverse bends on the uprights only.

Make all corner (sharp-angle) bends by securing the stock in vise jaws and using a wood block to push. The position of the stock relative to the jaws—given on the drawing—is critical. If you are careless, the unit won't fit together properly.

Assemble the unit in the following way: Clamp the uprights and feet together, then center-punch and drill the rivet holes through both pieces at once. Join these, using aluminum rivets. Next, join the ends of each shelf support with rivets and drill clearance holes for the shelf-supporting bolts. Then clamp each shelf support in place,

WROUGHT-IRON holder stores good supply of logs, as well as paper and kindling for starting fire.

drill rivet holes and install rivets the same way.

Apply primer and two coats of a semiflat black paint such as Krylon No. 1613. Cut the plywood shelves to fit, using measurements taken from each support. Seal each shelf with two thin coats of shellac on both sides and install them on the supporting bolts.

MATERIALS LIST—WROUGHT-IRON HOLDER

Key	No.	Size and description (use)
A	2	⅛ × 1 × 90″ hot-rolled mild steel (upright)
B	3	⅛ × 1 × 88″ hot-rolled mild steel (shelf support)
C	2	⅛ × 1 × 31½″ hot-rolled mild steel (foot)
D	3	¼ × 18¼ × 23¼″ plywood (shelf)
E	22	⅛″-dia. aluminum rivets
F	12	1½″ No. 8-32 rh screws and nuts
Misc.:		Primer, black spray paint, shellac.

log holders, continued

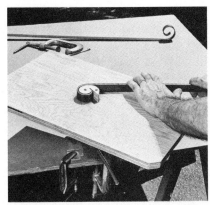

BENDING JIG is nailed to jig platform with 10d common nails. Grip projecting nail ends in vise (under platform), insert stock, make first bend.

NAIL SECOND block to jig as shown, then make reverse bend on uprights only.

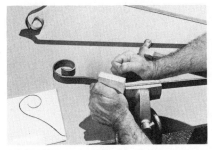

TO MAKE corner bends, clamp stock in vise and bend back, using wooden block. See drawing for position of vise jaws.

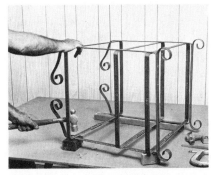

JOIN ALL of the pieces by drilling holes and inserting aluminum rivets. Flatten the rivets using a ballpeen hammer and a steel block.

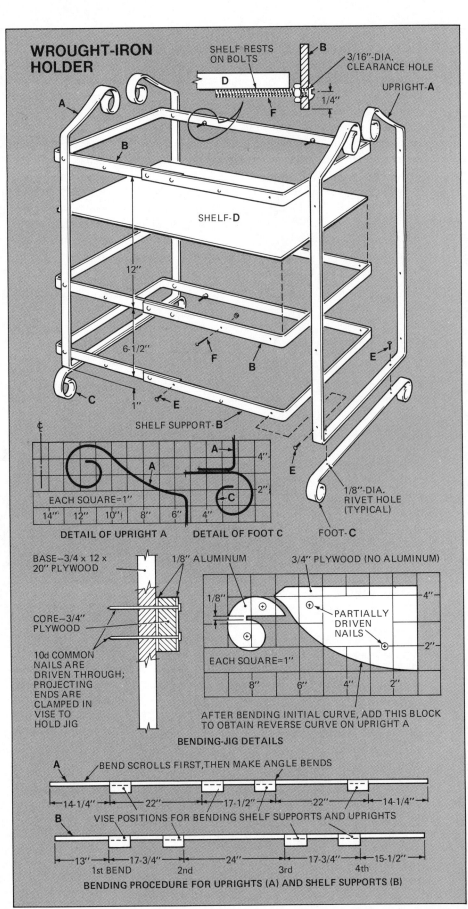

WROUGHT-IRON HOLDER

SHELF RESTS ON BOLTS

3/16"-DIA. CLEARANCE HOLE

1/4"

UPRIGHT-**A**

D

F

B

A

B

SHELF-**D**

12"

6-1/2"

F

B

E

C

E

1"

E

SHELF SUPPORT-**B**

1/8"-DIA. RIVET HOLE (TYPICAL)

FOOT-**C**

A

EACH SQUARE=1"

14" 12" 10" 8" 6" 4"

DETAIL OF UPRIGHT A

A

4"

2"

C

DETAIL OF FOOT C

BASE-3/4 x 12 x 20" PLYWOOD

1/8" ALUMINUM

3/4" PLYWOOD (NO ALUMINUM)

CORE-3/4" PLYWOOD

1/8"

PARTIALLY DRIVEN NAILS

10d COMMON NAILS ARE DRIVEN THROUGH; PROJECTING ENDS ARE CLAMPED IN VISE TO HOLD JIG

EACH SQUARE=1"

8" 6" 4" 2"

4"

2"

AFTER BENDING INITIAL CURVE, ADD THIS BLOCK TO OBTAIN REVERSE CURVE ON UPRIGHT A

BENDING-JIG DETAILS

A BEND SCROLLS FIRST, THEN MAKE ANGLE BENDS

14-1/4" 22" 17-1/2" 22" 14-1/4"

B VISE POSITIONS FOR BENDING SHELF SUPPORTS AND UPRIGHTS

13" 17-3/4" 24" 17-3/4" 15-1/2"

1st BEND   2nd   3rd   4th

BENDING PROCEDURE FOR UPRIGHTS (A) AND SHELF SUPPORTS (B)

THIS ADAPTABLE dining table/desk is built of hefty 1⅛-in. sugar pine and was given a clear finish.

A table for parties or homework

This handsome dining table seats four. Lower the drop leaf and you have a desk or sideboard.

The entire table is made from sugar pine

■ THIS ELEGANT contemporary table does triple duty. Besides serving as a dining table, it converts for use as a desk or sideboard when the leaf is down.

The table is made of ⁵⁄₄-in.-thick sugar pine. We used 15-in.-wide boards and added 3-in. strips, dowel reinforced, to make up the 18-in. slabs.

The legs are assembled with end half-lap joints. Arrange the leg members in proper order on a flat work surface and key all mating pieces. After the edges have been smoothed by jointing, trace against each butted piece directly to obtain the cutting lines.

Use a dado head to reduce the lap-joint areas to half thickness. When using a radial-arm saw, make a pass in a new section of the backup fence.

BY FOLDING DOWN one leaf, the table can serve as a writing desk or a sideboard for entertaining.

APPLY GLUE to mating leg surfaces. Use second coat on end grain (shoulders).

CLAMPING SETUP assures a true plane of boards when making dowel-hole center marks.

MATERIALS LIST—TABLE

Key	No.	Size and description (use)
A	2	1⅛ x 18 x 56″ sugar pine (tabletop and leaf) or assemble from: 2 pieces, 1⅛ x 15 x 56″ (A₁); 2 pieces, 1⅛ x 3 x 56″ (A₂); 10, ⅜″-dia. x 2″ dowels (A₃)
B	4	1⅛ x 5 x 17¼″ sugar pine (leg foot)
C	4	1⅛ x 4 x 28″ sugar pine (leg stile)
D	4	1⅛ x 4 x 17¼″ sugar pine (leg rail)
E	1	1½″ (open) x 55¼″ hinge
F	2	1½″ (open) x 27½″ hinge
G	4	3″ No. 12 fh wood screw
H	4	½″-dia. dowel plug
I	6	Nylon tack guide

Misc: white glue; 120- and 180-grit sandpaper, finish (see text).

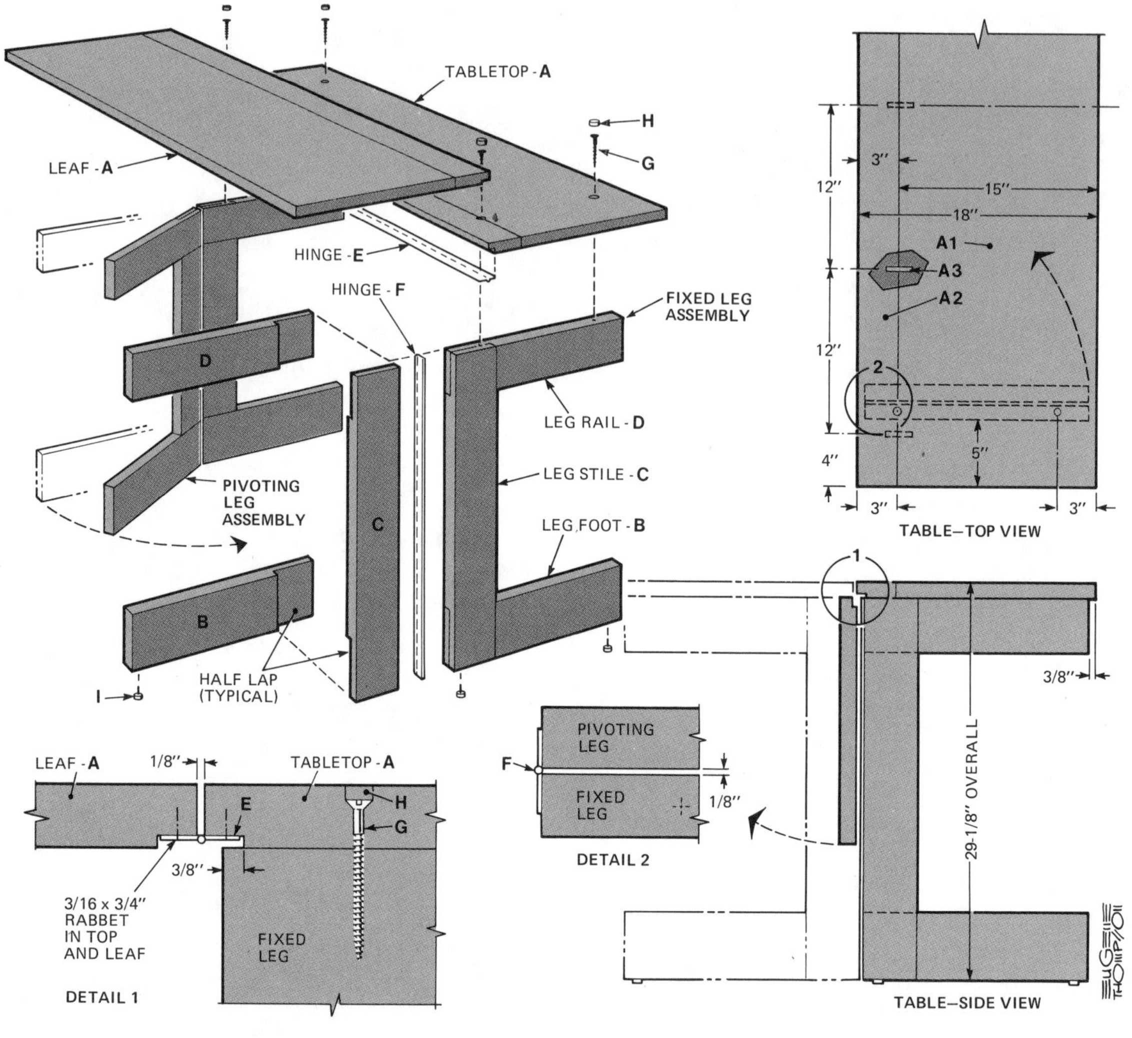

TABLETOP - **A**

LEAF - **A**

H

G

HINGE - **E**

HINGE - **F**

FIXED LEG ASSEMBLY

D

LEG RAIL - **D**

PIVOTING LEG ASSEMBLY

LEG STILE - **C**

C

LEG FOOT - **B**

B

I

HALF LAP (TYPICAL)

TABLE—TOP VIEW

3″

12″

15″

18″

A1

A3

A2

12″

2

4″

5″

3″   3″

DETAIL 1

LEAF - **A**   1/8″   TABLETOP - **A**

E

H

G

3/8″

3/16 x 3/4″ RABBET IN TOP AND LEAF

FIXED LEG

DETAIL 2

F

PIVOTING LEG

FIXED LEG

1/8″

1

3/8″

29-1/8″ OVERALL

TABLE—SIDE VIEW

TO EDGE, rabbet with the radial-arm saw. Use a spacing strip to position the work.

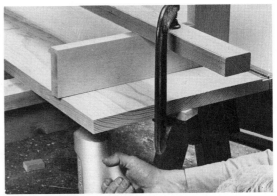

AFTER BORING screw holes in tabletop, clamp legs to it. Continue boring from below into legs.

Then align the joint line visually (on the work-piece) with the notch cut in the fence. Make one cut to establish the inside shoulder. Then make repeated cuts to remove the waste. If you use a table saw, cut a piece of scrap wood, then mark the cutting path on the table insert plate.

Note: Do not use a clamped limiting stop for making the cuts. A fixed stop won't compensate for variations in individual widths resulting from the sawing and jointing processes.

Partially drive a few thin nails when gluing the leg half laps to keep the parts from sliding during clamping. Allow room for clamp cushions. You can remove the nails and fill the holes afterward.

Now, adjust the jointer for a shallow cut and make a pass or two to trim the hinge edges of the leg stiles (C). Cut a small chamfer on each back corner before jointing to prevent end grain splintering. Use a belt sander to smooth the faces of the legs. Sand with the grain only.

If you must edge-join boards to make the top and leaf, use dowel centers to mark the hole centers before using a drill press. Bore the holes in one member, then insert the dowel centers. To align, clamp two pieces of wood over the joint at both ends of wood, using moderate clamp pressure. Then use two bar clamps to bring the pieces together just enough to transfer the center mark impressions. Or you can skip this step, if you use a portable drill with a doweling jig.

Cut a wide rabbet along the bottom edge of the leaf and top for the continuous hinge, so the legs can swing past it. You can make this cut with a dado head on the radial-arm or table saw. Or, use a router. To make the rabbet on the radial-arm saw, set up for in-ripping and feed the work *against* the rotation of the blade. Test-fit the leaf to the top with a hinge secured by screws. Later, disassemble parts to finish them.

To secure the fixed legs to the top, outline the

leg position on the underside of the top. Then use a drill guide to bore $\frac{1}{16}$ in.-dia. holes through the top for the screws. Clamp the legs in position with the table upside down on saw horses. Bore from below going through the original pilot holes into the legs. Remove the legs and enlarge the holes for the screws and plugs. Next, glue the legs in place. Join the pivoting and fixed legs with a hinge, leaving a $\frac{1}{8}$-in. gap between the legs.

We finished the table with a thinned water-white shellac sealer coat (two parts 3-lb.-cut shellac, one part alcohol), followed by two coats of Constantine's Wood Glo satin finish. We sanded lightly between coats with 220-grit garnet paper.

Note: It's somewhat more convenient to pivot the outside legs. If you wish, you can adapt our version by relocating the screw holes on top to fasten the inside legs. However, in this adaptation, the barrel of the hinge will be visible.

IN THIS VIEW of leaf and leg, hinge screw holes are clear of leg to permit removal of the pieces.

2 CUBE COFFEE TABLE is a relatively simple, contemporary project; it also can be used as an end table.

Four great projects for your home

Here are plans for four exciting projects you may be able to use in your own home. The two tables are made with plywood covered with plastic laminate. There's also a bar and a hanging glass rack

■ THESE ATTRACTIVE home-furnishing projects help you make the most of your living space. Following are plans and how-to tips on making the items.

Before the projects are assembled, fill all ex-posed edges of the plywood with wood filler. Then sand all parts with 100- or 120-grit abrasive paper. To assemble the projects, glue mating sur-faces together. Then drive and set nails to hold the work while the glue dries.

3 KEEP STEMWARE readily at hand—where it belongs logically—installed on the ceiling, directly over the service bar.
4 DECORATOR Debbie Seaburg, ASID, utilized wasted space for this bar/buffet unit for a family room.

1 SIZED TO SOFA height, the triangular table provides a surface to display favorite objects and satisfy storage needs.

STORAGE TABLE

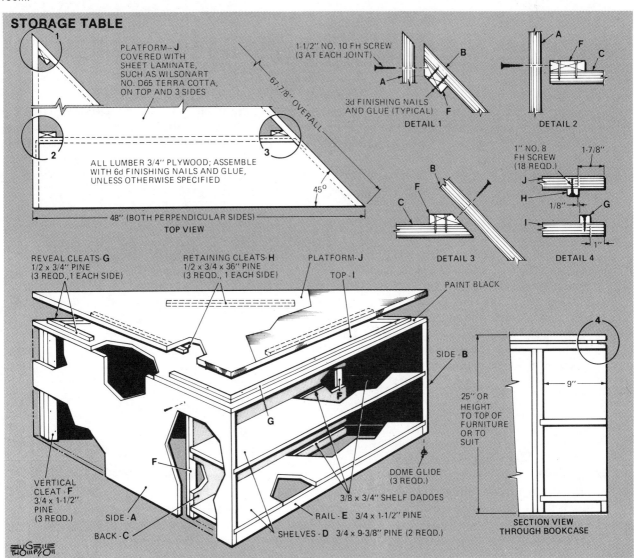

PLATFORM—J COVERED WITH SHEET LAMINATE, SUCH AS WILSONART NO. D65 TERRA COTTA, ON TOP AND 3 SIDES

1-1/2" NO. 10 FH SCREW (3 AT EACH JOINT)

3d FINISHING NAILS AND GLUE (TYPICAL)

DETAIL 1

DETAIL 2

61-7/8" OVERALL

ALL LUMBER 3/4" PLYWOOD; ASSEMBLE WITH 6d FINISHING NAILS AND GLUE, UNLESS OTHERWISE SPECIFIED

45°

48" (BOTH PERPENDICULAR SIDES)
TOP VIEW

1" NO. 8 FH SCREW (18 REQD.)
1-7/8"
1/8"
1"

DETAIL 3

DETAIL 4

REVEAL CLEATS-**G**
1/2 x 3/4" PINE
(3 REQD.,1 EACH SIDE)

RETAINING CLEATS-**H**
1/2 x 3/4 x 36" PINE
(3 REQD., 1 EACH SIDE)

PLATFORM-**J**

TOP - **I**

PAINT BLACK

SIDE - **B**

VERTICAL CLEAT-**F**
3/4 x 1-1/2" PINE
(3 REQD.)

SIDE - **A**

BACK - **C**

3/8 x 3/4" SHELF DADOES

DOME GLIDE (3 REQD.)

RAIL - **E**   3/4 x 1-1/2" PINE

SHELVES - **D**   3/4 x 9-3/8" PINE (2 REQD.)

25" OR HEIGHT TO TOP OF FURNITURE OR TO SUIT

9"

SECTION VIEW THROUGH BOOKCASE

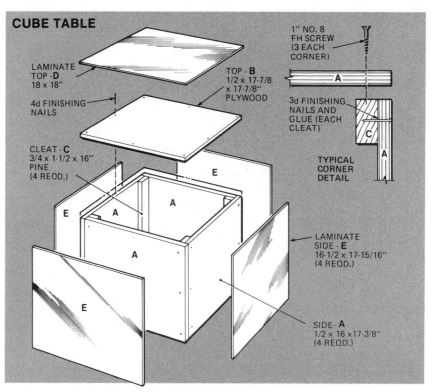

CUBE TABLE

LAMINATE
TOP - **D**
18 x 18"

4d FINISHING
NAILS

CLEAT - **C**
3/4 x 1-1/2 x 16"
PINE
(4 REQD.)

TOP - **B**
1/2 x 17-7/8
x 17-7/8"
PLYWOOD

1" NO. 8
FH SCREW
(3 EACH
CORNER)

3d FINISHING
NAILS AND
GLUE (EACH
CLEAT)

TYPICAL
CORNER
DETAIL

LAMINATE
SIDE - **E**
16-1/2 x 17-15/16"
(4 REQD.)

SIDE- **A**
1/2 x 16 x 17-3/8"
(4 REQD.)

1 TRIANGULAR STORAGE TABLE

■ BESIDES PROVIDING storage space and a display surface, this triangular table serves as a backup for a sofa. The table is topped by a platform supported by recessed cleats to give the visual effect of a floating top.

Study the drawing of the table, and cut the table sides, noting the edges that receive a 45° bevel. Notice that one end of each shelf is cut at a 45° angle. Plow dadoes in the table sides and shelf back to receive the shelves.

Join the sides with three vertical cleats; two of the cleats have beveled sides (see drawing details Nos. 1 and 3). After assembling the sides, shelves, rail and top, let the unit dry overnight.

In a well-ventilated room, away from cigarets, sparks and open flames, cover platform J with plastic laminate. Laminate the platform edges first, one at a time. Laminate the top after trimming edges with a router and straight carbide cutter.

Cut the laminate at least ¼-in. wider and longer than the surface to be covered. Apply the adhesive evenly to the laminate with a short-nap (mohair) paint roller or bristle brush; then coat the wood surface. When you can touch brown paper to the surface without it sticking, the adhesive is ready for bonding, usually in 20 to 30 minutes.

Place clean wood strips, dowels or brown Kraft paper over the plywood. Lower the laminate carefully, keeping it aligned with the plywood. When the pieces are aligned, slide out the first dowel or paper and press the laminate onto the plywood at one corner. Continue removing the separators and pressing the laminate in place.

To ensure good bonding, apply pressure over the entire surface with a wooden rolling pin. Use a router and a straight carbide cutter to trim off the overhanging waste material. Make sure the plywood edge that the router follows is straight. If any voids are present, fill them with wood filler and sand the spots smooth. Otherwise, the router will follow the irregularities and miscut the laminate.

Bevel all corner edges with a 22½° carbide cutter in a router, or use a plane with a sharp blade set for scant removal. Smooth edges with a file, applying pressure only on the downstroke. Remove excess contact cement with lacquer thinner. Attach retaining-spacer cleats to the platform.

Paint the rest of the table. First prime the plywood with a pigmented shellac such as Bin or Enamelac. Let it dry overnight, then paint with an alkyd or latex paint.

Position the platform on the table. The retaining cleats under the platform should fit within the reveal cleats on the tabletop.

2 CUBE COFFEE TABLE

■ YOU CAN BUILD this cube table in a single shop session and finish it with plastic laminate. This piece serves as a coffee, end or corner table.

Cut the plywood sides and top and the pine cleats to size, as shown. Fill any holes in the edges with a quality wood filler such as UGL's Wood Patch. Then sand all surfaces smooth and brush them off.

Begin assembly by gluing and nailing one cleat to each side. Position the cleats as shown in the drawing. When nailing, drive and set all nails and fill the holes with wood filler. Then join the corners with glue and screws. Finally, glue and nail the top in place.

Make sure all edges are smooth before laminating. For laminating tips, see the first project (triangular storage table).

3 HANGING GLASS RACK

■ THIS OVERHEAD STEMWARE rack has a "sculptured" look that is achieved by using your table saw. Begin by cutting the seven supports for the glasses and the three cross braces to length.

Set the table-saw blade to a ¼-in. elevation and the fence 1 in. from the blade to make the vertical cuts for each support. Then reset the table-saw blade at approximately a 20° angle and relocate the fence about ⅞ in. away on the other side of the blade. Test-cut in scrap wood, then turn the support on edge to cut out the waste.

Locate and bore screw and eyebolt holes in the braces on a drill press or with a portable drill.

Before assembly, sand parts smooth with 100-, then 120-grit abrasive paper; dust and wipe with a tack cloth. Space the supports, position the braces and mark the screw position on the braces. Then attach the supports to the braces. Mark the endpieces and cut them to length, using a band saw to create the "rounded" look on one side of the rack (see "top view" in the drawing).

Hang the rack temporarily, and brush on a primer, such as Bin or Enamelac. Follow this with coats of alkyd or latex paint to match decor. Allow adequate drying time between coats.

To install the rack, see the detail drawings.

4 BAR/BUFFET COUNTER

■ WE CONVERTED lally columns from obstructions to assets by framing around them to support this bar/buffet counter. The lally columns and counter base are framed with 2x3s, spaced 16 in. on center and assembled with 8d common nails. Use a level to check that framing is installed plumb.

The counter is a hollow-core door, covered with plastic laminate. First, laminate the counter edges, one at a time; then cover the top.

We used prefinished ¼-in. paneling from Georgia Pacific over the framing. Mark all stud locations on the floor and ceiling before installing panels, so you'll know where to nail.

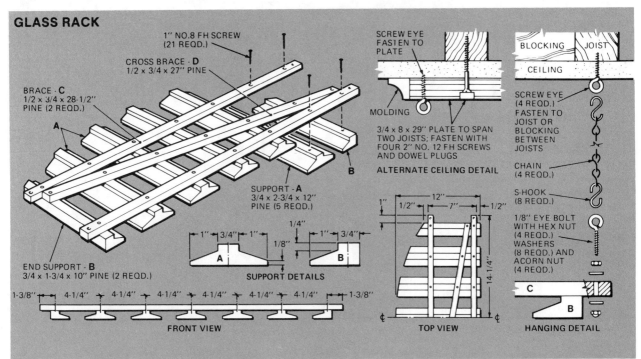

GLASS RACK

1" NO.8 FH SCREW (21 REQD.)

CROSS BRACE - D
1/2 x 3/4 x 27" PINE

BRACE - C
1/2 x 3/4 x 28-1/2"
PINE (2 REQD.)

SUPPORT - A
3/4 x 3/4 x 12"
PINE (5 REQD.)

END SUPPORT - B
3/4 x 1-3/4 x 10" PINE (2 REQD.)

SUPPORT DETAILS

1-3/8"   4-1/4"   4-1/4"   4-1/4"   4-1/4"   4-1/4"   4-1/4"   1-3/8"

FRONT VIEW

SCREW EYE FASTEN TO PLATE

MOLDING

3/4 x 8 x 29" PLATE TO SPAN TWO JOISTS; FASTEN WITH FOUR 2" NO. 12 FH SCREWS AND DOWEL PLUGS

ALTERNATE CEILING DETAIL

TOP VIEW

BLOCKING   JOIST

CEILING

SCREW EYE (4 REQD.) FASTEN TO JOIST OR BLOCKING BETWEEN JOISTS

CHAIN (4 REQD.)

S-HOOK (8 REQD.)

1/8" EYE BOLT WITH HEX NUT (4 REQD.) WASHERS (8 REQD.) AND ACORN NUT (4 REQD.)

HANGING DETAIL

First, install the paneling that will adjoin the counter on the inside of the columns. Fasten the countertop to the column studs with 3-in. lag-screws and finish paneling the column framing and counter base. Use 3d (1¼ in.) finishing nails or 1-in. brads every 6 in. along the edges and every 12 in. on intermediate studs. Set all nail-heads and conceal them with special crayon-like sticks. Or, use color-coated nails with a slight head. Such nails aren't set.

If you use panel adhesive, use fewer nails. Squeeze a bead of adhesive onto each stud face; nail the panel along the top edge only. Then wedge a scrap of 2x3 between the panel bottom and the studs to "air" the adhesive. After five minutes, remove the scrap wood and nail the panel to the studs.

Use prefinished corner guard to cover the paneling edges at the outside corners. If you use wooden corner guard, set the nailheads and conceal them with filler. Use only color-coated nails with vinyl corner guard.

To attach strips of mirrored sheet acrylic, bore oversize holes in each corner and center holes near the edge of each side of the strip. Secure acrylic to paneling with Phillips-head screws and cup washers.

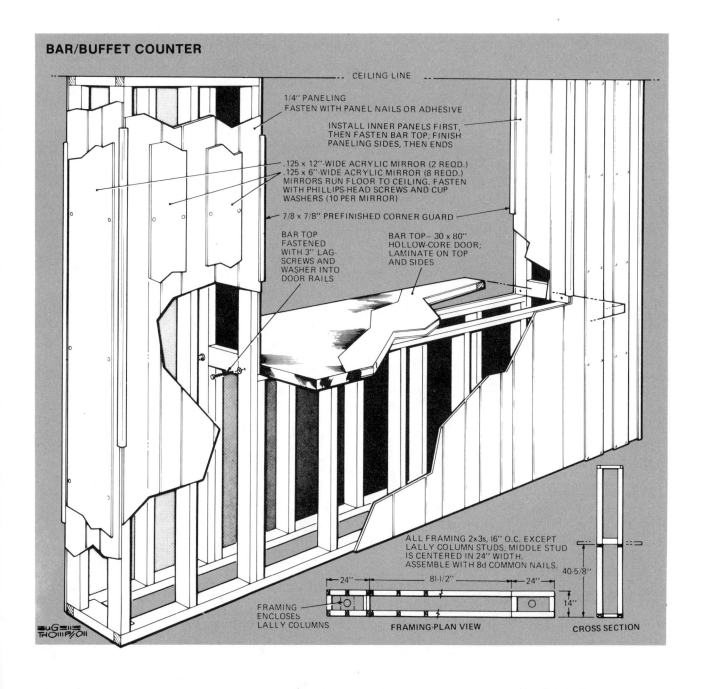

BAR/BUFFET COUNTER

CEILING LINE

1/4" PANELING
FASTEN WITH PANEL NAILS OR ADHESIVE

INSTALL INNER PANELS FIRST, THEN FASTEN BAR TOP; FINISH PANELING SIDES, THEN ENDS

.125 x 12"-WIDE ACRYLIC MIRROR (2 REQD.)
.125 x 6"-WIDE ACRYLIC MIRROR (8 REQD.)
MIRRORS RUN FLOOR TO CEILING. FASTEN WITH PHILLIPS-HEAD SCREWS AND CUP WASHERS (10 PER MIRROR)

7/8 x 7/8" PREFINISHED CORNER GUARD

BAR TOP FASTENED WITH 3" LAG-SCREWS AND WASHER INTO DOOR RAILS

BAR TOP— 30 x 80" HOLLOW-CORE DOOR; LAMINATE ON TOP AND SIDES

ALL FRAMING 2x3s, 16" O.C. EXCEPT LALLY COLUMN STUDS; MIDDLE STUD IS CENTERED IN 24" WIDTH. ASSEMBLE WITH 8d COMMON NAILS.

FRAMING ENCLOSES LALLY COLUMNS

24"   81-1/2"   24"

40-5/8"

14"

FRAMING-PLAN VIEW

CROSS SECTION

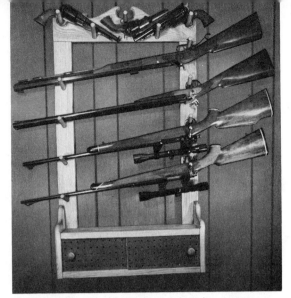

THIS GUN RACK is designed to hold four long guns and five handguns upside down. Oil from the barrel and action flows away from the wood stock and doesn't saturate and weaken it.

■ I DESIGNED THIS gun rack to hold guns upside down with their muzzles at the low point. This prevents oil from saturating and weakening the wood stock. The rack holds long guns and handguns by their trigger guards. The firearms hang on dowel pegs, which aren't likely to dent or scratch the stocks. Since there are no children in the household and I store ammunition elsewhere, I don't use trigger or cable locks.

Cut out a cardboard pattern using a 1-in. grid before you cut the top of the rack (part A). Then outline the pattern on the wood, bore out waste in the four circular curves with a ¾-in.-dia. bit and cut out the part on a band saw.

Join the rack sides and top with glue and screws in corner lap joints. Use a try square to lay out the parts and draw lines for the width of the lap cuts. Then use a table saw to make a ⅜-in.-deep shoulder cut; turn the stock on edge, set the rip fence and clear out the waste. The vertical legs of the rack are notched and rabbeted to receive the ends and bottom of the compartment. Mark the locations and bore ¾-in.-dia. x ⅝-in. deep holes at an angle for the rack pegs.

An 'oil-proof' gun rack

By GARY P. HANSEN

The compartment top, bottom, back and ends are cut of pine. The doors for the compartment are of perforated hardboard and they slide in grooves cut in the compartment top and bottom pieces. The top is notched to fit around the rack legs. The compartment's top fits into blind dadoes in the end pieces.

Test-fit the compartment parts, then sand them smooth with 120-grit abrasive, tack off and attach knobs to the doors before joining parts with carpenter's glue. Apply stain and finish as desired.

MATERIALS LIST—GUN RACK

Key	No.	Size and Description (use)
A	1	¾ x 5½ x 24″ pine (rack top)
B	2	¾ x 2¹¹/₁₆ x 41⅝″ pine (vertical members; rip a 1 x 6 in half)
C	2	¾ x 5½ x 23¼″ pine (compartment top, bottom)
D	2	¾ x 5½ x 11″ pine (compartment ends)
E	13	¾″-dia. x 4″ dowel (rack pegs)
F	2	¼ x 5¼ x 12″ perforated hardboard (doors)
G	2	1″-dia. wooden knobs
H	1	¾ x 5½ x 18⅝″ pine (compartment back)
I	*	⅜″ No. 10 fh wood screws

Misc.: Carpenter's glue; stain and finish.   *As required.

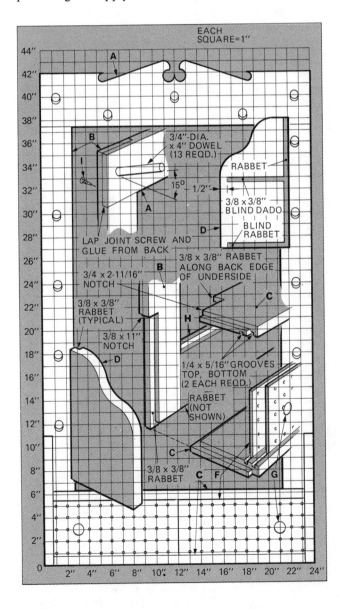

Build a New England stone fence

■ HANDSOME, mortarless stone walls, like those that still define and terrace the land of many New England farms and homesteads, can beautify your own home and garden. All it takes is patience, an assortment of readily available tools, some old-fashioned sweat and a few sensible rules laid down by oldtimers whose handiwork has survived two or more centuries.

There are three basic types of dry stone walls: free-standing, low terrace and high retaining wall. Construction techniques vary slightly for each.

most walls are plumb

A lot of arbitrary data have been published about how wide a dry stone wall should be for a given height, and whether or not it should taper from base to cap rock. Most old-time wall builders made the sides of their free-standing walls plumb, regardless of height. But the higher the wall, the wider they built it. Actually, 8 or 9 ft. is about as high as anyone would want to go with a dry wall. Any number of such walls (mostly in

By RICHARD F. DEMPEWOLFF

barn foundations)—about 4 ft. wide from top to bottom—still stand throughout the Northeast countryside.

Except for basic plans, the old-timers worked largely by eye, using common sense, a spirit level and, perhaps, a plumb bob. Nowadays, most experts agree that free-standing dry walls 3 ft. high or less require no taper. For anything taller than that, some wall builders recommend differing slope angles for stability. The diagram on page 44 provides a reasonable slope for the sides of free-standing dry walls. Rule of thumb calls for a base that is 6 in. wider than the top for each foot of height above 3 ft. There is no question that you'll use about one-third less rock—and less building time and effort—by tapering a high wall. And if it's properly constructed, its firmness and stability won't be impaired.

low and high walls

Low terrace stone walls, properly trenched and drained as shown, will stand solidly if built with plumb corners and sides. High retaining walls, also trenched and drained as shown, should lean toward the soil bank they hold in place (2 in. for every foot of height) to allow for frost heave. The base should also be wider than the top of the wall—1 in. for each foot of height—and the cap rocks should be a minimum width of 16 in.

construction tips

• The first step is to assemble the basic tools for the job: 3-lb. sledge with one beveled edge for chipping rocks, 10-lb. sledge, pinch bar and needlebar, cold chisels, star drill, steel shims and wedges (see page 44), mason's string, 3- or 4-ft. level, a pair of sturdy gloves, safety glasses to protect your eyes when chipping the stone, and heavy boots.

• Next, sketch a plan for the wall and lay it out on the site, as you would a building foundation. Stake the corners and string mason's line for height and level. Curving sections can be defined by running garden hose along desired contours.

3 TYPES OF STONE WALLS

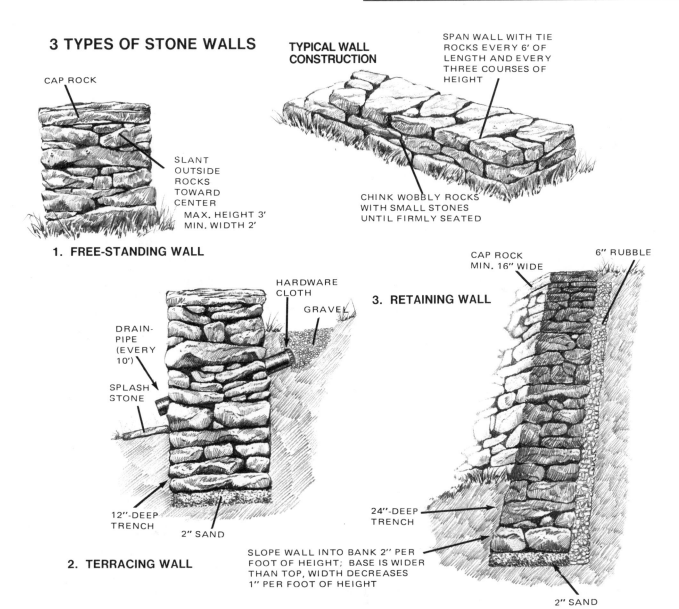

TYPICAL WALL CONSTRUCTION

SPAN WALL WITH TIE ROCKS EVERY 6' OF LENGTH AND EVERY THREE COURSES OF HEIGHT

CAP ROCK

SLANT OUTSIDE ROCKS TOWARD CENTER

MAX. HEIGHT 3' MIN. WIDTH 2'

CHINK WOBBLY ROCKS WITH SMALL STONES UNTIL FIRMLY SEATED

1. FREE-STANDING WALL

HARDWARE CLOTH

GRAVEL

DRAIN-PIPE (EVERY 10')

SPLASH STONE

12"-DEEP TRENCH

2" SAND

2. TERRACING WALL

3. RETAINING WALL

CAP ROCK MIN. 16" WIDE

6" RUBBLE

24"-DEEP TRENCH

SLOPE WALL INTO BANK 2" PER FOOT OF HEIGHT; BASE IS WIDER THAN TOP, WIDTH DECREASES 1" PER FOOT OF HEIGHT

2" SAND

calculate amount of stone

• Calculate the approximate cubic footage of stone you'll need by multiplying the length of the wall by the average width. Multiply this figure by the average height for the total.

• Nearly any kind of rock can be used in dry stone-wall construction, but some shapes, sizes and types are more adaptable than others. Angular-shaped rocks with flat surfaces are best. Rounded fieldstone can also be used, but you must chip it with a cold chisel and hammer to face and square the stone a bit so it will sit firmly in a wall. If possible, avoid this type, along with brook boulders. Igneous rock such as granite and basalt is fine, if you can find usable chunks. Large specimens that must be broken require hours of work with star drills, stone hammers, shims and wedges—not to mention trimming with a cold chisel or mason's hammer.

finding the rock

• Where do you find rock? In the Northeast, if you hike through any rural or exurban woodland, you won't go far before stumbling on an adequate supply. Old potato cellar foundations, played-out quarries with piles of discards and ancient stone rows that the oxen of pioneering farmers stone-boated to the periphery of hard-won fields are all excellent sources.

Frequently, the property owner will let them go for the asking, or for a small fee. In any case, make certain you get permission from the property owner *before* removing any stone from the land.

use quarry rubble

In almost any part of the country, some commercial quarry rubble is available. And in other areas with outcrops of layered sandstone, slate or

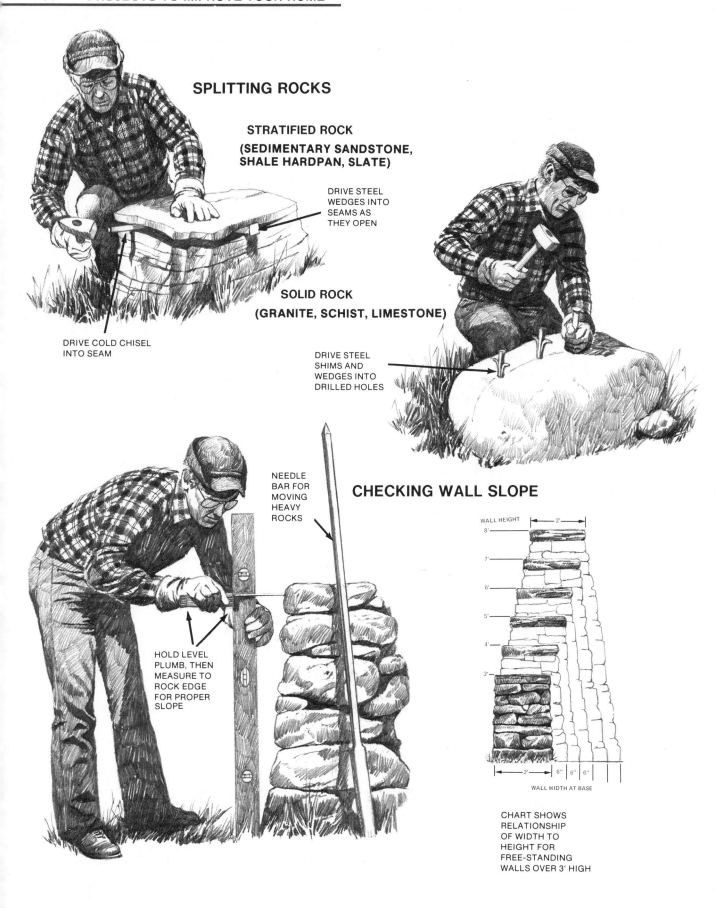

SPLITTING ROCKS

STRATIFIED ROCK
(SEDIMENTARY SANDSTONE, SHALE HARDPAN, SLATE)

DRIVE STEEL WEDGES INTO SEAMS AS THEY OPEN

SOLID ROCK
(GRANITE, SCHIST, LIMESTONE)

DRIVE COLD CHISEL INTO SEAM

DRIVE STEEL SHIMS AND WEDGES INTO DRILLED HOLES

NEEDLE BAR FOR MOVING HEAVY ROCKS

CHECKING WALL SLOPE

HOLD LEVEL PLUMB, THEN MEASURE TO ROCK EDGE FOR PROPER SLOPE

WALL HEIGHT

2'

8'
7'
6'
5'
4'
3'

2'   6'' 6'' 6''

WALL WIDTH AT BASE

CHART SHOWS RELATIONSHIP OF WIDTH TO HEIGHT FOR FREE-STANDING WALLS OVER 3' HIGH

STONE FENCE—CONSTRUCTION DETAILS

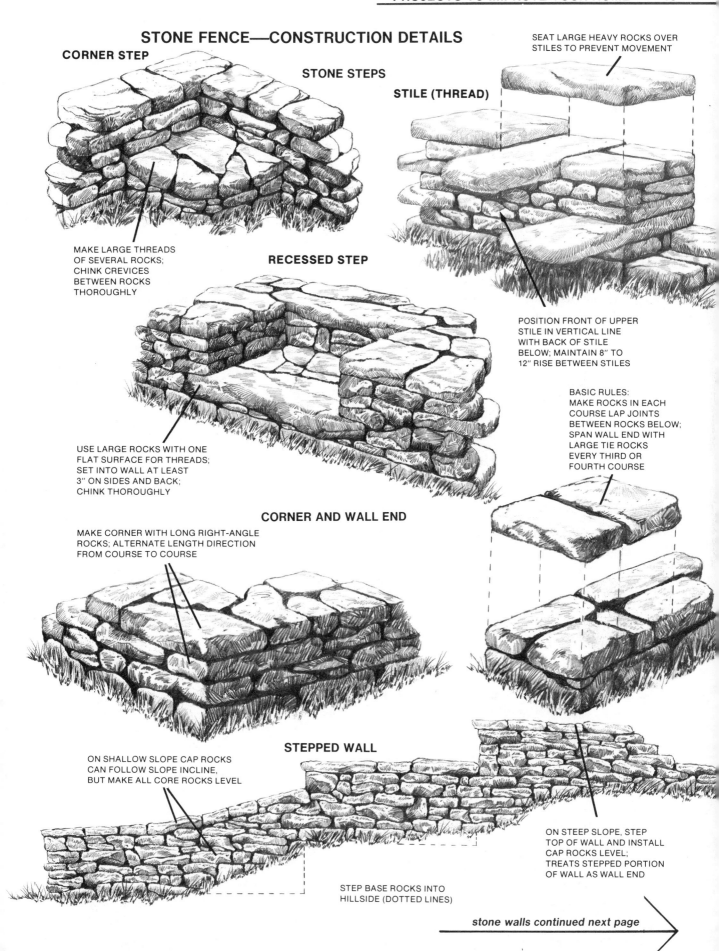

CORNER STEP

STONE STEPS

STILE (THREAD)

SEAT LARGE HEAVY ROCKS OVER STILES TO PREVENT MOVEMENT

MAKE LARGE THREADS OF SEVERAL ROCKS; CHINK CREVICES BETWEEN ROCKS THOROUGHLY

RECESSED STEP

POSITION FRONT OF UPPER STILE IN VERTICAL LINE WITH BACK OF STILE BELOW; MAINTAIN 8" TO 12" RISE BETWEEN STILES

USE LARGE ROCKS WITH ONE FLAT SURFACE FOR THREADS; SET INTO WALL AT LEAST 3" ON SIDES AND BACK; CHINK THOROUGHLY

BASIC RULES: MAKE ROCKS IN EACH COURSE LAP JOINTS BETWEEN ROCKS BELOW; SPAN WALL END WITH LARGE TIE ROCKS EVERY THIRD OR FOURTH COURSE

CORNER AND WALL END

MAKE CORNER WITH LONG RIGHT-ANGLE ROCKS; ALTERNATE LENGTH DIRECTION FROM COURSE TO COURSE

STEPPED WALL

ON SHALLOW SLOPE CAP ROCKS CAN FOLLOW SLOPE INCLINE, BUT MAKE ALL CORE ROCKS LEVEL

ON STEEP SLOPE, STEP TOP OF WALL AND INSTALL CAP ROCKS LEVEL; TREATS STEPPED PORTION OF WALL AS WALL END

STEP BASE ROCKS INTO HILLSIDE (DOTTED LINES)

stone walls continued next page

foliated schists, look for weathered slabs that have broken off and lie at the base of the rock face. These can be split easily at the seams and rough-cut into usable shapes with a cold chisel and hammer.

• Rock without stratification—igneous types and hard limestone—must be hand-drilled and wedged apart as illustrated. Score a line with a broad-edged cold chisel and bore a series of 4-in.-deep holes, about 8 in. apart, along it with a star drill and a hammer. Give the drill a one-eighth turn with each stroke. Insert steel shims and a wedge in each hole and tap the wedges until firmly embedded. Then whack each in turn with a 3-lb. hammer, repeating in series until a crack appears.

If further hammering doesn't cleave the rock, broad steel wedges, pinch bar and crowbar can be used to finish the job. Be careful not to drive a single wedge too hard and deep, or you'll break off a corner instead of splitting the rock down the line. (The steel wedges and shims shown are invaluable when it comes to splitting solid rock, but sometimes they can be difficult to find. If you can't get them through your local masonry supplier, contact Richard Pokrandt Manufacturing, RD 3, Box 182, Tamaqua, PA 18252.)

• The most practical way of hauling large blocks to the building site is on a stone boat (see the illustration on page 47). The rugged, sledlike device, used by early farmers to move rock from the fields, was much larger than the one shown here. But this smaller version, held together by lagscrews as illustrated, will handle just about any rock one man would care to wrestle.

hauling the sled

A garden tractor can haul the sled, or you can slip the tow line over the ball hitch of a station wagon or Jeep-type vehicle. Rocks up to 250 lbs. can be loosened with a crowbar and rolled aboard the low platform. And the 2x4 lip will keep the cargo from sliding or jouncing off en route to the site. (To build the stone boat, just follow the plans. You should be able to get a local blacksmith or welding shop to shoe the runners inexpensively.)

• In selecting stone, put aside pieces with a distinct right angle for corner blocks. Large, flat slabs should be saved for cap rocks to top off the finished structure—and for step treads if you plan stairs. Large, heavy rocks make a good base; the more of these you use in the first course, the fewer you'll have to *lift* into position later.

• For walls less than 3 ft. high, a shallow trench

2 or 3 in. deep, leveled with sand, will provide enough footing in firm soil. Higher free-standing walls, terracing walls and retaining walls should be started at least 1 ft. below the surface, on a sand bed as shown. First-course rocks become a guide for the rest of the wall, so take care to align them with reasonable precision.

• Free-standing walls that climb a slope call for special foundation tricks. For proper strength and integrity, the courses of rock in the wall must run horizontally. Where the slope rises, the wall is stepped (see page 45), with base courses set into the hillside as shown. On gentle inclines, the cap rocks may follow the slope contour, but all the core rocks must be laid in the horizontal plane.

• Rough stone doesn't form the same kind of nice, even courses as brick or concrete block. Some rocks will be inches higher than others. So before you start the next course, select rocks to fill low spots and gaps. For this purpose, keep a pile of smaller pieces, slivers and wedge-shaped stones on hand. You'll need them in all succeeding courses to shim and chink the "wobblers." It is particularly important in dry-stone construction that each rock be seated firmly in position. One large, wobbly rock can make a whole section of wall come tumbling down.

• The construction of succeeding courses calls for a few simple rules. First, use a spirit level and mason's line to keep courses running true. Rough stonework tends to dip and rise sneakily. Make sure that the joints between rocks in one course are lapped by rocks in the next. Some flush joints are unavoidable, but in no case should they extend beyond two courses.

weak points

An extended vertical division, where rocks don't tie each other together, creates a weak point where the entire structure can separate and, eventually, tumble. A New England wall-builder credo states: "One over two; two over one." Actually, there's nothing wrong with one over three or four and vice versa. The main point is to ensure that most joints are lapped from course to course.

• Along the same lines, dry stonework less than 3 ft. wide requires "tie rocks" every 6 ft. along the wall's length, staggered in every third successive course (see page 43). These rocks span the width of the wall, tying the side faces together for transverse integrity. They are particularly important every second or third course at the ends of a freestanding wall.

• For appearance sake, the flattest edge of all

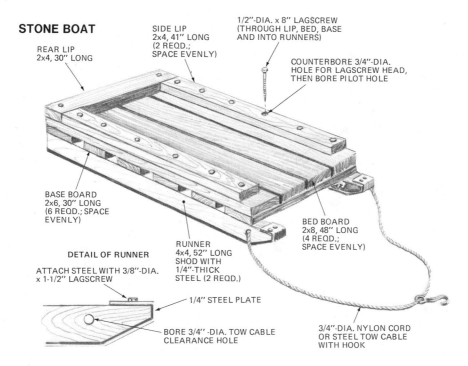

STONE BOAT

REAR LIP
2x4, 30" LONG

SIDE LIP
2x4, 41" LONG
(2 REQD.;
SPACE EVENLY)

1/2"-DIA. x 8" LAGSCREW
(THROUGH LIP, BED, BASE
AND INTO RUNNERS)

COUNTERBORE 3/4"-DIA.
HOLE FOR LAGSCREW HEAD,
THEN BORE PILOT HOLE

BASE BOARD
2x6, 30" LONG
(6 REQD.; SPACE
EVENLY)

BED BOARD
2x8, 48" LONG
(4 REQD.;
SPACE EVENLY)

DETAIL OF RUNNER

ATTACH STEEL WITH 3/8"-DIA.
x 1-1/2" LAGSCREW

RUNNER
4x4, 52" LONG
SHOD WITH
1/4"-THICK
STEEL (2 REQD.)

1/4" STEEL PLATE

BORE 3/4"-DIA. TOW CABLE
CLEARANCE HOLE

3/4"-DIA. NYLON CORD
OR STEEL TOW CABLE
WITH HOOK

rocks should be on the wall's face. Some roughness is inevitable, of course, and provides the characteristic appeal of dry-stone construction. But an "averaged out" alignment of the wall faces is important to the overall firmness and strength of the structure. Smaller rocks used along the face should be set level, by shimming if necessary, or they should slope slightly toward the center of the structure—not outward toward the face.

positioning wedge-shaped stones

For the same reason, any wedge-shaped shimming stones should be positioned with the thick edge toward the wall center so it is locked in. Outward-sloping rock surfaces eventually work loose due to freeze-and-thaw action. If they fall out, they weaken the structure and provide a starting point for disintegration.

• Terrace-wall steps should be built into the structure, rather than tacked on later. Pick the largest, flattest rocks for the top tread piece of each step. It should tie into the side walls of the stair slot at least 3 to 4 in. (see page 45).

Every rock in a stair section should be absolutely firm and immovable. If you hear the slightest click or grinding sound when you walk on the steps, there's movement. Continued traffic eventually will work the rocks loose and the stair will be rendered unsafe and useless.

• Wide, shallow steps, semicircular corner steps and other sophisticated landscaping techniques rarely feature single rocks for the whole tread,

since such steps are usually too large. For these applications, the pieces abutting the wall should still be part of the wall structure. Individual rocks making up the tread platforms should be thick, heavy slabs with a broad, flat surface. Small stones for chinking are hammered into the crevices between tread rocks to keep them from shifting position.

building a stile

• Free-standing walls once used as livestock enclosures on farms often had stiles (cantilevered steps), rather than stairs. Most animals can figure out how to manipulate conventional stairs. But steps created with rocks or timbers projecting from the sides of a wall are a little too complex for anything but a goat.

Such stiles can be an attractive adjunct to a long stretch of dry stone wall. They can be easily incorporated when the wall is being built (see page 45). Be careful to pick flat-surfaced rocks that are long enough to span the width of the wall and project beyond it about 1 ft. Laid into the structure, like tie rocks, these units must be buried under large, heavy rocks in the next course to prevent movement. If the person using the stile is heavier than the rocks holding the stile in place, the stepper is apt to raise the entire top section of the wall and bring it sliding down.

Despite all the foregoing tips and cautions, remember that the rough, uneven texture of a dry stone wall is the very thing that provides its beauty and character.

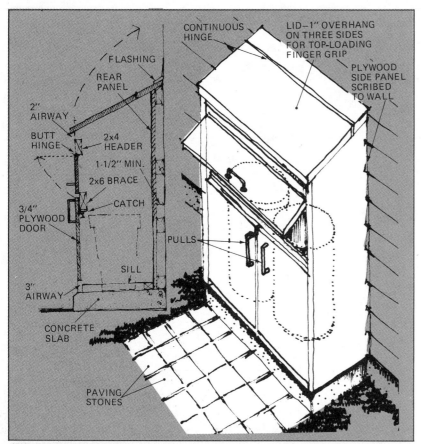

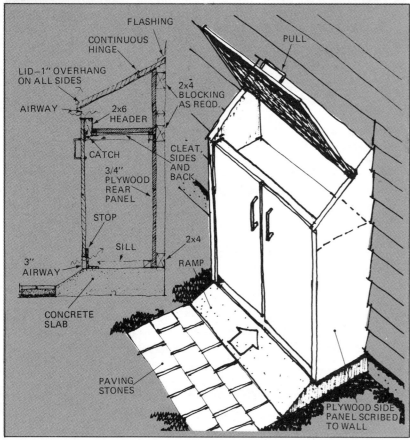

Little sheds

If your garage is already full and your back-yard is too precious for a yard building, get the storage you need with one of these sheds designed by Ira Grandberg, A.I.A.

TOOL STORAGE SHED

Accessibility is the most impressive feature of this shed. Miscellaneous small tools or the unwieldy garden hose can be stored in the upper bin, while heavy equipment can be rolled up the ramp and into the lower area.

Decide on the dimensions that will suit your storage needs. Then excavate for the concrete slab and footings. Remember that footings must be below the area frostline.

Notice that the ramp is part of the slab and is angled at about 25°. Construct the slab form of plywood and incorporate the ramp into the form. Secure forms with stakes and backfill soil outside between the stakes. This will provide added bracing for the form.

Before the concrete sets, bury the heads of three lagbolts (¼-in.-dia. x 5 in.) along the sides of the slab for securing the sill. Leave the threaded end of the bolt extending up about 2 in. Make sure it is plumb.

This shed does not have a frame. The doors are hinged directly to the side panels and the panels are attached to headers and to the sills which are bolted to the slab. The floor of the upper bin provides rigidity for the structure.

TRASH CAN HIDEAWAY

You may be enjoying your yard more than ever before, but you'll take even greater pride in the view if you can manage to hide away unsightly garbage cans.

This shed does the job without sacrificing accessibility to the cans. Regardless of the size of the cans you choose to keep in the shed, they can be easily removed through the doors below for trash disposal.

The upper doors allow for easy trash deposit, whether in large quantities (top door) or small scraps through the upper front door.

Pour a rectangular concrete slab, using plywood forms. Install the anchor bolts for the sill.

for your yard

The "lean-to" design allows for construction without a frame because the house wall provides structural support. Note that the shed dimensions must be based on the size of your trash cans.

It's important that you remember to leave clearance for easy removal of the cans through the bottom doors.

All of the sheds in this collection may be finished to match your house. Whether you use textured or smooth-surfaced plywood, you should make certain that the plywood you select is rated for outdoor use.

GARDEN SUPPLY SHED

Use the lower shelves for garden supplies and small tools, and the upper shelves for plants. The acrylic allows the sunshine in, but it protects plants from heavy frost. In the spring, you can make room in your hotbed for delicate garden plants by moving the hardier ones (pepper, cabbage, onion) into the cold frame at the top of this shed. Chrysanthemums and geraniums will continue to bloom in here long after autumn frosts have killed most other plants.

Remember that concrete footings must extend below the frostline in your area. Building suppliers carry a variety of ready-made concrete footing forms. Use ¼-in. or ⅜-in.-dia. lagscrews 2 ft. on center to secure the shed frame to the house frame. Screws should be long enough to penetrate the siding and studs.

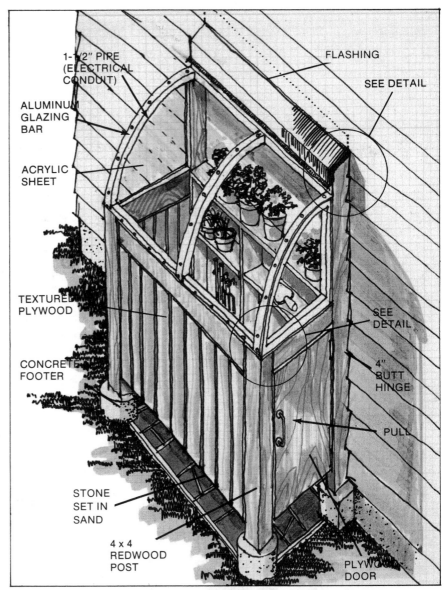

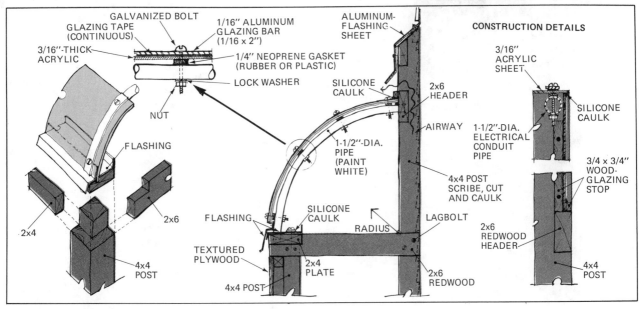

Enlarge and facelift your kitchen

**When you remodel your kitchen,
you can visually connect the new to the old with
shop-built cabinets that match**

By HARRY WICKS

■ AMERICAN HOMEOWNERS are staying put and improving what they already own. For some, home improvement may mean adding a bedroom in the attic or basement. For others, a new family room may be needed. For many, there is a need to create a bigger kitchen and possibly, an eat-in area in that room.

We enlarged the kitchen shown by knocking out a section of an exterior kitchen wall after relocating several appliances. We built new cabinets which matched the originals in the existing kitchen, thereby creating a smooth visual transition. And we covered the walls with rough-sawn

AN OLD TABLE, simply freshened with glossy-finish latex-alkyd paint, makes a totally new dining center.

planking and fitted the ceiling with false beams to achieve a country look.

The room's designer, Shirley Regendahl, ASID, also pulled the rooms together visually by using a careful combination of colors. For the colors used, see the list on page 54.

adding a room

Once you've decided upon the location and size of your addition, you must determine whether the wall to be removed is a bearing wall (one which supports the load imposed by the roof). If you lack the know-how to determine joist run and how a roof is supported, play it safe: Call in a professional engineer and follow his advice.

If it is a bearing wall, install a temporary wall, located about 1 ft. inside the house wall, to support the joists overhead during the tearing out and rebuilding. Use 2x4s for the plates and studs for the temporary wall, and drive shims beneath the bottom plate, if necessary, to assure the wall being wedged securely in place. The building codes and zoning laws in many communities require a permit before the building lines of a residence may be altered. So check with your local building department before you put a saw to the wall.

At this time, determine whether there are any water or heat pipes, or electrical wires in the wall. If there are, take every precaution to avoid damaging them during the rip-out operation. To be

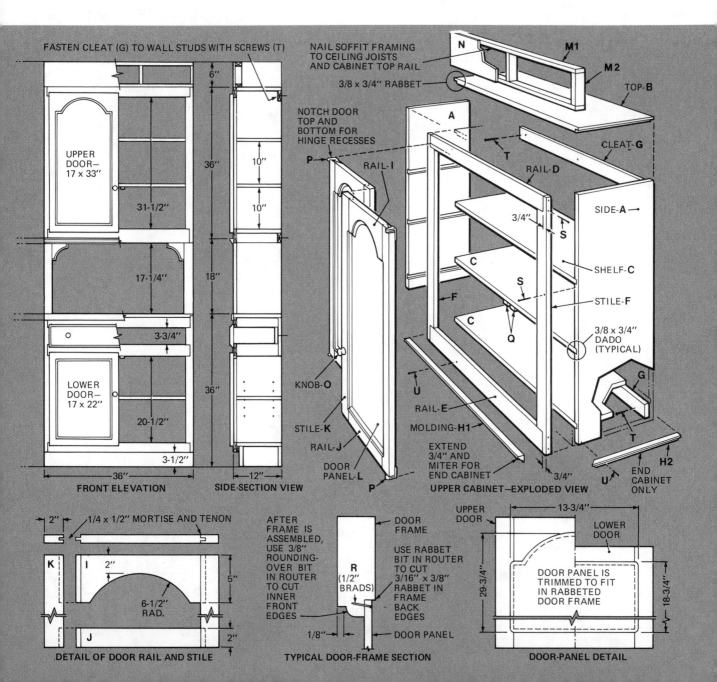

FASTEN CLEAT (G) TO WALL STUDS WITH SCREWS (T)

UPPER DOOR— 17 x 33"

LOWER DOOR— 17 x 22"

6"
36"
31-1/2"
17-1/4"
3-3/4"
36"
20-1/2"
3-1/2"
36"

FRONT ELEVATION

10"
10"
18"
12"

SIDE-SECTION VIEW

NAIL SOFFIT FRAMING TO CEILING JOISTS AND CABINET TOP RAIL

3/8 x 3/4" RABBET

NOTCH DOOR TOP AND BOTTOM FOR HINGE RECESSES

RAIL-I

KNOB-O

STILE-K

RAIL-J

DOOR PANEL-L

N   M1   M2   TOP-B

A

RAIL-D   CLEAT-G

T

SIDE-A

3/4"   S

SHELF-C

S   STILE-F

C

Q

3/8 x 3/4" DADO (TYPICAL)

G

F

U

RAIL-E

MOLDING-H1

EXTEND 3/4" AND MITER FOR END CABINET

3/4"   U

T

H2

END CABINET ONLY

UPPER CABINET—EXPLODED VIEW

2"   1/4 x 1/2" MORTISE AND TENON

K   I   2"

6-1/2" RAD.

J

5"

2"

DETAIL OF DOOR RAIL AND STILE

AFTER FRAME IS ASSEMBLED, USE 3/8" ROUNDING-OVER BIT IN ROUTER TO CUT INNER FRONT EDGES

1/8"

DOOR FRAME

R (1/2" BRADS)

USE RABBET BIT IN ROUTER TO CUT 3/16" x 3/8" RABBET IN FRAME BACK EDGES

DOOR PANEL

TYPICAL DOOR-FRAME SECTION

UPPER DOOR

13-3/4"

LOWER DOOR

29-3/4"

DOOR PANEL IS TRIMMED TO FIT IN RABBETED DOOR FRAME

18-3/4"

DOOR-PANEL DETAIL

safe, turn off water to water pipes, electricity to electric lines, and so on before starting.

Locate your opening and use a large-diameter bit in your drill to mark the upper corners of the cutout. Next, go outside and pinpoint the interior floor elevation on the outside wall, using the holes to guide you.

Your footings and block wall (or slab) must be installed before you make the wall cutout—but first you must know the floor elevation.

knocking out a wall

Remove the siding, then use your spirit level to mark the horizontal and vertical lines to be cut. Set your saw blade to cut to a depth of about ⅞ in. (standard siding thickness is ¾ in.) and make the cut. *Caution:* Only an experienced saw user should make this type of wall cutout with a portable circular. There is a great possibility of kick-back—especially when moving the saw overhead.

Take off the sheathing below, then remove the interior wall, in the same fashion. Finally, cut out the studs. Next, install the appropriate-size header and posts to support it. If it's not a bearing wall, you can use a pair of 2x6s, spiked together. If the wall carries weight from above, ask the local building department, or a professional engineer, to calculate the size header needed.

If you plan to build the addition yourself, you'd be wise to buy a good carpentry reference book. I recommend *Modern Carpentry*, by Willis H. Wagner, published by The Goodheart-

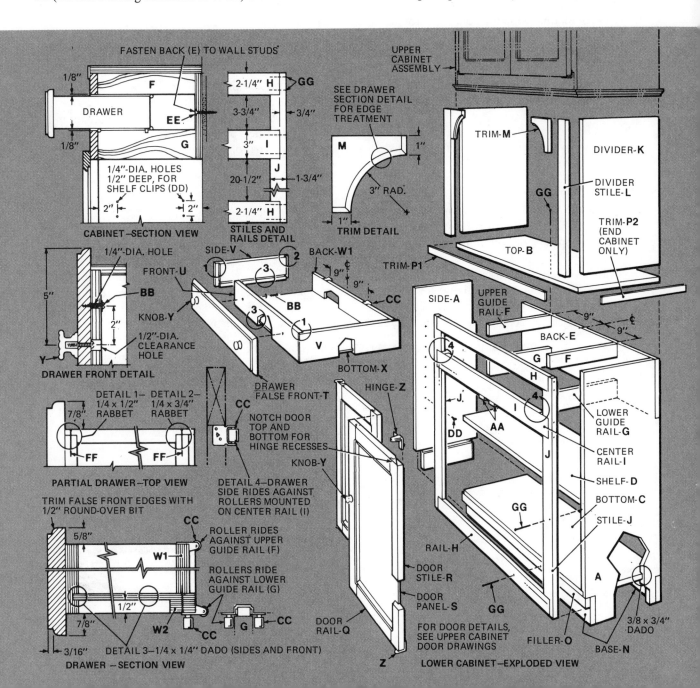

Willcox Co. Inc., South Holland, IL. It's available at bookstores, or write the publisher for availability and price.

making an add-on work

There's an important design consideration when planning a house addition—how it will look both outside and inside. The shape of the add-on, plus the materials used for siding, roof, windows and so on should blend perfectly with what is already there. New windows should match the old in style and should be installed at the same elevation as the existing ones.

Inside, it's important to create a finished room that feels as though it has always been there. Color is an effective device here: A careful selection of paints and wallpapers can make an add-on compatible with any connected room.

This kitchen's walls were skinned with rough-sawn planking—brand-new stock from the lumberyard—which was coated with paint to achieve a barn-board effect. (Using solid wood on the walls also makes it easier to hang the new wall cabinets.)

The beams overhead are false (hollow), installed over furring strips that are nailed to the joist undersides.

PM's cupboard

As can be seen in the drawings, the cupboard is built in base- and wall-cabinet modules. No exotic woodworking techniques are used here; the cabinets are built using the straightforward methods employed in many cabinet shops.

Use white glue throughout for all joinery. Since you're working with pine stiles and rails, you can secure joints with 6d and 8d finishing

nails. The nails should be set and hidden with wood filler. When nailing near a board end, pre-bore a head hole to avoid splitting the wood member.

We suggest you build the cabinets in your shop, then haul them to your new room for installation. Install the cabinets by securing them to wall cleats nailed to wall studs. Be absolutely certain that you build the cabinets in your run with a "scribe." A scribe is simply an over-wide outside stile. Thus, the stile that abuts the wall should be cut and installed on the cabinet so that it extends about 2 in. beyond the cabinet's side. This extra material can then be scribed to the wall, using a divider to ensure a perfect fit. If there's any gap between the end of the cabinet run and the wall, conceal it with a narrow molding.

painting the cabinets

Though it takes a little more time, it's better to paint the cabinets after they are up. This way, you can patch, sand and conceal any damage that may have occurred during their installation. To speed the job somewhat, however, apply the prime coat of paint while the cabinets are still in the shop.

Painting the two colors on the molding detail (bead shape on door fronts) takes both time and a steady hand.

These accent colors should be added after the cabinet has been painted and you have allowed ample time for it to dry.

To avoid wavy lines, use masking tape on both sides of the molding detail. Make certain that you press down the edge securely so the paint won't bleed underneath.

MATERIALS LIST—UPPER CABINET

Key	No.	Size and description (use)
A	2	¾ × 11¼ × 36⅜″ plywood (side)
B	1	¾ × 11¼ × 36″ plywood (top)
C	3	¾ × 11¼ × 35¼″ plywood (shelf)
D	1	¾ × 2¼ × 34½″ pine (rail)
E	1	¾ × 3 × 34½″ pine (rail)
F	2	¾ × 1¾ × 36¾″ pine (stile)
G	2	¾ × 2¼ × 34½″ pine (wall cleat)
H1	1	¾ × ⅞ × 36″ solid crown molding
H2	1	¾ × ⅞ × 12¾″ solid crown molding
I	2	¾ × 5 × 14″ pine (upper door rail)
J	2	¾ × 2 × 14″ pine (lower door rail)
K	4	¾ × 2 × 33″ pine (door stile)
L	2	¼ × 13¾ × 29¾″ plywood (door panel)
M1	2	¾ × 1½″, length to suit, furring strips (soffit plates)
M2	*	¾ × 1½″, length to suit, furring strips (soffit studs)
N	*	½″ drywall
O	2	1½″-dia. wooden knob
P	2 pr.	Vertical, stile-mounted pivot hinge for overlay door
Q	2	Magnetic catch
R	*	½″ brad
S	*	8d finishing nail
T	*	3″ No. 12 fh screw
U	*	2d finishing nail

*As required.

MATERIALS LIST—LOWER CABINET

Key	No.	Size and description (use)
A	2	¾ × 11¼ × 35¼″ plywood (side)
B	1	¾ × 12 × 36″ plywood (top)
C	1	¾ × 11¼ × 35¼″ plywood (bottom)
D	1	¾ × 11 × 34″ plywood (adjustable shelf)
E	1	¾ × 9 × 36″ plywood (rail)
F	2	¾ × 2¼ × 10½″ pine (upper guide rail)
G	2	¾ × 3 × 10½″ pine (lower guide rail)
H	2	¾ × 2¼ × 34½″ pine (face rail)
I	1	¾ × 3 × 34½″ pine (face rail)
J	2	¾ × 1¾ × 32½″ pine (stile)
K	2	¾ × 11¼ × 17¼″ plywood (divider)
L	2	¾ × 2 × 17¼″ pine (divider stile)
M	2	¾ × 4 × 4″ pine (trim)
N	2	¾ × 5 × 36″ pine (base)
O	1	¾ × 1½ × 36″ pine (filler)
P1	1	¼ × 1⅜ × 36″ pine lattice (trim)
P2	1	¼ × 1⅜ × 12¼″ pine lattice (trim)
Q	4	¾ × 2 × 14″ pine (door rail)
R	4	¾ × 2 × 22″ pine (door stile)
S	2	⅛ × 13¾ × 18¾″ plywood (door panel)
T	1	¾ × 5 × 24″ pine (drawer face)
U	1	½ × 3½ × 31¾″ plywood (drawer front)
V	2	½ × 3½ × 9¾″ plywood (drawer side)
W1	1	½ × 2¾ × 31¾″ plywood (drawer back)
W2	2	½ × 1 × 3″ pine (roller cleat)
X	1	¼ × 9½ × 31¾″ plywood (drawer bottom)
Y	4	1½″-dia. wooden knob
Z		Two pair of vertical, stile-mounted pivot hinges for overlay door
AA	2	Magnetic catch
BB	2	1″ No. 8 fh screw and washer
CC	2	Plastic roller set*
DD	4	Shelf support clip
EE	3	3″ No. 12 fh screw
FF	**	2d finishing nail
GG	**	8d finishing nail

*Roll-eez drawer rollers are available from Albert Constantine and Son Inc., 2050 Eastchester Rd., Bronx, N.Y. 10461
**As required.

KITCHEN COLORS

Floors: D4757 Bituminous
Walls in kitchen area: M3192 Coral Reef
Countertop in kitchen: M3427 Lunar Green
Cupboard shutters under sink cabinets: P2484 Vanilla Cream
Cabinet trim: M3192 Coral Reef and Lunar Green
Ceiling, planked walls: M3756 Mariner's Grey
Beams: P2185 Precious Peach
Table: Lunar Green
Chairs: Precious Peach
All paints are latex alkyd from Pittsburgh Paints' DesignaColor System.

Our mobile kitchen island rolls where you want it

■ KITCHEN ISLANDS have long been design favorites of people fortunate enough to have large kitchens. Such cabinets provide additional storage and counter space at the center of the room, while serving as an impromptu gathering area for socializing with family or house guests.

If you've always wanted more counter space in your kitchen, but you don't have room for an island, here's a fine solution: a kitchen island containing a bar unit which folds when not in use

THIS ATTRACTIVE roll-about kitchen island can be painted with colors customized to your home.

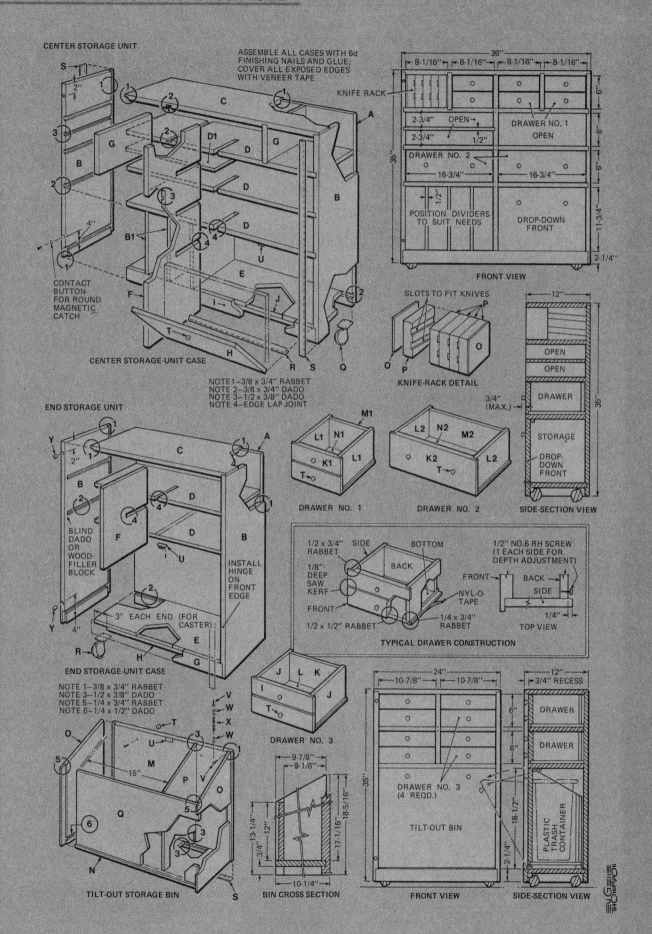

CENTER STORAGE UNIT

ASSEMBLE ALL CASES WITH 6d FINISHING NAILS AND GLUE; COVER ALL EXPOSED EDGES WITH VENEER TAPE

KNIFE RACK

CONTACT BUTTON FOR ROUND MAGNETIC CATCH

CENTER STORAGE-UNIT CASE

NOTE1—3/8 x 3/4" RABBET
NOTE 2—3/8 x 3/4" DADO
NOTE 3—1/2 x 3/8" DADO
NOTE 4—EDGE LAP JOINT

FRONT VIEW

36"
8-1/16" 8-1/16" 8-1/16" 8-1/16"
6"
2-3/4" OPEN
DRAWER NO. 1 OPEN
35"
2-3/4" 1/2"
6"
DRAWER NO. 2
16-3/4" 16-3/4"
6"
1/2"
POSITION DIVIDERS TO SUIT NEEDS
DROP-DOWN FRONT
11-3/4"
2-1/4"

SLOTS TO FIT KNIVES
KNIFE-RACK DETAIL

3/4" (MAX.)
12"
OPEN
OPEN
DRAWER
35"
STORAGE
DROP-DOWN FRONT
SIDE-SECTION VIEW

END STORAGE UNIT

BLIND DADO OR WOOD-FILLER BLOCK

INSTALL HINGE ON FRONT EDGE

3" EACH END (FOR CASTER)

END STORAGE-UNIT CASE

NOTE 1—3/8 x 3/4" RABBET
NOTE 3—1/2 x 3/8" DADO
NOTE 5—1/4 x 3/4" RABBET
NOTE 6—1/4 x 1/2" DADO

DRAWER NO. 1

DRAWER NO. 2

TYPICAL DRAWER CONSTRUCTION

1/2 x 3/4" SIDE RABBET
1/8"-DEEP SAW KERF
FRONT
1/2 x 1/2" RABBET
BOTTOM
BACK
NYL-O-TAPE
1/4 x 3/4" RABBET
1/2" NO.6 RH SCREW (1 EACH SIDE FOR DEPTH ADJUSTMENT)
FRONT BACK SIDE
1/4"
TOP VIEW

DRAWER NO. 3

TILT-OUT STORAGE BIN

BIN CROSS SECTION
9-7/8"
9-1/8"
13-1/4" 12"
18-5/16"
17-1/16"
3/4"
10-1/4"

FRONT VIEW
24"
10-7/8" 10-7/8"
6"
6"
35"
DRAWER NO. 3 (4 REQD.)
TILT-OUT BIN
18-1/2"
2-1/4"

SIDE-SECTION VIEW
12"
3/4" RECESS
DRAWER
DRAWER
PLASTIC TRASH CONTAINER

Now we've taken this good idea and made it better. With help from Armstrong World Industries designers, we have created a movable kitchen island that adapts quickly to suit work and decorating needs. Because all three cabinet sections are castermounted and connected with hinges, several different configurations, as well as room positions, are possible. The unit includes space for knives, flatware, paper and canned goods, plus a unique bar cabinet that lets you corral ice, glasses and spirits in one spot.

Complete plans and how-to-build instructions are presented on the following pages. Materials lists for all three units are provided on page 59. Study them carefully. You may be able to save yourself some expense if you purchase the wood for all three units at the same time. It's a good idea to have all parts and materials on hand before you begin construction of the island.

starting the job

Before cutting anything, study all of the drawings carefully. There is nothing terribly sophisticated about the woodworking techniques employed here, but there are many details that you must observe. The layout of all the dadoes, rabbets and half-lapped joints must be precise, otherwise, the cabinet could be assembled out of square. If that happens, it will never open and close properly.

It's best to use plywood that is good on both sides (A-A) for this project, because many of the parts are visible from both sides. If the additional cost of this grade is prohibitive, use stock that's good on one side only (A-D) and fill all surface voids on the poor side. Also, try to construct the cases so that the poorer (D) surfaces face down or in.

center storage unit

To build the center storage unit, cut the top, back, bottom, sides, shelves and dividers to size. Then lay out all the rabbets, dadoes and half-lapped joints shown in the drawing on page 56. Next, glue and nail together the sides, top and back, then install the bottom, toe kick (I) and support cleat (J). Check the cabinet for square.

If you've been careful cutting the parts to size—especially the back—the cabinet should be square and no adjustment will be necessary. However, if the case is slightly out of square, you must force (i.e., wrack) it until it's square and hold it that way with tacked-on braces until the glue dries. Leave the squared and braced cabinet clamped overnight.

tape sides of drawers

Preassemble the knife rack and drawers as shown, then insert them into the case. The self-sticking nylon tape on each side of the drawer bottom assures that the drawers will slide easily without drawer guides. (This nylon tape, called Nyl-O-Tape, is available from The Woodworkers' Store, 21801 Industrial Blvd., Rogers, MN 55374. It is approximately $\frac{1}{32}$ in. thick and is used on all the drawers in both the end and center storage units.) This tape also allows minor adjustments in the up and down position of the drawer, relative to the drawer opening. If your drawer is slightly out of square, place a double thickness of tape on the appropriate side.

The stop points of the drawers can also be adjusted. Simply turn the depth-adjustment screws on the back of each drawer until the drawer front is properly aligned in the closed position.

Cut the drop-down front panel to size and attach it to the top edge of the toe kick using a continuous hinge. Install the magnetic catch and contact plate for this door, then finish-sand the entire unit, ending up with 150-grit sandpaper. Remove the dust with a brush and tack cloth.

end storage unit

There is one major difference between the end storage unit and the center unit which can be seen on the side-section view on page 56: The drawers and the tilt-out bin on the end unit are recessed ¾ in. from the front edge of the cabinet case. This recess is needed to provide clearance for the drawer and bin pulls when the two units are closed together. Because of this, be sure to use pulls which project no more than ¾ in. from the drawer and bin fronts.

cut the dadoes

Also note the blind shelf dadoes on the case sides of this unit. Cut these with a dado head in your table saw or with a router using either of the following methods:
• Plow the dado all the way across the side and then glue in a small filler block.
• Stop the dado just short of the appropriate point and clean out the curved corners with a sharp chisel.

Install the shelves and divider and let the assembly dry overnight.

Before cutting the parts for the tilt-out bin, measure the case opening and make dimension adjustments if necessary. Test-fit the bin front with the hinge installed; when satisfied with fit, remove the front and assemble the entire bin with

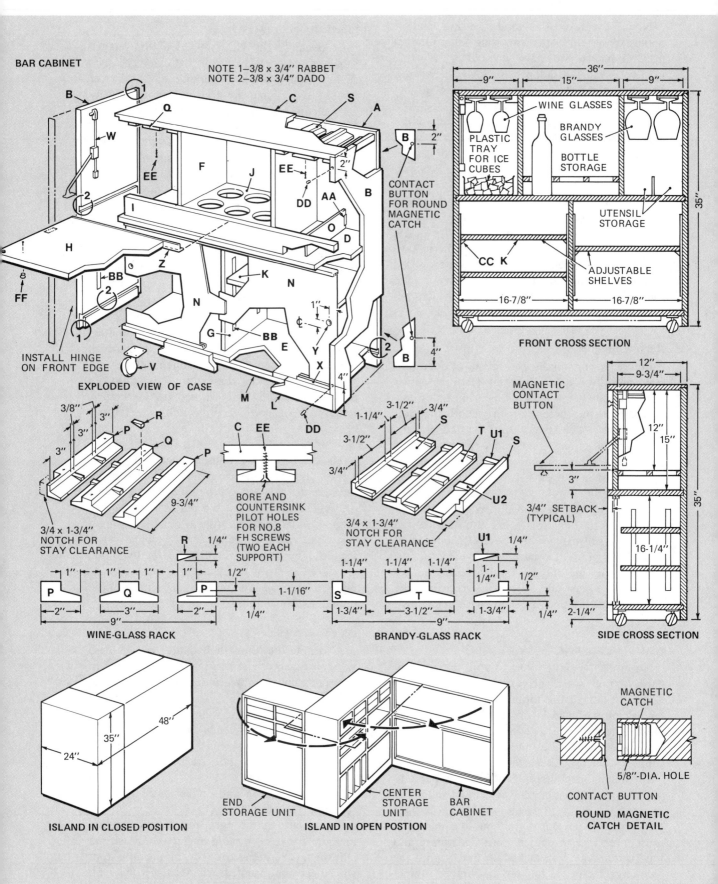

BAR CABINET

NOTE 1–3/8 x 3/4'' RABBET
NOTE 2–3/8 x 3/4'' DADO

CONTACT BUTTON FOR ROUND MAGNETIC CATCH

INSTALL HINGE ON FRONT EDGE

EXPLODED VIEW OF CASE

FRONT CROSS SECTION

WINE GLASSES
BRANDY GLASSES
BOTTLE STORAGE
PLASTIC TRAY FOR ICE CUBES
UTENSIL STORAGE
ADJUSTABLE SHELVES

3/4 x 1-3/4'' NOTCH FOR STAY CLEARANCE

BORE AND COUNTERSINK PILOT HOLES FOR NO.8 FH SCREWS (TWO EACH SUPPORT)

3/4 x 1-3/4'' NOTCH FOR STAY CLEARANCE

MAGNETIC CONTACT BUTTON

3/4'' SETBACK (TYPICAL)

WINE-GLASS RACK

BRANDY-GLASS RACK

SIDE CROSS SECTION

ISLAND IN CLOSED POSITION

END STORAGE UNIT
CENTER STORAGE UNIT
BAR CABINET

ISLAND IN OPEN POSTION

MAGNETIC CATCH
5/8''-DIA. HOLE
CONTACT BUTTON

ROUND MAGNETIC CATCH DETAIL

MATERIALS LIST—BAR CABINET UNIT

Key	No.	Size and description (use)
A	1	3/4 × 34 5/8 × 35 1/4″ plywood (back)
B	2	3/4 × 12 × 34 5/8″ plywood (side)
C	1	3/4 × 12 × 36″ plywood (top)
D	1	3/4 × 11 5/8 × 35 1/4″ plywood (shelf)
E	1	3/4 × 10 7/8 × 35 1/4″ plywood (bottom)
F	2	3/4 × 9 3/4 × 15″ plywood (top divider)
G	1	3/4 × 9 1/2 × 16 1/4″ plywood (bottom divider)
H	1	3/4 × 11 13/16 × 34 3/8″ plywood (door)
I	1	3/4 × 3 × 34 1/2″ plywood (rail)
J	1	3/4 × 9 3/4 × 15″ plywood (bottle shelf)
K	3	3/4 × 9 1/2 × 16 3/8″ plywood (adjustable shelf)
L	1	3/4 × 2 1/4 × 35 1/4″ plywood (toe kick)
M	1	3/4 × 3/4 × 30″ pine (cleat)
N	2	1/4 × 15 13/16 × 17 3/4″ plywood (sliding door)
O	1	1/4 × 3 × 9 5/8″ plywood (divider)
P	2	1 1/16 × 2 × 9 3/4″ pine (end support)
Q	1	1 1/16 × 3 × 9 3/4″ pine (center support)
R	8	1/4 × 3/8 × 1″ pine lattice (glass divider)
S	2	1 1/16 × 1 3/4 × 9 3/4″ pine (end support)
T	1	1 1/16 × 3 1/2 × 9 3/4″ pine (center support)
U1	8	1/4 × 3/4 × 1 1/4″ pine lattice (glass divider)
U2	4	1/4 × 1 1/4 × 1 1/4″ pine lattice (glass divider)
V*	4	Shepherd 2 1/2″ flat plate ball caster No. 9360
W**	2	Constantine No. 55F14 flap stay
X	1	Plastic track for overlapping 1/4″ doors
Y	2	1″-dia. finger pull
Z	1	1 1/2 × 34 1/4″ continuous hinge
AA**	2	Constantine No. 211S26 zip clip
BB	8	12″ shelf standard
CC	12	Shelf clips
DD**	2	Constantine No. 55F25 round magnetic catch
EE	12	1 1/2″ No. 8 fh screws
FF	2	3/4″-dia. × 3/4″-long porcelain knob

Misc.: 6d finishing nails, glue, veneer tape.
*Shepherd Products U.S. Inc., 203 Kerth St., St. Joseph, Mich. 49022
**Constantine, 2050 Eastchester Rd., Bronx, N.Y. 10461

MATERIALS LIST—CENTER UNIT

Key	No.	Size and description (use)
A	1	3/4 × 34 5/8 × 35 1/4″ plywood (back)
B	2	3/4 × 12 × 34 5/8″ plywood (side)
B1	3	1/2 × 11 1/4 × 11 3/4″ plywood (divider)
C	1	3/4 × 12 × 36″ plywood (top)
D	3	3/4 × 11 1/4 × 35 1/4″ plywood (shelf)
D1	1	1/2 × 11 1/4 × 17 5/8″ plywood (shelf)
E	1	3/4 × 10 7/8 × 35 1/4″ plywood (bottom)
F	1	3/4 × 11 1/4 × 32″ plywood (divider)
G	2	3/4 × 6 3/4 × 11 1/4″ plywood (divider)
H	1	3/4 × 11 9/16 × 16 3/4″ plywood (door)
I	1	3/4 × 2 1/4 × 35 1/4″ plywood (toe kick)
J	1	3/4 × 3/4 × 30″ pine (cleat)
		DRAWER No. 1
K1	3	3/4 × 5 7/8 × 7 15/16″ plywood (front)
L1	6	1/2 × 5 5/8 × 10 3/4″ plywood (side)
M1	3	1/2 × 5 3/8 × 6 7/16″ plywood (back)
N1	3	1/2 × 7 15/16 × 10 3/4″ plywood (bottom)
		DRAWER No. 2
K2	2	3/4 × 5 7/8 × 16 3/4″ plywood (front)
L2	4	1/2 × 5 5/8 × 10 3/4″ plywood (side)
M2	2	1/2 × 5 3/8 × 15 1/4″ plywood (back)
N2	2	1/2 × 10 3/4 × 16 3/4″ plywood (bottom)
		KNIFE RACK
O	2	1/4 × 6 × 7 1/4″ pine (filler block)
P	5	1 1/2 × 6 × 7 1/4″ fir (notched block)
		HARDWARE
Q*	4	Shepherd 2 1/2″ flat plate ball caster No. 9360
R	1	1 1/2 × 16 5/8″ continuous hinge
S	2	1 1/2 × 35″ continuous hinge
T	12	3/4″-dia. × 3/4″-long porcelain knob
U	1	Magnetic catch with strike

Misc.: 6d finishing nails, glue, veneer tape.
*Shepherd Products U.S. Inc., 203 Kerth St., St. Joseph, Mich. 49022.

MATERIALS LIST—END STORAGE UNIT

Key	No.	Size and description (use)
A	1	3/4 × 23 1/4 × 34 5/8″ plywood (back)
B	2	3/4 × 12 × 34 5/8″ plywood (side)
C	1	3/4 × 12 × 24″ plywood (top)
D	2	3/4 × 10 1/2 × 23 1/4″ plywood (shelf)
E	1	3/4 × 10 7/8 × 23 1/4″ plywood (bottom)
F	1	3/4 × 10 1/2 × 12 3/4″ plywood (divider)
G	1	3/4 × 2 1/4 × 23 1/4″ plywood (toe kick)
H	1	3/4 × 3/4 × 18″ pine (cleat)
		DRAWER No. 3
I	4	3/4 × 5 7/8 × 10 3/4″ plywood (front)
J	8	1/2 × 5 5/8 × 10″ plywood (side)
K	4	1/2 × 5 3/8 × 9 1/4″ plywood (back)
L	4	1/2 × 10 × 10 3/4″ plywood (bottom)
		TILT-OUT BIN
M	1	3/4 × 18 5/16 × 22 3/8″ plywood (front)
N	1	1/2 × 9 7/8 × 21 3/8″ plywood (bottom)
O	2	1/2 × 9 7/8 × 18 5/16″ plywood (side)
P	1	1/2 × 9 1/8 × 17 1/16″ plywood (divider)
Q	1	1/2 × 12 × 21 3/8″ plywood (back)
		HARDWARE
R*	4	Shepherd 2 1/2″ flat plate ball caster No. 9360
S	1	1 1/2 × 22 1/4″ continuous hinge
T	10	3/4″-dia. × 3/4″-long porcelain knob
U	1	Magnetic catch with strike
V	2	Screw eye
W	2	S-hook
X		12″ chain (cut to length)
Y**	2	Constantine No. 55F25 round magnetic catch

Misc.: 6d finishing nails, glue, veneer tape.
*Shepherd Products U.S. Inc., 203 Kerth St., St. Joseph, Mich. 49022.
**Constantine, 2050 Eastchester Rd., Bronx, N.Y. 10461

glue and nails. Let the assembly dry overnight.

Install the magnetic catch and contact plate. Then assemble and install the drawers as described earlier. Attach the restraining-chain assembly and finish-sand the whole unit.

bar cabinet

Assemble the bar cabinet in the same manner as the other units and attach the shelf standards (BB) to the sides and the lower compartment divider. Next, install the upper dividers and the bottle storage rack, and fabricate and install the two glass racks as shown in the drawing on page 58. The wedge-shaped cleats on these racks were designed to prevent the glasses from hitting each other when the island is opened, closed or being rolled around the room.

complete the assembly

Install the plywood rail (I) and the utensil divider, then cut the drop-down door to size and attach it with a continuous hinge. Add both stays (W) for this door and the magnetic catch plates. Then install the sliding-door tracks and doors for the lower compartment; bore the holes for the finger pulls. Don't install the pulls yet; wait until after the case has been painted. Apply the veneer tape to the exposed edges, finish-sand the entire unit, then dust and wipe with a tack cloth.

paint and hardware

Before priming and painting the cases, position and bore the holes for the four round magnetic catches as shown. These serve to hold the three units together in the closed position. Remove the catches and their corresponding contact buttons and reinstall them after you've finished the painting.

Temporarily install the continuous hinges that join the cabinet units to make certain the units fit as they should. At this time, you should also install the casters to check the unit for roll.

When you're satisfied that all the carpentry is satisfactory, remove the cabinet-joining hinges and cover the casters with masking tape, then paint.

After the paint dries, the units can be reassembled with the continuous hinges and the protective tape can be removed from the casters.

Double-deck porch adds two party rooms

The upper deck is great for sunbathing and entertaining guests. Lighting lets you enjoy this area on warm evenings. You can use the lower porch night and day, in any season

■ THE PM DOUBLE-DECK porch extends the living space on both floors of this home. With sliding doors of the first-floor porch open, the adjoining living room doubles in size. The second-floor master bedroom has a panoramic view through the doors of its adjoining upper deck.

Several considerations were included in designing the two-level space: First, the structure had to blend with the American colonial house—the home of artist Ed Valigursky. Second, we wanted to employ the newest construction materials and design ideas. Third, we wanted to join the deck and porch with a stairway fitting the de-

UPPER-LEVEL sundeck (above) is a delightful vantage point for surveying the scenery while sunning, having lunch or entertaining guests. For evening entertaining, you might prefer moving downstairs to the screened-in room (left). It has an open, airy feeling, yet it's near the kitchen and living room. The room has window panels that seal it for use during cold weather.

GALVANIZED spiral stairway (far left) joins the two levels for convenient back-and-forth traffic. Outdoor lights (near left) make this double-deck porch an ideal spot to invite your friends for nighttime parties.

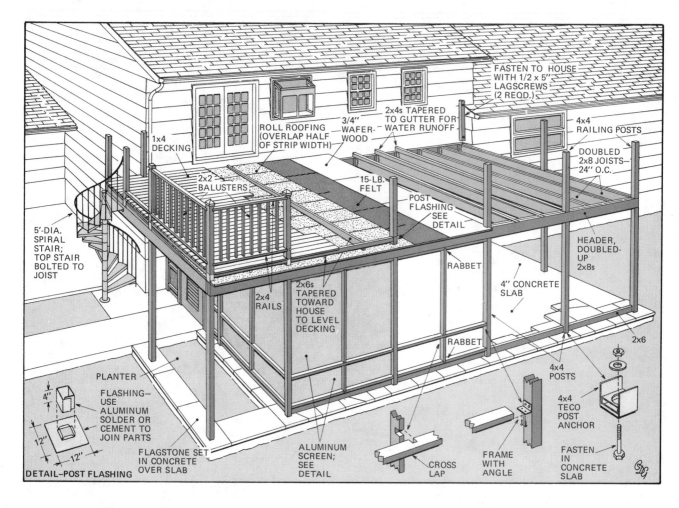

FASTEN TO HOUSE WITH 1/2 x 5" LAGSCREWS (2 REQD.)

4x4 RAILING POSTS

DOUBLED 2x8 JOISTS— 24" O.C.

2x4s TAPERED TO GUTTER FOR WATER RUNOFF

ROLL ROOFING (OVERLAP HALF OF STRIP WIDTH)

3/4" WAFER-WOOD

1x4 DECKING

2x2 BALUSTERS

POST FLASHING SEE DETAIL

15-LB. FELT

HEADER, DOUBLED-UP 2x8s

RABBET

4" CONCRETE SLAB

5'-DIA. SPIRAL STAIR; TOP STAIR BOLTED TO JOIST

2x4 RAILS

2x6s TAPERED TOWARD HOUSE TO LEVEL DECKING

RABBET

2x6

4x4 POSTS

PLANTER

FLASHING— USE ALUMINUM SOLDER OR CEMENT TO JOIN PARTS

4"

12"

12"

DETAIL—POST FLASHING

FLAGSTONE SET IN CONCRETE OVER SLAB

ALUMINUM SCREEN; SEE DETAIL

CROSS LAP

FRAME WITH ANGLE

4x4 TECO POST ANCHOR

FASTEN IN CONCRETE SLAB

sign scheme. Fourth, the porch had to be as open as possible for summer enjoyment, yet enclosed for cold-weather use. Fifth, the porch/deck needed a lighting system.

To maintain the colonial feeling, we gave the deck an open look with railings made of simple 2x2 balusters between posts. Hinged French doors with grille inserts give a multipaned colonial look. Several relatively new design features and materials include: a window greenhouse, decay-resistant, pressure-treated Wolmanized wood, metal construction connectors for strong

SUPPORT POSTS and joists are the only framing members installed in this view. Note the temporary diagonal bracing on the posts at this stage.

FRAMING OF the lower porch is complete in this view. The railing posts on the upper deck are in place and the roll roofing has been installed.

THE DETAIL (far left) shows two upper rails joining a capped post. Detail (near left) shows metal post-and-beam tie. Note corner of joist hanger (top left in photo).

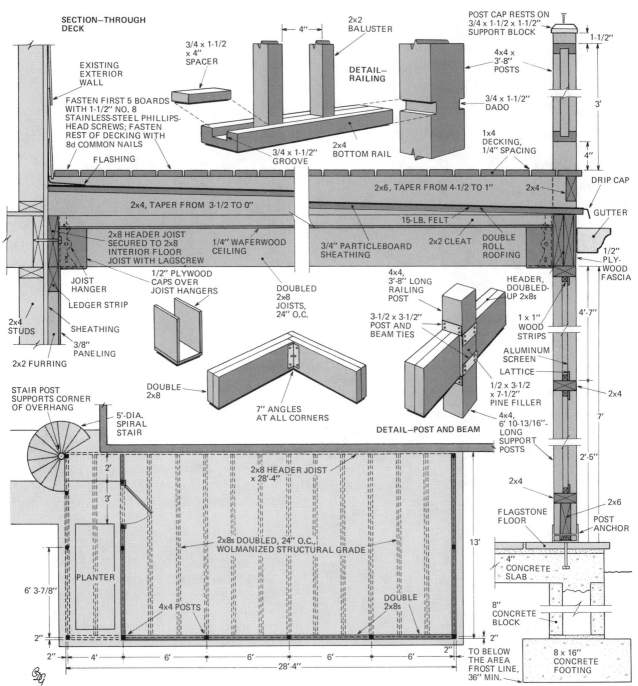

SECTION—THROUGH DECK

EXISTING EXTERIOR WALL

FASTEN FIRST 5 BOARDS WITH 1-1/2" NO. 8 STAINLESS-STEEL PHILLIPS-HEAD SCREWS; FASTEN REST OF DECKING WITH 8d COMMON NAILS

FLASHING

2x4, TAPER FROM 3-1/2 TO 0"

2x8 HEADER JOIST SECURED TO 2x8 INTERIOR FLOOR JOIST WITH LAGSCREW

1/4" WAFERWOOD CEILING

JOIST HANGER

LEDGER STRIP

2x4 STUDS

SHEATHING

3/8" PANELING

2x2 FURRING

1/2" PLYWOOD CAPS OVER JOIST HANGERS

DOUBLED 2x8 JOISTS, 24" O.C.

DOUBLE 2x8

3/4 x 1-1/2 x 4" SPACER

3/4 x 1-1/2" GROOVE

2x2 BALUSTER

4"

DETAIL—RAILING

2x4 BOTTOM RAIL

3/4 x 1-1/2" DADO

3/4 particleboard SHEATHING

2x6, TAPER FROM 4-1/2 TO 1"

15-LB. FELT

2x2 CLEAT

DOUBLE ROLL ROOFING

4x4, 3'-8" LONG RAILING POST

3-1/2 x 3-1/2" POST AND BEAM TIES

7" ANGLES AT ALL CORNERS

DETAIL—POST AND BEAM

POST CAP RESTS ON 3/4 x 1-1/2 x 1-1/2" SUPPORT BLOCK

1-1/2"

4x4 x 3'-8" POSTS

3'

4"

1x4 DECKING, 1/4" SPACING

2x4

DRIP CAP

GUTTER

1/2" PLYWOOD FASCIA

HEADER, DOUBLED-UP 2x8s

1 x 1" WOOD STRIPS

4'-7"

ALUMINUM SCREEN

LATTICE

1/2 x 3-1/2 x 7-1/2" PINE FILLER

4x4, 6' 10-13/16" LONG SUPPORT POSTS

2x4

7'

2'-5"

STAIR POST SUPPORTS CORNER OF OVERHANG

5'-DIA. SPIRAL STAIR

2'

3'

PLANTER

6' 3-7/8"

2"

4x4 POSTS

2x8 HEADER JOIST x 28'-4"

2x8s DOUBLED, 24" O.C., WOLMANIZED STRUCTURAL GRADE

DOUBLE 2x8s

13'

2x4

2x6

FLAGSTONE FLOOR

POST ANCHOR

4" CONCRETE SLAB

8" CONCRETE BLOCK

2"

TO BELOW THE AREA FROST LINE, 36" MIN.

8 x 16" CONCRETE FOOTING

2"   4'   6'   6'   6'   6'   2"

28'-4"

PLAN VIEW—PORCH AND DECK FRAMING

SECTION—POST AND FOOTING

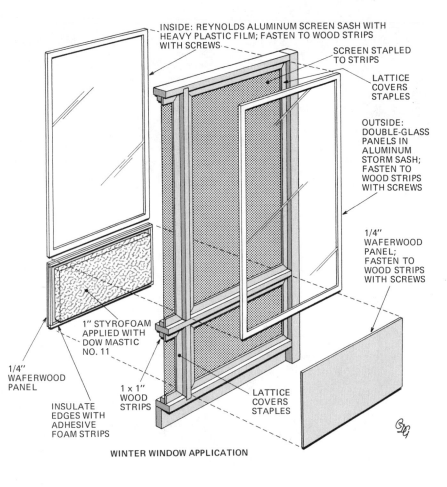

INSIDE: REYNOLDS ALUMINUM SCREEN SASH WITH HEAVY PLASTIC FILM; FASTEN TO WOOD STRIPS WITH SCREWS

SCREEN STAPLED TO STRIPS

LATTICE COVERS STAPLES

OUTSIDE: DOUBLE-GLASS PANELS IN ALUMINUM STORM SASH; FASTEN TO WOOD STRIPS WITH SCREWS

1/4" WAFERWOOD PANEL; FASTEN TO WOOD STRIPS WITH SCREWS

1" STYROFOAM APPLIED WITH DOW MASTIC NO. 11

1/4" WAFERWOOD PANEL

INSULATE EDGES WITH ADHESIVE FOAM STRIPS

1 x 1" WOOD STRIPS

LATTICE COVERS STAPLES

WINTER WINDOW APPLICATION

WINTERIZING porch includes fastening particleboard over lower windows. Panel is secured with screws through each edge of panel into a wood strip.

SLIDING PATIO DOOR leads to living room. Stationary window (center) lets light in. "Winter windows" and space heater prepare porch for cold weather.

joints; roof sheathing and finished ceiling panels of Waferwood particleboard. To join the two spaces, one side of the deck overhangs the porch and neatly accommodates a spiral stairway.

For minimal obstruction to the view, the enclosed porch has a series of windows—the space between each pair of posts is framed into two larger windows on top and two smaller windows directly below; yet permanent screens ensure protection from insects. For cooler times, storm windows made in the shop using bronze-finished aluminum sash are applied over the upper porch windows and fastened in place with screws. Screened openings at the floor are covered from the outside with particleboard panels. During the coldest weather, interior storm windows of PVC film in aluminum sash are applied to the upper windows; interior particleboard panels backed with polystyrene insulation cover the lower openings. A portable kerosene heater warms occupants.

Our night lighting system includes mushroom lights for the walkways and a spotlight on the deck.

The concrete slab and flagstone floor on top were already in place. If you must begin by pouring footings and a concrete slab, any good reference book on concrete should provide the necessary information to do this job correctly.

locating the header joist

Lay out the header joist along the house wall. If you have access to the deck from the second level, position the header joist so the finished decking will be 2 to 3 in. below the sill of the doorway to the house. In this case, the center of the joist should be about 12 to 13 in. below the proposed sill to allow for decking, tapered boards and roofing materials. Make sure the header joist is level by snapping a level chalkline along the house where the top of the header joist will be.

Strip away siding or shingles so the header can be installed flush against the sheathing and re-snap the level chalkline on the sheathing. Also remove siding to attach the two adjacent posts to the house studs with 6-in. lagscrews. Resnap the vertical chalklines; use a spirit level to ensure that the lines are plumb and level. Run a bead of caulk along the chalkline. Lagscrew header to second-floor joist header. Apply aluminum flashing over the sheathing and lap it on the header.

At each post location, bore an oversize hole through the flagstone into the concrete for a bolt to secure the post anchor bracket. Secure the bolt with patching cement. Slip the bracket over the bolt and secure it with a washer and nut. Set the post in the anchor. Secure the post with nails through predrilled holes on the bracket. Brace posts with two diagonal 2x4s until framing is done.

Lay out locations of the rail-post fasteners on the header joists. Install the joist hanger hardware. Then measure, cut and fasten joists to posts with metal post-and-beam connections. You must use a ½-in. pine filler between posts with the connector (see detail on page 63).

putting in the stairway

The spiral stair post supports a corner of the deck overhang. Erect the stairway at this point and fasten it in place. We bolted the top step to the joist.

Next, cut posts for the deck railing to size. Cut dadoes for top and bottom rails; install posts in metal connectors already placed.

To finish the ceiling, we nailed 2x2 cleats near the top of the joists; then fastened ¼-in. particleboard panels to the cleats.

After framing porch windows, we nailed 1x1-in. strips around each frame and used heavy-duty, galvanized staples to fasten screening permanently to the strips. Lattice strips cover the staples.

For proper drainage of the deck level, we attached 2x4s cut on a skew (to direct water to the rain gutter) to the joists. Over this we fastened ¾-in. particleboard sheathing with panels staggered to avoid any long seams.

Then we applied 15-lb. roofing felt (tarpaper) parallel to the house wall. Each layer should overlap the preceding one 12 in., starting at the lower edge. Next, we installed 30-lb. mineral roll roofing, sealing it with asphalt cement. Each strip laps the upper half of the previous strip to get a double thickness over the deck.

The next step is to flash the railing posts (see post flashing detail, page 62). Solder the two-part aluminum flashing together or join in with plastic cement.

leveling the surface

To level the deck surface, we positioned 2x6s tapering toward the house. Space the 2x6s 24 in. on centers; temporarily tack some 1x4 decking on top of them to hold position. When they are set, begin to nail decking at the railing; work toward the house, staggering the joints.

To avoid splitting, prebore 1x4 decking for fasteners, especially near edges. Trim board ends after nailing deck to ensure a straight line.

The deck railing has 2x4 top and bottom rails between posts with 2x2 balusters 4 in. apart. Using a circular saw, cut baluster grooves centered the length of each rail (see railing detail, page 63). Cut balusters to length, test-fit and assemble rails and balusters with resorcinol glue and 6d galvanized nails. Install 4-in. spacers between balusters on the bottom rail to fill the groove, then the railing sections between posts, and finally the post-cap support blocks and caps.

We wanted to stain the lumber a rich brown, but we have to wait six months to let salts leach out.

In the meantime, you can work on the window treatments (see winter window application drawing on facing page). An indoor-outdoor porch like ours is sure to increase your enjoyment of the outdoors and encourage you to entertain.

Three easy home improvements

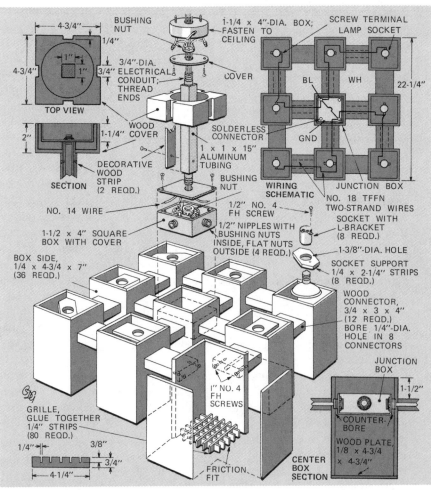

Labels in diagram:
4-3/4"
BUSHING NUT
1/4"
1-1/4 x 4"-DIA. BOX; FASTEN TO CEILING
SCREW TERMINAL LAMP SOCKET
4-3/4"
1"
1"
3/4"-DIA. ELECTRICAL CONDUIT; THREAD ENDS
3/4"
COVER
BL   WH
22-1/4"
TOP VIEW
WOOD COVER
SOLDERLESS CONNECTOR
GND
2"
1-1/4"
1 x 1 x 15" ALUMINUM TUBING
SECTION
DECORATIVE WOOD STRIP (2 REQD.)
BUSHING NUT
WIRING SCHEMATIC
JUNCTION BOX
NO. 18 TFFN TWO-STRAND WIRES
NO. 14 WIRE
1/2" NO. 4 FH SCREW
SOCKET WITH L-BRACKET (8 REQD.)
1-1/2 x 4" SQUARE BOX WITH COVER
1/2" NIPPLES WITH BUSHING NUTS INSIDE, FLAT NUTS OUTSIDE (4 REQD.)
1-3/8"-DIA. HOLE
BOX SIDE, 1/4 x 4-3/4 x 7" (36 REQD.)
SOCKET SUPPORT 1/4 x 2-1/4" STRIPS (8 REQD.)
WOOD CONNECTOR, 3/4 x 3 x 4" (12 REQD.) BORE 1/4"-DIA. HOLE IN 8 CONNECTORS
JUNCTION BOX
1-1/2"
1" NO. 4 FH SCREWS
COUNTER-BORE
GRILLE, GLUE TOGETHER 1/4" STRIPS (80 REQD.)
WOOD PLATE, 1/8 x 4-3/4 x 4-3/4"
1/4"   3/8"   3/4"
4-1/4"
FRICTION FIT
CENTER BOX SECTION

1 CONTEMPORARY LIGHT FIXTURE

■ THIS TEAK FIXTURE consists of eight light boxes surrounding a ninth box which holds an electrical junction box. Holes bored in wood connectors contain the wiring.

The wood parts consist of: nine wood boxes; 12 wood connectors with ¼-in.-dia. holes through eight of them; eight socket supports, each with a center hole for a lamp socket such as Leviton's No. 005-3152-F porcelain L-bracket socket. The egg-crate grilles are strips of wood, slot-joined and glued together, then friction-fitted in place. A decorative wood cover at the ceiling encloses the upper electrical box; use a router to make the hole for the box. This cover is held at the ceiling by two decorative wood strips attached to Reynolds do-it-yourself aluminum tubing with screws.

Lay out box parts and wood connectors. Prebore screw holes in 12 connectors, ½-in. on center (o.c.) from each side, centered top to bottom; prebore screw holes in the box sides, 1⅜-in. o.c. from each side, and 1⅛-in. o.c. from top.

Next, glue the box parts together, except for

the center wood box. For strong joints, glue box sides around a wood form shielded with wax paper, consisting of two wood blocks whose dimensions equal the inside dimensions of the light boxes. Clamp the assembly with web clamp or rope.

Before assembling the wood box at center around the junction box, counterbore for the nipples and nuts; also bore and attach the four wood-block connectors that adjoin this box with glue and screws. Install the junction box; glue and clamp the wood sides with a web clamp around the junction box area. Glue the bottom plate. (Note: For extra strength, double these four connectors.)

Join the four light boxes to the connectors already attached to the center box, using a stubby screwdriver. Attach remaining connectors and corner boxes.

Install each socket support ½ in. down from the top of each box with glue and brads. Install the sockets. Then wire the fixture with No. 18, two-strand TFFN (Thermoplastic Fixture Flexible Nylon) wire from the junction box (see schematic). At the junction box, join fixture wire to No. 14 wire and secure with solderless connectors; fasten ground wire to its screw.

Bore a center hole in the junction box cover. Secure the conduit to the box cover with a bushing nut. Run No. 14 wire through this conduit, then screw the cover to the junction box. Bore

VINYL-TAPE GRAPHIC adds visual impact to this bedroom. Tape comes sandwiched between paper. Remove the paper from the adhesive side, press tape to wall and peel off the top paper as shown above.

screw holes for the teak-strip attaching screws in the aluminum tubing and get some assistance to install the whole fixture. First slip the aluminum tubing over the conduit, then the wood cover over the tubing. Attach conduit to the upper electrical box cover with a bushing nut and connect wires with solderless connectors. Then screw the box cover to the box. Slip the wood cover in place and secure the supporting wood strips. Install low-wattage lamps and grilles.

2 TAPE WALL GRAPHIC

■ AN EASY, inexpensive way to perk up a room is with tape stripes—the same type used on vans and four-wheel-drive vehicles. Automotive paint stores often stock these bright, multicolored stripes.

The graphic in this attic bedroom was made with a 50-ft. roll of a 10-in. wide, tricolor stripe called ProStripe Maxiroll. Installation took an hour.

The tape is double-backed. Peel away the paper protecting the adhesive side, lay the stripe

in place, and rub the outer protective paper with a supplied nylon squeegee. The tape successfully covers textured walls. Angled bends other than 90° present a problem. However, if they're only slightly more or less, you *can* lap pieces of tape.

For information on ProStripe, write: Spartan Plastics Inc., Box 67-PM, Holt, MI 48842.

3 POT-AND-PAN RACK

■ THIS POT-AND-PAN rack is made of fir. Round the top corners of the 2x4 with a block plane and sandpaper. Locate the wall studs (probably 16 in. on center) and secure the 5-ft. spacer (2x2) to three studs, countersinking the screws. Space the screws, attaching the 2x4 to the spacer evenly. Countersink the screws and plug the holes with dowels. Stain the rack; finish with semigloss polyurethane.

You can make the rail hooks of ⅜-in.-dia. Reynolds do-it-yourself aluminum rod. Cut a 12-in. length and mark bends (see drawing). Make a rod holder of two pieces of ¾x¾x3-in. hardwood, clamped into a ¾x1½x3 in. block. Bore a ⅜-in.-dia. hole centered on mating surfaces of blocks through shortest dimension. Then secure blocks between vise jaws. Insert the rod with the 2¼-in. section centered. Tighten the jaws *firmly*. Slip an 8-in. length of ½-in.-dia. iron pipe over the rod until the pipe end aligns at the first bend mark; lift up on the pipe to bend. Then make the second bend. Use the bending jig shown in the drawing to make the third bend. Cut off waste *after* making the bends.

POT-AND-PAN rack holds kitchen utensils at hand. Traditionally, the movable rail hooks are used in the meat-packing industry.

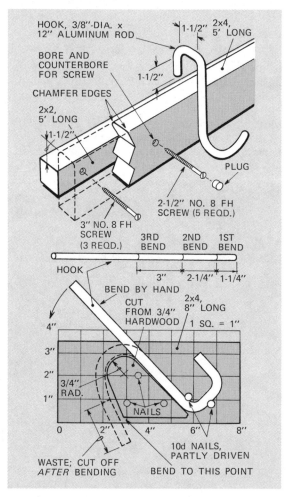

Tile the wall behind your stove

You can provide additional safety for your wood-burning stove and increase its efficiency at the same time. The secret is in the use of ceramic tile, with its good looks and high reflectivity

■ ENERGY-EFFICIENT, wood-burning stoves are growing in popularity, as are the increasing number of styles and designs offered to meet homeowners' needs. The beauty, safety and efficiency of any stove can be enhanced by surrounding it with ceramic tile. Choosing a combination of stove and tile for your home can be an enjoyable experience. And you'll be surprised to discover how easy it is to install the tile yourself in combination with "Wonder-Board," a glass-mesh, concrete-reinforced shield made by Modulars Inc., Box 216, Hamilton, OH 45012. The stove shown is the Moravian Parlor Stove by Quaker Stove Co. Inc., Box E, Kumry Rd., Trumbauersville, PA 18970. For information

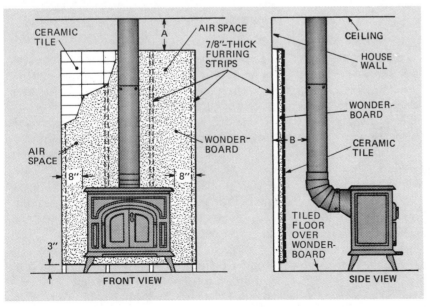

WONDER-BOARD'S UL listing allows its use as a wall shield to provide a 50 percent reduced clearance (as specified by stove maker) from a combustible wall surface. Drawing shows minimum clearances. Clearance (A) may be 1½ to 12 in. for rear-flue-exit stoves, but the shield need not extend higher than 8 in. above the top of a top-flue-exit stove. UL-approved clearance is 3 in. Clearance (B) may vary as specified by stove maker, but it always applies to the flue for rear-flue and to the back of the stove for top-flue-exit stoves. See text for information regarding floors.

NAIL 2-in.-wide, double-thickness wallshield furring strips to wall, 16 in. on center. Double thickness provides the UL-required ⅞-in.-air space between the wall shield and the combustible wall.

FASTEN PANELS with 4-in. nails or dry-wall screws. A double furring strip is needed at all angles, since the shield isn't flexible. Leave a ⅛-in. gap between the panels when you hang them.

APPLY TILE over ⅛ in. of latex-modified portland cement mortar (thin set) mixed with sand. Use spacers for uniformity. To prevent slippage, attach plywood strips to shield bottom with C-clamps.

AFTER PLYWOOD strips are removed from shield bottom, bottom tile course may be set. Apply cement with a square-notch trowel. Use the ¼ x ⅜-in. notches. Allow wall to cure for two days before grouting.

about styles and colors of tile, write to American Olean Tile Co., 1000 Cannon Ave., Lansdale, PA 19446.

We show how to install the shield and tile on a wall behind a stove, according to UL specifications, which require an air space between the shield and the combustible wall. Installing the floor is an even simpler procedure, since the shield may be laid down directly on the subfloor without provisions for an air space. Check your stove maker's installation instructions for the minimum area required for floor protection. Then lay the tile on the floor shield, following the same procedure we describe for applying the tile over the wall shield.

You may attach the wall shield to existing plaster or dry wall in any area you choose, but the clearances as shown in the drawing must not be compromised. Study the drawing for minimum clearances for top- and rear-flue stoves.

Note that we show a rear-flue-exit stove in the drawing. Because the rear clearance applies to the flue in this stove design, these stoves require more space, regardless of the use of wall shields. If your primary interest in wall shields is to save space, then you should buy one of the top-flue-exit stoves; or consider replacing your old rear-flue-exit stove.

You can become a pro at working with Wonder-Board in a short time. As it is concrete-reinforced, this kind of shield is heavy (about 4 pounds per sq. ft.) and durable, but easy to cut.

FILL ALL JOINTS (UL specifications require ⅛-in. spacing between panels) with latex-modified portland cement mortar mixed with sand. Embed glass-fiber tape; cover with more mortar. Trowel the joints flush.

THE COMPLETED wall-shield installation shows a clearance (3 in. from completed floor) between floor and the bottom edge of the shield. Leave at least 1½ in. between the top edge and the ceiling.

APPLY GROUT (various colors available) with a rubber-faced trowel. Work grout in and over spacers, using a diagonal movement. Follow all package directions carefully, as some grouts set very quickly.

Score through the "membrane" on either side with a carbide-tipped scoring tool. Snap the panel along the scored line and then cut the membrane on the other side with one quick run of the tool. You can also use a masonry saw, but this is much more time consuming and produces some dust.

Try not to damage or disturb the surface of the shield in handling, as the adhering quality of cements may be affected. The manufacturer of these shields recommends using a "sanded latex-modified portland cement mortar, applied with a notched trowel to provide a layer of mortar at least ⅛ in. thick over the entire surface to be tiled." The notches in the trowel provide the ⅛-in thickness in patterns of parallel lines. Let the tool

do the work. The mortar will be spread evenly as tiles are pressed into it.

Apply your tile carefully, pushing each tile gently into the mortar and then tapping it lightly to align with adjacent tiles and cross-shaped spacers. This will bring tiles flush with the finished surface.

The bottom left photo on page 70 shows a technique (using C-clamps and plywood strips) for stabilizing the lower courses of tile as you work from bottom up. Don't skip this procedure. Even though the mortar may seem tacky enough to hold the tiles firmly in place, whole areas of tile can slip before you realize it. Thus, this precautionary step is well worth the effort. It's also an easy way to align your first course. By working from the bottom up, you use gravity to help get a good snug fit between tiles.

After the tile is in place, the wall must be allowed to cure for several days before grouting. Whether or not you have experience grouting, make certain you read the manufacturer's instructions to find out the proper working consistency. A little practice will show you that a diagonal stroke is the most effective for working the grout in between the tiles. Continue stroking in a combination diagonal and circular motion until all grout on the surface is distributed in an ever-widening area from the point where you began. Neatness during this step saves effort at cleanup.

After grout starts to set, but before it begins drying to a lighter color, you may want to run over the grout with a finishing tool for a neat finish. Inquire about this procedure and the tool at your tile supplier.

Quick and easy front-door replacement

Installing a new front door used to be a big job, sometimes one only a professional carpenter could handle. Stanley's new steel replacement entry door changes all that

By ROBIN NELSON

1 Take care when removing interior trim so you can reinstall it over metal door frame. Or install new moldings.

2 Remove and discard old threshold. A new one comes with door frame. Make cut through so you can remove it.

6 After all fitting adjustments are made, lay a zigzag bead of caulk across the sill. Then install the frame.

7 Nail the door frame to the jamb, using 1-⅞-in. nails provided in the kit. Pre-drilled holes make this easy.

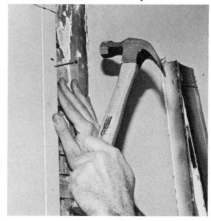

8 Retainer brackets hold unit firm for installation. Remove bracket screws. If frame is square, door opens easily.

■ INSTALLING A NEW front door is usually a job for a professional carpenter. But the Stanley Works, best known for its popular line of hand tools, recently began offering steel replacement entry doors which are engineered to fit existing wood jambs. Both frame and door are steel, with the latter having a foam core, plus both magnetic-strip and compression-type weatherstripping for improved insulation.

Our test installation of a replacement door took approximately six hours, not including installation of new interior trim and final painting of both door and trim. Since the house is over 40 years old, the jamb had become distorted through settling and overpainting. Refitting such jambs is necessary, using a Surform tool or plane and shims supplied with the door. This may add approximately one hour to the time the door installation might normally require.

The photos on these pages show the basic steps for installing a replacement door system.

The step shown in photo No. 5 requires the most care. As the door jamb must be square, use a level to check the vertical jamb members for plumb. Use shims to bring the sides to plumb, as explained in the instruction booklet. Some shimming may also be required of the header and sill in order to make these planes level.

All shimming must be done with the final checks made on the door frame itself, with a spirit level, before you begin to do any of the frame nailing.

Stanley offers the replacement door in two sizes: 2 ft., 8 in. by 6 ft., 8 in. and 3 ft. by 6 ft., 8 in. The doors are sold by Stanley Door Systems, 1225 East Maple Rd., Troy, MI 48084.

All doors are precut for standard lock and deadbolt hardware (not included in price).

3 Use a Surform tool or plane to remove irregularities in the old door jamb that might inhibit a correct fit.

4 Nail furring strips to an unrabbeted jamb. The outside edge of the new door frame then abuts these strips.

5 Use shims between jamb and frame to ensure a snug fit and to bring the jamb plumb. Nail shims over mortises.

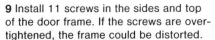

9 Install 11 screws in the sides and top of the door frame. If the screws are over-tightened, the frame could be distorted.

10 Nail weatherstripped stops (provided in kit) over furring strips with stripping compressed against door face.

11 Weatherstripping should expand as door is opened. Install it sufficiently compressed to make a tight seal.

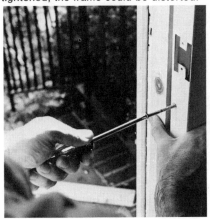

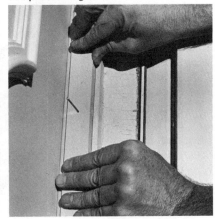

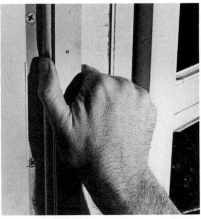

CARPORT AND POTTING shed with storage shelves becomes a boat cover and workshop. A translucent cover gives solar heat and protection for year-round use. It's easily assembled and knocked down thanks to the clamps used.

Back-yard shelter in one afternoon

A boat cover, garage or greenhouse
can be erected quickly with the help of
these clever new clamps

By BILL MCKEOWN

■ IT STARTED AS a plan to build a quick winter cover for a small 12-foot skiff. We ended up with a 10x20-foot boathouse that's a greenhouse offseason—spring, summer and fall—plus a garage and storage shed with shelves, as well.

The construction method was so simple, moderately priced and easy that we just kept on going—like assembling an Erector set. Cost, with

PREBENT FRAMES are quickly assembled and dropped into pipes driven in the ground for a firm footing. An assistant makes the job go faster.

cover, was under $500. Time? One busy afternoon—and it can be disassembled and stored away in less time and with equal ease.

The secret ingredients were clever fittings called Kover Klamps (Box 1628, New Rochelle, NY 10802). They hold together standard thin-wall electrical conduit. It's ¾-inch-inside diameter EMT tubing that comes in 10-foot lengths and is available everywhere at electrical supply outlets and numerous hardware stores.

There are other devices similar to these clamps. But this one can be secured at any angle. The two metal pieces with rubber gasket in between are tightened with one simple socket wrench. Our only other tools were a metal cutter and tubing bender, plus a tape measure and level. We had planned to rent them. But we quickly found that the system was so easy to use that, for $28, we bought the tools so that we could build fast shelving for a basement storage room, as well.

A small boat in winter and a snowmobile in summer can be covered with one set of eight Kover Klamps, five lengths of 10-foot tubing, eight couplings for straight runs and seven rubber crutch tips. This makes a custom-fitted shed. A large power or sailboat may mount a winter cover on deck with rubber crutch tips on the ends of the pipe uprights and the framing clamped to lifeline stanchions or tied down, just as a makeshift wooden frame would be. But come spring,

bits of colored tape can color-code the uprights, ribs and ridgepole so that the complete set can be taken down, stored compactly and reassembled once again in the fall. Because the tubing can be curved and the Kover Klamps have no sharp edges, the cover ties snugly over the frame. Spots where chafing might occur can be protected with tape or carpet scraps tied on.

We used translucent plastic that has bonded-in filaments and great resistance to tearing. Supplied with grommeted edges from Weathermate (Box 4447, Salem, MA 01970), the greenhouse cover with two separate end panels was just under $100; a dark plastic of similar strength would cost approximately $30 less.

For our carport boatshed, we drove lengths of pipe into the ground about four feet apart along each side and bolted prebent conduit uprights to them, although the structure could also have been just set on the ground. The ridgepole had light fixtures fitted into it with wiring threaded through the tubing. Each segment was carefully leveled this first time up. Next time, the setup might be twice as fast.

Because the frames are light, one worker can readily erect a boatshed or garage single-handed. One socket wrench tightens down the single nut that secures each Kover Klamp, and the framework gains rigidity as it is assembled. Diagonal members may be added for extra strength, if desired.

ONE NUT is loosened so Kover Klamp can be swiveled and then tightened to hold two electrical-conduit tubing lengths together in any position.

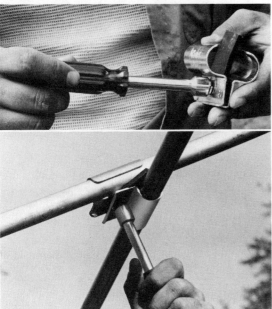

SHAPING CONDUIT into a custom curve is simple with a standard pipe bender. This gives rounded corners that won't chafe the cover.

Carpet you install yourself

MARKET COURT is one of six patterns in 12-ft-wide, do-it-yourself carpet.

■ INSTALLING wall-to-wall carpet used to be a job left strictly to pros. Now a carpet collection called the Sculptured Touch is geared for do-it-yourself installation. Made by Armstrong World Industries Inc., the carpet comes in 12-ft.-wide rolls and cost under $13 per sq. yd. at the time this was written.

The carpet is 100-percent nylon and comes with its own foam backing, so you don't have to buy extra padding. The backing has improved resistance to cracking and crumbling. It also resists mold and mildew, so you can install the carpet in a basement or over a concrete slab. The only installation tools you need are double-faced adhesive tape, shears, and crayon or chalk.

The 10 embossed patterns offered include, among others: a basket weave brick, an octagon look, a parquet and three medallion designs.

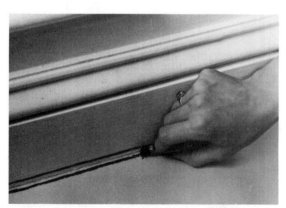

RUN A CRAYON or chalk line around the room's perimeter. Mark the floor and the wall.

PRESS CARPET firmly into the floor-wall joint to transfer the chalk marks. Then cut along the lines.

ROLL THE CARPET onto the floor; allow a few inches of excess to run up the wall.

USE DOUBLE-FACE tape at seams and doors to ensure that the carpet stays flat at the edges.

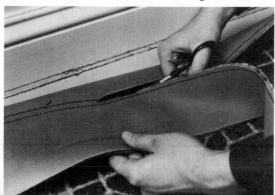

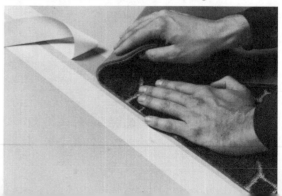

Faucet you install with a screwdriver

ENTIRE FAUCET body is installed from above sink. Plastic tubing connects directly to water-shutoff valves.

■ THIS NEW FAUCET by Fillpro Div. of JH Industries is unique in its method of installation and the mechanical means by which water is turned on and off.

Made of chromed zinc alloy, the entire faucet body installs from above the sink with the use of only a screwdriver. For supply risers it utilizes two 20-in. long sections of flexible Tygon tubing (a plastic material with embedded polyester cord for reinforcement). This tubing connects directly to the water shutoff valves underneath the sink through the compression fittings on the top of the valves.

Endura is available at home centers and hardware stores for about $40. Made by JH Industries, 980 Rancheros Dr., San Marcos, CA 92069.

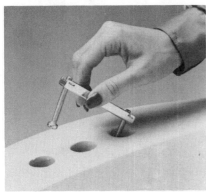

INSERT ONE side of U-shaped tiebar assembly in outside hole. Maneuver until screw comes up other hole.

PUSH FLEXIBLE tubing through holes and set faucet flush on base plate. Fasten with screw through plate front.

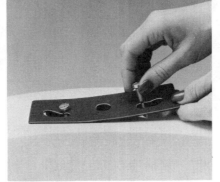

SLIDE GASKET underneath the screwheads to seal the faucet and prevent the tiebar from falling.

THE END of the flexible tubing goes directly into the compression fitting on the shutoff valve.

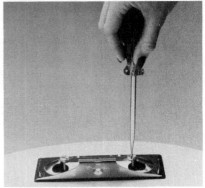

PUT BASE PLATE over gasket and slide holes under screwheads. Fingertighten, then draw tight.

HANDLE opens and closes flow by pinching or releasing the flexible tubing. No washers, seals or valves are used.

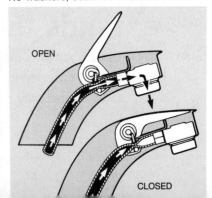

OPEN

CLOSED

Greenhouse with cold frame extends the growing season

You can grow beautiful plants indoors in this greenhouse/cold-frame combination that lets you enjoy juicy red tomatoes, cucumbers, squash and other vegetables fresh from your garden much earlier than they usually ripen. Here also are plans for building the potting bench

GREENHOUSE/COLD-FRAME addition is built of stock parts, except for window next to the door and a duplicate on the opposite wall; these can be made by a glazier. Dick Raymond shows off seedlings in the cold frame (below) where they harden before he moves them outdoors for final planting.

■ YOU CAN SOW the seeds for your vegetable garden early in the season inside this greenhouse. You can then harden the seedlings by moving them to the attached cold frame, before planting them outdoors when weather permits.

The combination structure allows master gardener Dick Raymond to start his planting season to ensure a good yield early—and throughout the planting season. The structure, built of readily available parts, can also be used to maintain flowering plants and lush foliage during the coldest winter months, when you'll be most grateful for the greenery.

A system of thermostatically controlled exhaust fans vents air from the greenhouse to the house and outdoors. This provides the house with solar heat on sunny days and guards against the greenhouse overheating. These shutter-mounting exhaust fans are readily available; those shown are Dayton fans by W.W. Grainger Inc., 5959 Howard St., Chicago, IL 60648.

For good heat retention, the greenhouse is glazed with 1-in.-thick double-glazed, patio-door replacement panels. Those on the roof are pitched at an angle to gain maximum solar benefits in the winter when the sun angle is low. The foundation is insulated with 2-in. Styrofoam as shown.

After determining the greenhouse location, lay out the exterior building lines using mason's line and pointed stakes; check corners for square. Determine the depth of the frostline for your area.

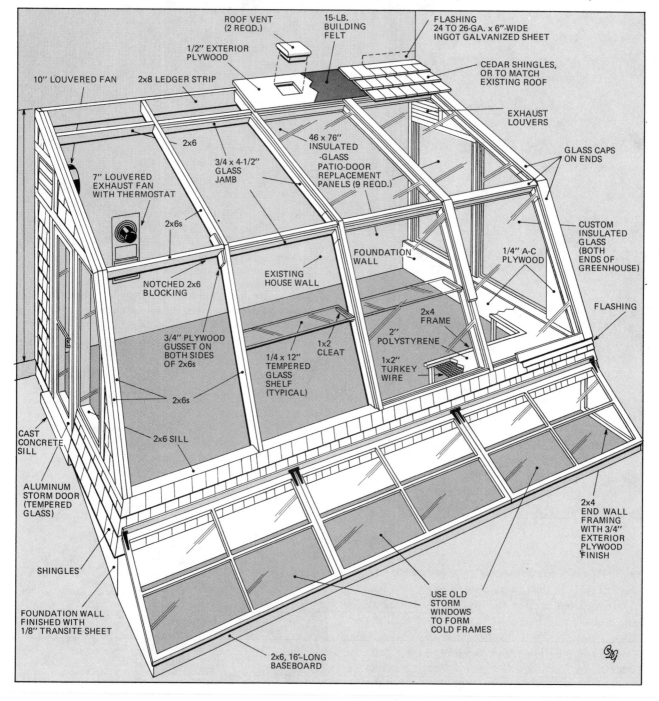

Excavate for the footings and foundation walls. You probably won't need forms to pour the footing. Simply dig a neat trench to required depth and width. The following foundation block wall is insulated, then covered by transite board.

The greenhouse floor consists of 6 in. of sand covered with 2 in. of gravel. If you prefer, install a brick-in-sand floor covering. Just make certain that the 6-in. layer of sand is well compacted at the correct elevation. The sill is sealed and anchored to the cement blocks.

The greenhouse is framed with 2x6s, using conventional framing methods. Later, the framing members are clad with ¾-in. pine stock. Gussets are used on both sides of all sidewall roof joints.

Since the roof pitch may vary from that shown, complete all of the framing before measuring the two openings for the custom insulated glass. The eight other glass areas utilize standard patio-door replacement panes.

Install the ¾-in. pine jambs over the framing after the glass is in place and caulked. (In this design the interior jamb serves as the glass bead

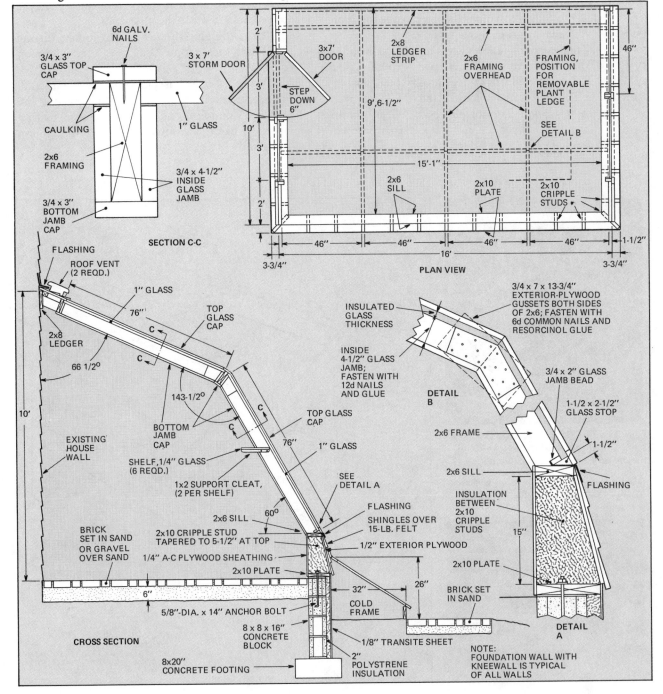

stops.) Important: Make certain the glass-wood joints are sealed, *both inside and out,* with caulking.

To make maximum use of the sunny space, you can install glass shelves as shown. Dick Raymond opted to install a ¼x12x46-in. tempered glass shelf across each of the six vertical glass areas. Each is supported by two 1x2 cleats 14 in. long.

The greenhouse also contains portable plant ledges propped on cement blocks. The ledges are framed with 2x4s to which 1x2-in. turkey wire has been fastened with 2-in. heavy-duty staples. Two-in.-thick Styrofoam is placed over the frame to insulate transplanting flats.

Soil-warming cables are simply laid in place. The cables are from Easy-Heat Wirekraft, U.S. 20 East, New Carlisle, IN 46552.

The cold frame is constructed of 2x4 end walls sheathed with exterior plywood. A 2x6 board is installed between the end walls; used storm windows are hinged in place.

potting bench

This sturdy redwood potting bench will give you an indoor work center for planting activities.

The work surface is a comfortable 35¼ in. from the floor. However, you may want to shorten it to suit the user's height. Its legs are notched to receive the stretchers and rails, and it can be assembled with common nails. But ¼-in. carriage bolts, washers and nuts give a stronger bench.

Check the corners with a square before the glue dries. Wrack the unit square, if necessary, and tacknail diagonal strips from the legs to the top to hold it while the glue dries.

Before the glue dries, cut 1x6s to size for the shelf and benchtop. Attach with 6d common nails.

The splashboard is cut from 1x10 material. The sides and back are simply butt-joined at the corners. Round the ends on the sidepieces using a sabre or band saw; attach parts by 6d common nails and glue.

FAN AT LEFT draws cool air in; stacked pair at right (bottom fan not visible) moves air from greenhouse to house.

DOUBLE ROOF vents draw off warm air from greenhouse by convection. Both are sealed in winter.

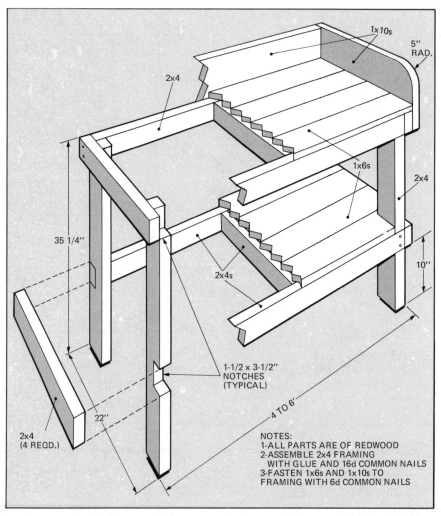

By **WILSON G. WALTERS**

A collapsible leaf cart

■ BEAUTIFUL shade trees around your house are a blessing in the summer, but they present an almost unmanageable situation when fall comes. Here's my solution: a leaf cart with three collapsible sides that holds well over 100 bushels of dry leaves.

To make the cart, begin by assembling the joint for the rear uprights and the base supports. Position the top of the notch 36⅛ in. from the top of the upright. Because I was using 6-in.-dia. wheels, I bored the axle hole 1¾ in. from the bottom of the upright. If you use different wheels, allow clearance so when sides are dropped they won't hit wheels.

After the joint is complete, attach the cross-pieces to the base supports and rear uprights, then install the hitch assembly as shown. Next, assemble the three folding sides and attach the hinges. The detail shows how to build sides and front so they meet compactly.

You'll have to experiment to position the hinges on the front base crosspieces. I accomplished this by having the hinges overlap slightly. When folded up, the sides are splayed slightly because the upper rails (H) butt against the outside edge of the rear uprights.

Install the chicken wire with staples, using one continuous strip for the back, bottom and front, and one 8-ft. piece on each side. Nail the lattice over the wire for extra support; install 2-in. hooks and eyes on all four corners. Finally, bend 6d nails into small loops to act as clips that join the wire on the sides to that on the bottom.

MATERIALS LIST—LEAF CART

Key	No.	Size and description (use)
A	2	1½ × 1½ × 96″ fir (base rail)
B	2	1½ × 3½ × 42″ fir (rear upright)
C	1	¾ × 4½ × 36″ fir (crosspiece)
D	2	½ × 5 × 10″ plywood (gusset)
E	1	¾ × 2½ × 36″ fir (crosspiece)
F	4	¾ × 2½ × 36″ fir (side upright)
G	4	¾ × 2½ × 35¼″ fir (front corner upright)
H	2	¾ × 2½ × 96¾″ fir (side rail)
I	6	¼ × 1½ × 34″ lattice (cleat)
J	4	2″ hook and eye
K	4	¾ × 2½ × 32″ fir (base crosspiece)
L	8	2″ double-hole utility hinge
M	2	1½ × 1½ × 40″ fir (A-arm)
N	2	¾ × 1½ × 5″ fir (spacing block)
O	1	1½ × 3½ × 20″ fir (hitch tongue)
P	1	½ × 5″ carriage bolt, nut, washer (hitch pin)
Q	1	⁵⁄₁₆ × 4″ carriage bolt, nut, washer
R	2	¼ × 3½″ carriage bolt, nut, washer
S	2	¼ × 2″ carriage bolt, nut, washer
T	2	¼ × 2¾″ carriage bolt, nut, washer
U	2	¼ × 4″ carriage bolt, nut, washer
V		36″-wide chicken wire, about 32′ long
W	2	6″-dia. wheels with nylon bushings
X	2	6½″ × dia. to suit, machine bolt, nut and spacing washers
Y	2	¼ × 4½″ carriage bolt, nut, washer
Z	10	2″ No. 8 fh wood screws

Misc.: 4d nails, ⅝″ U-shaped staples

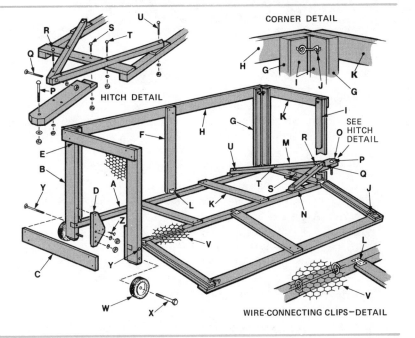

CORNER DETAIL

HITCH DETAIL

SEE HITCH DETAIL

WIRE-CONNECTING CLIPS—DETAIL

A bountiful harvest with little work

By DEREK FELL

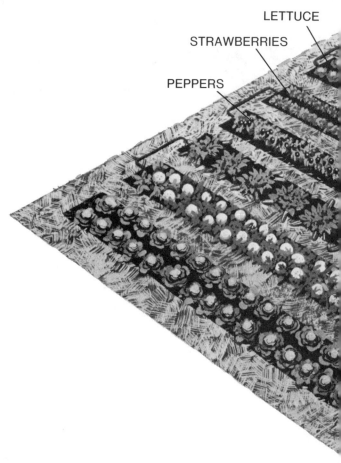

LETTUCE

STRAWBERRIES

PEPPERS

■ HOW WOULD you like to grow a vegetable garden in which there are no weeds and no serious pest damage; where there is no digging after the first year and no manual watering? Yet, despite the minimal effort, the garden is highly productive, beginning early in the season.

I have tended such a garden the past three years. A system of mulching that utilizes black plastic prevents weeds from growing. After the first year's digging to make raised growing rows, I simply replenish the soil each year with compost. Instead of hosing or sprinkling, inexpensive drip irrigation makes watering automatic and efficient. Organic pest controls keep pests away.

The garden shown is 15x41 ft. You can dig your own site in spring and divide it into 2-ft.-wide by 4-to-5-in. high raised rows, with 1-ft.-wide walkways. To raise the rows, rake the soil from the walkways or use compost. Level them on top.

Midway at the garden edge lay two 150-ft. lengths of polyflex drip irrigation hose with 2-ft. emitter spacings, along the middle of the rows, in opposite directions, snaked up one row and down the next. Connect the two hoses to a water spigot with a Y-valve. Every inch of row can be watered in 30 minutes.

Next, cover the raised beds with 3-ft.-wide rolls of black plastic, leaving a 1- to 2-in. lip along the walkway for soil anchorage. On the walkways

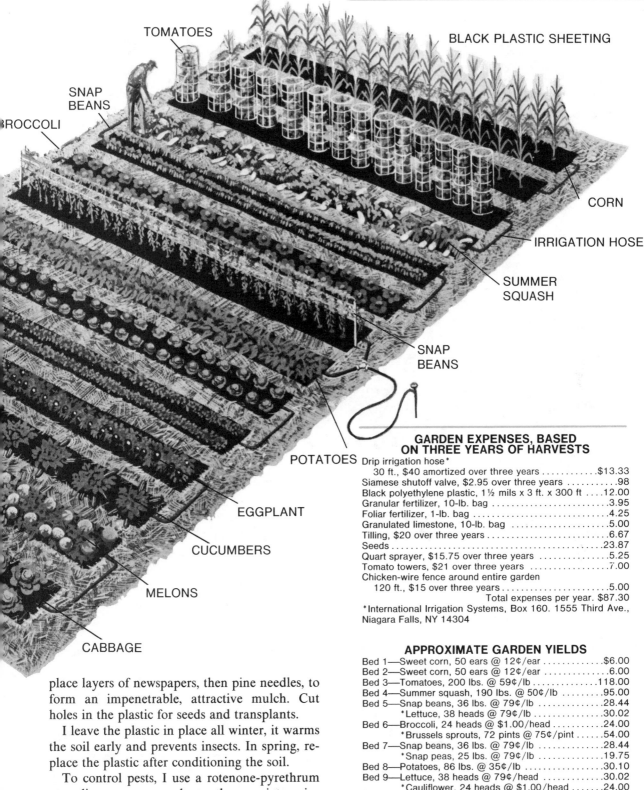

TOMATOES

BLACK PLASTIC SHEETING

SNAP
BEANS

BROCCOLI

CORN

IRRIGATION HOSE

SUMMER
SQUASH

SNAP
BEANS

POTATOES

EGGPLANT

CUCUMBERS

MELONS

CABBAGE

place layers of newspapers, then pine needles, to form an impenetrable, attractive mulch. Cut holes in the plastic for seeds and transplants.

I leave the plastic in place all winter, it warms the soil early and prevents insects. In spring, replace the plastic after conditioning the soil.

To control pests, I use a rotenone-pyrethrum or a diatomaceous earth-pyrethrum mixture insecticide. Both are made from natural compounds that leave no residue. Apply insecticide *early* to keep pests at bay. Also, clean up dead vegetation in fall to prevent pests from wintering.

To maintain nutrient levels, I use compost with bone meal added. For tomatoes, peas and heavy feeders, I also use liquid fertilizer.

GARDEN EXPENSES, BASED ON THREE YEARS OF HARVESTS

Drip irrigation hose*

30 ft., $40 amortized over three years	$13.33
Siamese shutoff valve, $2.95 over three years	.98
Black polyethylene plastic, 1½ mils x 3 ft. x 300 ft	12.00
Granular fertilizer, 10-lb. bag	3.95
Foliar fertilizer, 1-lb. bag	4.25
Granulated limestone, 10-lb. bag	5.00
Tilling, $20 over three years	6.67
Seeds	23.87
Quart sprayer, $15.75 over three years	5.25
Tomato towers, $21 over three years	7.00
Chicken-wire fence around entire garden	
120 ft., $15 over three years	5.00
Total expenses per year.	$87.30

*International Irrigation Systems, Box 160. 1555 Third Ave., Niagara Falls, NY 14304

APPROXIMATE GARDEN YIELDS

Bed 1—Sweet corn, 50 ears @ 12¢/ear	$6.00
Bed 2—Sweet corn, 50 ears @ 12¢/ear	6.00
Bed 3—Tomatoes, 200 lbs. @ 59¢/lb	118.00
Bed 4—Summer squash, 190 lbs. @ 50¢/lb	95.00
Bed 5—Snap beans, 36 lbs. @ 79¢/lb	28.44
*Lettuce, 38 heads @ 79¢/lb	30.02
Bed 6—Broccoli, 24 heads @ $1.00/head	24.00
*Brussels sprouts, 72 pints @ 75¢/pint	54.00
Bed 7—Snap beans, 36 lbs. @ 79¢/lb	28.44
*Snap peas, 25 lbs. @ 79¢/lb	19.75
Bed 8—Potatoes, 86 lbs. @ 35¢/lb	30.10
Bed 9—Lettuce, 38 heads @ 79¢/head	30.02
*Cauliflower, 24 heads @ $1.00/head	24.00
Bed 10—Strawberries, 36 pints @ 90¢/pint	32.40
Bed 11—Peppers, 24 heads @ 50¢/lb	12.00
Eggplant, 50 lbs. @ 50¢/lb	25.00
Bed 12—Cucumbers, 84 @ 45¢ each	37.80
Bed 13—Cantaloupes, 42 @ $1.00 each	42.00
Bed 14—Cabbage, 24 heads, 6 lbs. each, 20¢/lb	28.80
Chinese cabbage, 24 heads @ 79¢/head	18.96
Spaghetti squash (growing on fence) 35 at 5 lbs. each @ 50¢/lb	87.50

TOTAL YIELD: $778.23 EXPENSES: $87.30
* Second Planting PROFIT: $690.93

TEMPERATURE-CONTROLLED root cellar provides a place to store all your raw and canned vegetables.

Build a root cellar for your harvest

■ AFTER YOU'VE harvested a blue-ribbon yield from your garden, the next step may be to provide storage for your bumper crop, so you'll have fresh vegetables throughout the winter. Master gardener Dick Raymond accomplished this with a root cellar that he built in a corner of his basement.

This cold cellar is a modern version of the traditional root cellar, an underground pit which was usually covered with earth. It can store root crops and other vegetables, as well as canned goods.

We've further updated the root cellar by devising a means of cooling it when needed, using outside air. The controlling device in this cooling system is a differential temperature thermostat. By means of sensors, this thermostat keeps tabs on the temperature outdoors and the temperature in the root cellar.

You can set the thermostat to activate a fan when the temperature outdoors is 5° F. cooler than the temperature in the root cellar. The fan draws this cool air into the root cellar to cool the vegetables. The fan turns off automatically when the temperature in the root cellar is within 2½° F. of the outdoor temperature. (For supplier information on the thermostat and other items, see the list on page 89.)

An additional freeze cutoff sensor mounted in the root cellar keeps the fan from running when the temperature in the root cellar falls below 42° F. Then the cellar is cooled by natural airflow.

Root crops are preserved best in colder temperatures, between 32° and 40° F. Although the cellar is largely below grade and, therefore, shielded from temperature extremes, in areas with severe winters, there is some danger of freezing temperatures in the cellar. In these areas, it is wise to keep a thermometer in the cellar; if the temperature drops near 32° F., you can seal the intake vent. When you seal the intake vent, however, be sure to use the manual override on the thermostat, so the fan in the sealed vent isn't activated when the inside temperature rises.

Sufficient humidity keeps produce from shriveling. Humidity should generally be above 60 percent of most vegetables; many thrive in 90 percent humidity. Ideally, you should keep a hygrometer in the cellar to measure humidity. Or you can check the vegetables from time to time to see if moisture is needed.

Locate the root cellar on a north wall, if possible, away from heat pipes. You can replace the glass of a cellar window with ½-in. plywood and install a ventilation system for the root cellar in the plywood. Cover any other window panes in the space to keep out light.

If there are no windows at the location, you must break through the foundation, or cut through at or above the sill, to install the air-intake and exhaust system. Use a cold chisel and a hammer to break through concrete block.

Study the drawing of the root cellar on page 88. Conventional framing is constructed of 2x4 studs spaced 16 in. on center (O.C.) and assembled with 8d nails to the sole and top plates. The top plate is toenailed to the joists of the floor above. (See Sections 3 and 4 for framing the door.) Use a level to check that the framing is square.

Fasten paneling to the framing on the basement side of the walls before wiring the differential temperature thermostat. Mark all stud locations on the floor and ceiling before you install the panels, so you'll know where to nail.

Use 1½-in. casing or finishing nails every 6 in. along the edges and every 12 in. on intermediate studs. Or attach the paneling with panel adhesive and use fewer nails. Squeeze a bead of adhesive onto each stud face; nail the panel along the top edge only. Press the panel in place, swing the bottom out and prop the panel away from the adhesive for five minutes before nailing the panel to the stud. Finally, apply corner guard.

If you use Aspenite wall panels, attach them with nails. Before applying, bevel the vertical edges or round them off with a rasp plane to make a neat V-joint; or cover the panel joints with moldings.

the venting system

Install the blower assembly and exhaust duct, and wire for the differential thermostat and sensors before insulating and sheathing the interior of the root cellar. Use the wiring diagram for the air-intake system on page 88 as a guide.

Mount the differential thermostat on the newly

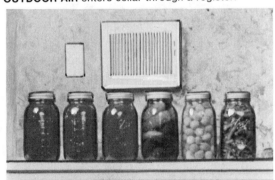

OUTDOOR AIR enters cellar through a register.

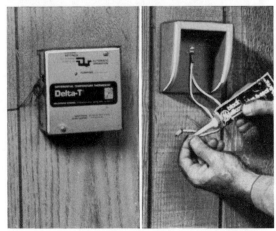

THERMOSTAT outside the cellar activates fan. Right, a temperature sensor is placed outdoors.

ALL WALLS of the root cellar are insulated to keep produce at the proper temperature for storage.

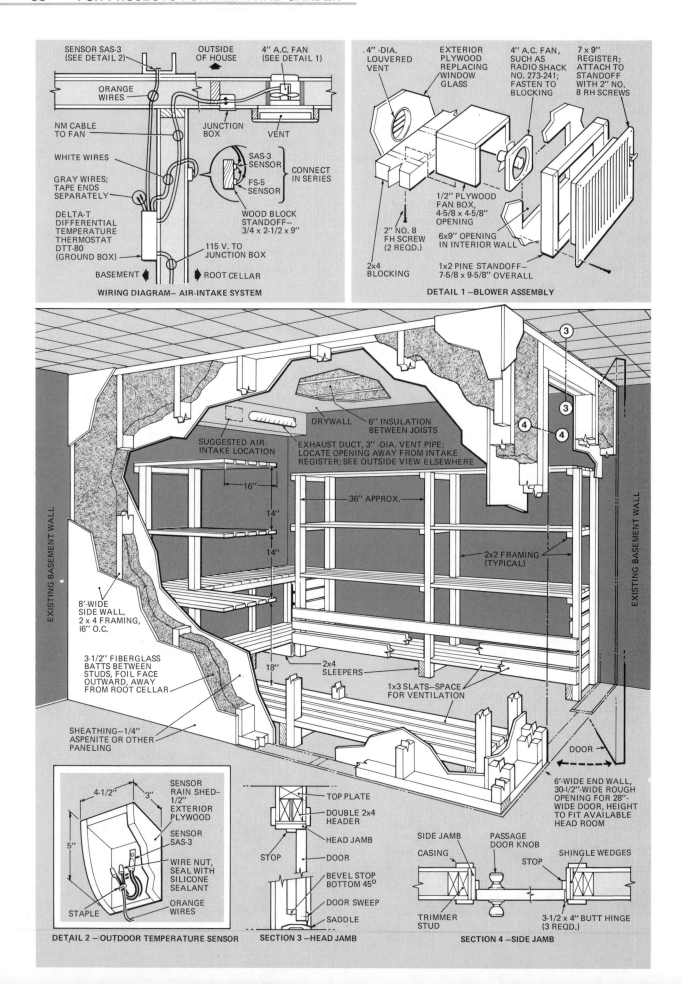

WIRING DIAGRAM— AIR-INTAKE SYSTEM

SENSOR SAS-3 (SEE DETAIL 2)

OUTSIDE OF HOUSE

4" A.C. FAN (SEE DETAIL 1)

ORANGE WIRES

NM CABLE TO FAN

JUNCTION BOX

VENT

WHITE WIRES

SAS-3 SENSOR

FS-5 SENSOR

CONNECT IN SERIES

GRAY WIRES; TAPE ENDS SEPARATELY

DELTA-T DIFFERENTIAL TEMPERATURE THERMOSTAT DTT-80 (GROUND BOX)

WOOD BLOCK STANDOFF— 3/4 x 2-1/2 x 9"

115 V. TO JUNCTION BOX

BASEMENT   ROOT CELLAR

DETAIL 1 —BLOWER ASSEMBLY

4"-DIA. LOUVERED VENT

EXTERIOR PLYWOOD REPLACING WINDOW GLASS

4" A.C. FAN, SUCH AS RADIO SHACK NO. 273-241; FASTEN TO BLOCKING

7 x 9" REGISTER; ATTACH TO STANDOFF WITH 2" NO. 8 RH SCREWS

1/2" PLYWOOD FAN BOX, 4-5/8 x 4-5/8" OPENING

2" NO. 8 FH SCREW (2 REQD.)

6x9" OPENING IN INTERIOR WALL

2x4 BLOCKING

1x2 PINE STANDOFF— 7-5/8 x 9-5/8" OVERALL

DRYWALL

6" INSULATION BETWEEN JOISTS

SUGGESTED AIR-INTAKE LOCATION

EXHAUST DUCT, 3" -DIA. VENT PIPE; LOCATE OPENING AWAY FROM INTAKE REGISTER; SEE OUTSIDE VIEW ELSEWHERE

16"

14"

36" APPROX.

14"

2x2 FRAMING (TYPICAL)

EXISTING BASEMENT WALL

EXISTING BASEMENT WALL

8'-WIDE SIDE WALL, 2 x 4 FRAMING, 16" O.C.

3-1/2" FIBERGLASS BATTS BETWEEN STUDS, FOIL FACE OUTWARD, AWAY FROM ROOT CELLAR

18"

2x4 SLEEPERS

1x3 SLATS—SPACE FOR VENTILATION

DOOR

SHEATHING—1/4" ASPENITE OR OTHER PANELING

6'-WIDE END WALL, 30-1/2"-WIDE ROUGH OPENING FOR 28"-WIDE DOOR, HEIGHT TO FIT AVAILABLE HEAD ROOM

DETAIL 2 —OUTDOOR TEMPERATURE SENSOR

4-1/2"   3"

SENSOR RAIN SHED— 1/2" EXTERIOR PLYWOOD

5"

SENSOR SAS-3

WIRE NUT, SEAL WITH SILICONE SEALANT

STAPLE

ORANGE WIRES

SECTION 3 —HEAD JAMB

TOP PLATE

DOUBLE 2x4 HEADER

HEAD JAMB

STOP

DOOR

BEVEL STOP BOTTOM 45°

DOOR SWEEP

SADDLE

SECTION 4 —SIDE JAMB

SIDE JAMB

PASSAGE DOOR KNOB

CASING

STOP

SHINGLE WEDGES

TRIMMER STUD

3-1/2 x 4" BUTT HINGE (3 REQD.)

sheathed basement wall. Ground the box by fastening the green wire to the inside of the box. The thermostat is wired to the air-intake fan with No. 16 nonmetalic (NM) cable joined in a junction box located near the intake vent. You can use conduit if you prefer to surface-wire the connection. Bore a hole through the paneling for the cable. Seal around the cable with silicone sealant.

Cut a hole in the plywood covering the window for the louvered vent and attach it in place (see Detail 1—Blower Assembly). The fan frame is secured to blocking attached in the window. A box encloses the fan, and a 1x2 pine frame standoff allows clearance for the register louvers.

Join the fan and thermostat wiring at the junction box. Hook the thermostat at 115-v. power via another junction box.

The air from the cellar is exhausted via a 3-in.-dia. flexible clothes dryer exhaust duct, which ends outside at a clothes dryer wall cap. The air intake and exhaust are separated outdoors by a plywood baffle (see outside view drawing of vent system on page 89). Inside the root cellar, locate the opening of the exhaust duct away from the air-intake vent and near the ceiling to vent the warmer air.

SOURCE LIST—ROOT CELLAR

Differential temperature thermostat: The unit shown is model DTT-80 which has two SAS-3 sensors included. An additional FS-5 freeze cutoff sensor is an added purchase. They are available at solar-product suppliers or from the manufacturer: Heliotrope General, 3733 Kenora Dr., Spring Valley, CA 92077.

Vent register: 7x9-in. vent register is made by American Metal Products, Masco Corp., 6100 Bandini Blvd., Los Angeles, CA 90040.

Vegetable storage information: For additional information on storing vegetables, send for: *Storing Vegetables and Fruits in Basements, Cellars, Outbuildings and Pits*, bulletin No. 119, U.S. Dept. of Agriculture; from Superintendent of Documents, U.S. Government Printing Office, Washington, DC 20402.

Hygrometer: These instruments are used to measure the absolute or relative amount of moisture in the air. They are available by mail from Edmund Scientific, 101 East Gloucester Pike, Barrington, NJ 08007.

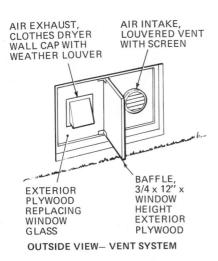

AIR EXHAUST, CLOTHES DRYER WALL CAP WITH WEATHER LOUVER

AIR INTAKE, LOUVERED VENT WITH SCREEN

EXTERIOR PLYWOOD REPLACING WINDOW GLASS

BAFFLE, 3/4 x 12" x WINDOW HEIGHT EXTERIOR PLYWOOD

OUTSIDE VIEW— VENT SYSTEM

ends outside at a clothes dryer wall cap. The air intake and exhaust are separated outdoors by a plywood baffle (see outside view drawing of vent system on page 89). Inside the root cellar, locate the opening of the exhaust duct away from the air-intake vent and near the ceiling to vent the warmer air.

Use 18- to 24-ga. zip or bell wire to connect the sensor leads to the thermostat. Orange wires from the thermostat go to the SAS-3 temperature sensor located outdoors (see Detail 2). Both the outdoor sensor and the connection to it should be shielded from the elements. It may be easier in some homes to snake these wires out through the first floor.

The gray-wired sensors on the thermostat aren't used in this application. Tape their ends separately to prevent their coming in contact and causing a short.

The indoor temperature SAS-3 sensor located in the root cellar is connected to the thermostat with white wires. An additional sensor (FS-5 freeze cutoff sensor) is also located in the cellar. Both should be located well away from the cold

CELLAR VENTILATION system is set up in a basement window. In the top photo, plywood replaces glass. The louvered vent is ready for installation and junction box is ready for fan hookup. Horizontal blocking supports the fan. Below, the fan hookup is complete.

air intake vent. Staple them to a wood block or a block of rigid foam insulation which won't conduct heat, after the interior sheathing is applied. Seal the holes in the wall and the wire nuts with silicone sealant.

The root cellar must be well insulated from the basement to retain its cool air. Use 3½-in. fiberglass batt insulation between studs. Face the foil vapor to the warm (basement) side of the wall.

For the most part, the storage racks in this root cellar are 2x2 framing (posts) nailed to sleepers with 1x3 slats spaced for ventilation. However, you can also use lumber from your scrap pile.

Since it's coolest nearest the floor, store crops that need the coldest temperatures there. Store canned items nearer the ceiling.

STACKING BOXES TO CARRY YOUR GARDEN PRODUCE

To carry his harvest of vegetables from the garden to the root cellar, master gardener Dick Raymond uses these easy-to-build stacking boxes. They help keep vegetables from becoming bruised, damaged, or otherwise unfit for storage by the time they get to the root cellar.

The big handles make the boxes easy to carry and they let you haul a full week's supply from the root cellar to the kitchen, or carry freshly canned products from the kitchen back to the root cellar.

The boxes also come in handy for storing an odd squash or a handful of potatoes that won't fit into a bin or on a shelf. This overflow of vegetables might otherwise end up on the floor, to be kicked or stepped on accidentally. You can also stack the boxes to save floor space. You can even use them for vegetable storage elsewhere—in a pantry, a cool closet or on a porch, for instance.

The boxes shown are made from the remains of an old packing crate, and assembled with 4d and 6d nails. You could also use pine, fir or other available stock to build them. Each box measures 11½x16½x24 in., and holds about a bushel of produce. However, you can modify these dimensions so the boxes will fit in a vacant spot in your root cellar.

Begin work by cutting the six different types of parts to size. Center the nesting cleats on the end members and fasten them with 4d nails. Fasten the ends to the sides, using butt joints with 6d nails. Check that the corners are square.

Position the bottom boards, leaving about ⅝-in. spacing between them. Again, check the box carefully for square and then fasten the bottom boards to the endpieces with 6d nails.

Fasten the handles to the handle supports with 4d nails. Then position the handle supports in the box; fasten them to the box ends and to the sides with 4d nails.

EASY TO BUILD and easy to carry, these stacking boxes go from the garden, piled high with vegetables, to nest in an unused corner of the root cellar.

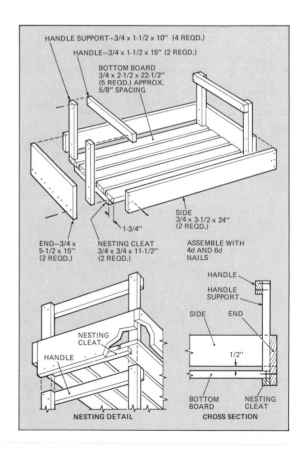

Build a heavy-duty garden cart

This 14-cu.-ft. plywood trailer has floating-axle suspension to distribute the weight. It uses standard building materials and hardware

By DICK ROBERTS

■ HITCHED TO MY garden tractor, this trailer cart satisfies my need for a large-payload, light-weight cart that's relatively rustproof and rot-resistant. The aluminum-edged, plywood cart holds an impressive 14 cu. ft. of material.

First, on a 4x8 sheet of ⅝-in. CDX plywood lay out the bottom, sides and ends of the cart according to the materials list on page 93. After the parts have been cut, treat them with a wood preservative and then glue and tack them together, omitting the tailgate end.

Next, cut the drawbar (D in materials list) and the T-stabilizer (E). Cross-lap join them as shown in the drawing. Fit the assembly flush to the sides and open rear of the cart's bottom; secure them in place with stovebolts (T) countersunk flush with the cart bed.

Now cut the spacer (G) for the undercarriage mounts. Cut a 1½-in.-deep x 2½-in.-wide dado in the spacer for the drawbar; the spacer should be flush with the bottom of the cart when installed.

Cut four hanger mounts (F), test-fit them with the spacer onto the cart bottom, and nail them to the spacer with 10d common nails. Then nail the assembly to the drawbar with 8d common nails. Secure the mounts to the cart with 2¼-in. wood screws (T2) from inside the cart.

Next, cut the sheet aluminum for the cart bed (C1). Using the pattern as a guide, notch the corners and fold as indicated by the dotted lines. Fit the covering into the bed and fasten it temporarily with tacks through the folded tabs.

To make the guide channels for the tailgate and the edging for the cart panels, you'll need about 76 in. of 2x2-in. aluminum angle and 29 ft. of ¾x¾-in. aluminum angle. Hacksaw two 17⅜-in. lengths of the latter for the inner tailgate channel guides (W); cut two 18-in. lengths of 2x2-in. angle for the outer channel guides (X).

Set the tailgate and the guides in place, clamp the guides to the sides of the cart and remove the tailgate. Drill holes and bolt the channel guides together through the cart sides using 1-in. stove-bolts, washers, lock washers and nuts (T3).

Finish edging the top of the tailgate with angle (W1), centered and secured with ½-in. aluminum

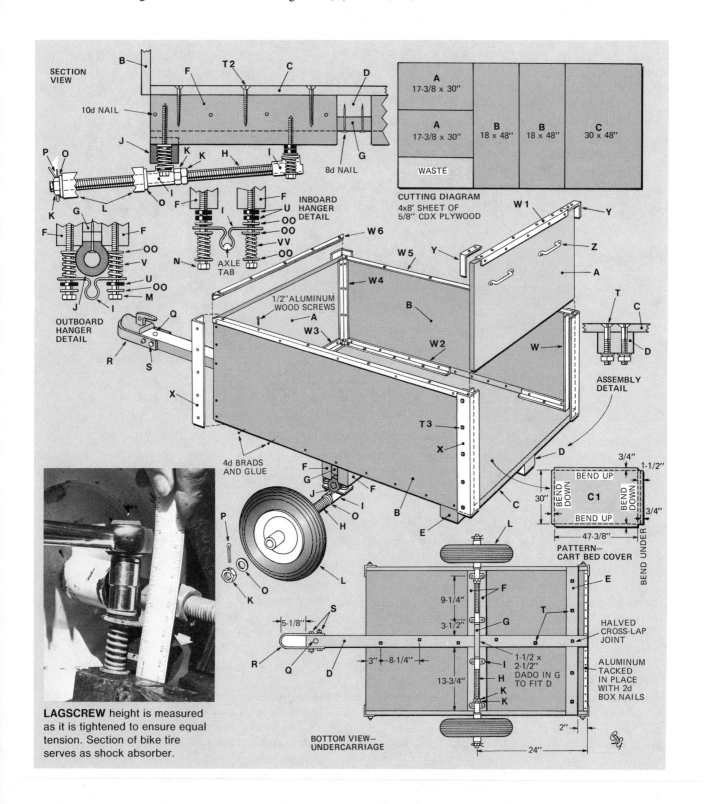

CUTTING DIAGRAM
4x8' SHEET OF
5/8" CDX PLYWOOD

A 17-3/8 x 30"			
A 17-3/8 x 30"	B 18 x 48"	B 18 x 48"	C 30 x 48"
WASTE			

LAGSCREW height is measured as it is tightened to ensure equal tension. Section of bike tire serves as shock absorber.

BOTTOM VIEW—
UNDERCARRIAGE

wood screws countersunk flush to the outside.

Secure the locking hasps to the ends of the rail with wood screws. Then secure the two aluminum handles.

Miter cut the inside edging (W2 and W3) and bolt it through the floor and sides with ¼-in.-dia. x 1-in. roundhead machine screws and nuts. Miter cut and install top edging (W5 and W6) with ½-in. aluminum flathead screws.

Finish the edging by cutting the front vertical pieces (X and W4). Fit and bolt parts in place with ¼-in.-dia. x 1-in. roundhead machine screws and nuts.

Flop the cart so you can work on its undercarriage. Begin work on the inboard hanger (see detail) by hacksawing the axle tabs (stops) off two of the four axle housings.

Then, begin assembly by running two nuts near the center of one axle rod. Slide one of the open-ended axle housings down to the nuts. Add a flat metal washer, a wheel, another flat washer and another nut. Adjust this assembly by setting the nuts so ⅛ in. of the rod protrudes beyond the nut at the wheel end of the rod. Make sure that the wheel spins freely.

Begin assemblying the inboard hanger onto the axle rod by slipping a close-ended axle housing onto the other end of the rod and running it up to the axle tab. Lay the completed assembly on the cart's axle mounts; then locate and mark positions of the four lagscrews that secure the assembly in place. Repeat the steps with the other wheel assembly. You will need two pairs of heavy-duty springs (valve springs from an old engine are ideal) for the outboard hanger assemblies, and two pairs of lighter springs (available at hardware stores) for the inboard assemblies. Feed the necessary washers onto the lagscrew of the outboard hanger. Slip the screw through the axle-hanger lip; then add a heavy-duty spring. Add another washer and temporarily secure the assembly with a clamp. Repeat the procedure on the opposite lip of the hanger. Then run both screws into their holes, leaving 1¾ to 2¾ in. of shank showing.

Complete the inboard assembly with washers, lagscrews and light springs. Run screws into the mounting holes; leave 1¾ in. protruding.

Mount the opposite wheel assembly in the same manner. Then test to see that the axles float freely and evenly between the compressed springs when weight is applied. Adjust if needed.

TAILGATE slides smoothly up and down between channels. Angle hasps at top of gate securely lock it in place.

AXLES FLOAT between two sets of springs. This tends to adjust the load and steady the cart over rough terrain.

MATERIALS LIST—GARDEN CART

Key	No.	Size and description (use)
A	2	⅝ × 17⅜ × 30″ CDX plywood (front, back gate)
B	2	⅝ × 18 × 48″ CDX plywood (sides)
C	1	⅝ × 30 × 48″ CDX plywood (bottom)
C1	1	.025 × 31½ × 49⅝″ sheet aluminum (liner)
D	1	1½ × 2½ × 61½″ fir (drawbar)
E	1	1½ × 2½ × 31¼″ fir (drawbar T-stabilizer)
F	4	1½ × 3½ × 13¾″ fir (hanger mounts)
G	1	¾ × 2½ × 30″ fir (axle spacer)
H	2	⅝″-dia. × 18″ threaded rods (axles)
I	4	Axle housings (from cast-off wheelbarrows)
J	2	2″ bike-tire sections (shock cushions)
K	6	⅝″-i.d. nuts (axle assembly)
L	2	4.00-8 (4″ wide × 8″-dia. hub) tubeless wheelbarrow wheels
M	4	⅜ × 5″ lagscrews (outboard hangers)
N	4	⅜ × 4″ lagscrews (inboard hangers)
O	4	⅝″-i.d. washers (axle assembly)
OO	20	⅜″-i.d. washers (hangers)
P	2	2″ cotter pins (axle assembly)
Q	1	¼″-dia. × 2″ carriage bolt
R	1	Tractor hitch
S	2	½″-dia. × 3″ capscrew, washer, lock washer, nut
T	10	⅜″ × 3″ stovebolts, washers, lock washers, nuts

Key	No.	Size and description (use)
T2	12	2¼″ No. 14 flathead screws
T3	as reqd.	¼″-dia. × 1″ rh stovebolts, washers, lock washers, nuts
U	12	Rubber washers
V	4	Stiff compression springs
VV	4	Light-duty compression springs
W	2	⅛ × ¾ × ¾ × 17⅜″ angle (inside gate guide)
W1	1	⅛ × ¾ × ¾ × 27½″ aluminum angle (gate edging)
W2	2	⅛ × ¾ × ¾ × 46″ aluminum angle
W3	1	⅛ × ¾ × ¾ × 30″ aluminum angle
W4	2	⅛ × ¾ × ¾ × 16⅜″ aluminum angle
W5	2	⅛ × ¾ × ¾ × 47⅜″ aluminum angle
W6	1	⅛ × ¾ × ¾ × 31¼″ aluminum angle
X	4	⅛ × 2 × 2 × 18″ aluminum angle
Y	2	⅛ × ⅝ × 2 × 2″ aluminum angle
Z	2	handles

Misc.: ½″ aluminum wood screws, wood preservative, ¼″-dia. rh machine screws and nuts, 4d brads, 8d and 10d common nails, waterproof glue, primer, heavy-duty exterior paint, lithium grease.

Bring in fresh air without losing heat

Superinsulated, tightly sealed homes conserve heat and energy, but they retain stagnant air, too. Air exchangers are the practical solution

By JOHN INGERSOLL

■ HIGH FUEL PRICES have driven many homeowners to add more insulation, block out drafts, caulk cracks, install tighter windows and generally seal up their houses. The object of this exercise is to contain skyrocketing heating costs.

All of these procedures work, but now some homeowners are finding that they have done too good a job. Sure, they're saving on fuel bills, but they're also finding that the odor of Uncle Oscar's cigar lingers not for hours, but for days.

Steam from the shower collects as condensate on windows. Yesterday's burned beans continue to haunt you. In short, the stale air inside the house remains inside instead of filtering out through the cracks.

The solution to this indoor air pollution problem is obvious—ventilate. But the difficulty is that you ventilate your expensive heat right out the window or open door.

There is a way to ventilate while retaining up

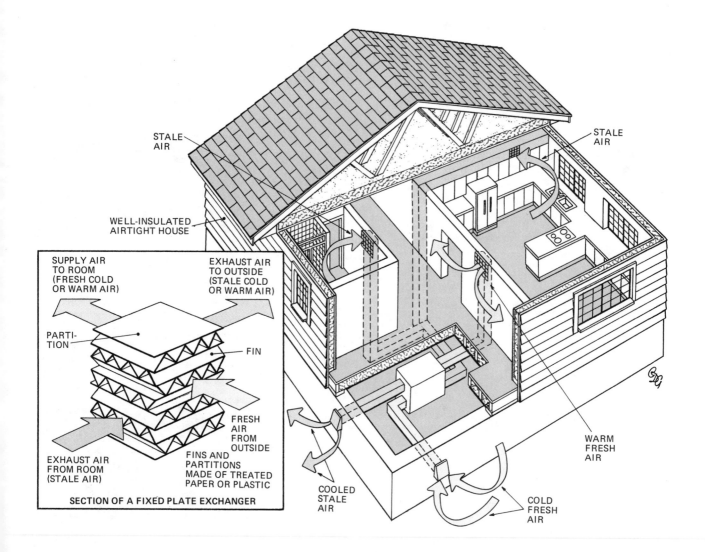

STALE
AIR

STALE
AIR

WELL-INSULATED
AIRTIGHT HOUSE

SUPPLY AIR
TO ROOM
(FRESH COLD
OR WARM AIR)

EXHAUST AIR
TO OUTSIDE
(STALE COLD
OR WARM AIR)

PARTI-
TION

FIN

FRESH
AIR
FROM
OUTSIDE

EXHAUST AIR
FROM ROOM
(STALE AIR)

FINS AND
PARTITIONS
MADE OF TREATED
PAPER OR PLASTIC

SECTION OF A FIXED PLATE EXCHANGER

COOLED
STALE
AIR

WARM
FRESH
AIR

COLD
FRESH
AIR

to 80 percent of the heat that would otherwise exit with the stale air. Air-to-air heat exchangers have been around on a commercial scale for more than a generation, but smaller models for residential use are new.

Air-to-air heat exchangers ventilate the whole house effectively, while handling the heat-loss problem efficiently. Efficiencies up to 80 percent save most of the heat which would otherwise be lost, while changing indoor air frequently enough to keep it both pleasant and healthy.

latent heat

Some new air exchangers also transfer latent heat—the heat trapped in the water vapor held by the warm stale air. Condensing this water out of the stale air reclaims still more heat.

By exchanging both heat and vapor, the total energy content—called enthalpy—of the incoming clean air can be raised so it's from 70 to 80 percent of that in the outgoing stale air. This helps to maintain a comfortable temperature and humidity level inside the house.

When indoor relative humidity stays between 40 and 50 percent, your feeling of comfort prods you to turn down the thermostat by a few degrees—a step that makes a noticeable difference in fuel bills. It also keeps your furniture from drying out to the point where glue joints crack and walking on your rugs produces sufficient static electricity to cause shocks.

they work in summer, too

Air-to-air heat exchangers work equally well in summer to conserve your air-conditioned cool air. The principle is the same, but the direction of the heat and moisture exchange is reversed. Stale but cool indoor air (whether air-conditioned or not) is vented to the outside, taking the heat and excess moisture from the warmer incoming air with it. Enthalpy air-to-air heat exchangers also extract water vapor from the warmer incoming air, while cooling it to keep your house from the clammy feeling of excess humidity.

So much for the pluses. Even enthalpy air exchangers have their minuses. For one, unless your house is supertight, with an air change rate of 0.5 or less (one change every two hours), they do no good. In fact, a house that changes its air once an hour without help will only lose excessive amounts of heat no matter how efficient its air exchanger may be.

freeze-ups may occur

The other problem with air exchangers, especially enthalpy models, is freeze-ups. Most are plagued by freeze-ups on the incoming airstream side when the outside temperature drops below 10° F. Ice forms, blocking up the openings. Most soon thaw from the warmth of outgoing air. Some have electric heaters, but these have their own energy expenses. Still, ice dams do lower the efficiency of some enthalpy air-to-air heat exchangers.

FIVE TYPICAL air exchangers go in basement or attic to ventilate superinsulated houses and reclaim heat from outgoing stale air. Four—vanEE (1), Enercon (2), Air Changer (4) and E-Z-Vent (5)—are "sensible" designs (see text), which warm incoming fresh air by passing it through a heat exchanger next to outgoing stale air. Econofresher (3) is a rotary enthalpy design that conserves latent heat, resists freeze-up and rehumidifies. For a more complete comparison of features on these models, see the chart on the next page.

types of exchangers

Different types of air exchangers react differently to freeze-ups. Here's a quick rundown on the three main types of air-to-air heat exchangers: the fixed-plate "sensible" models, fixed-plate enthalpy designs, and rotary enthalpy exchangers.

Fixed-plate sensible heat exchangers get their name from your being able to sense the heat in the incoming air. They contain a series of non-porous separators mounted so that incoming and outgoing air travel through side-by-side channels; that way, the heat from one can warm the other without contaminating it. Heat is transferred through the separator. Two small fans pull in outside air and push out indoor air.

shut down the fan

When a freeze-up occurs, a sensor can shut down the fan on the incoming side, or you've got to do so yourself. Then, outgoing warm air continues to transfer heat to the iced-up incoming channels, melting the ice. At about 20° F. outside, this is claimed to take only a minute or two. Down at 0° F. or below, it takes longer.

A very tight house collects vapor from cooking and bathing, which can steam up windows in cold weather. An air exchanger also removes this excess moisture quite rapidly, while bringing in only small amounts of humidity with the colder outside air in winter.

humidifier may be required

Some air exchangers require a humidifier to replace the moisture removed with the stale air. This is a separate operation and is not incorporated in most models, so you may have to add a humidifier to the cost of an air exchanger. The need is most important on cold days.

Fixed-plate enthalpy exchangers work the same way as sensible models. The difference is in the separators. These are water absorbent, so they filter the moisture out of the stale air and pass it through to the clean incoming air. Thus, these models pass through both sensible and latent heat.

fixed-plate models pass water vapor

By passing the water vapor through with the outside air, these models help to maintain the relative humidity balance in the house. However, they still lose some moisture to the outside, though markedly less than with a sensible design.

Rotary enthalpy exchangers are, at this writing, only available under the Econofresher name. In this design, a honeycombed wheel transfers heat and vapor from the outgoing warm air to the incoming cold air. Since the surface of the wheel is exposed to both cold and warm air, it appears to have overcome the freeze-up problem effectively. No single set of ducts is constantly exposed to freezing temperatures, so ice never builds up. Company literature claims frost-free operation down to 5° F. In summer, it's claimed to work well in keeping interiors cool and humidity balanced at a comfortable level.

HOW AIR EXCHANGERS COMPARE

	Price (Approx.)	Size (in.)	Weight (lbs.)	Latent Heat?	Airflow (c.f.m.)	Energy Draw (w.)
Air Changer	$760[1]	54 × 22 × 14	75	No	150	70
Air-X-Changer	$235	7 × 7 × 14	13	No	60 to 135	1,500[2]
Econofresher	$300	22 × 12 × 8	21	Yes[3]	30 to 55	40
Enercon	$1,250	48 long × 20 dia.	85	No	150	150
E-Z-Vent	$550	62 × 16 × 14	90	No	100 to 200	200
Lossnay[4]	$350	22 × 16 × 12	29	Yes	40 to 63	52
Memphremagog	$700[5]	50 × 28 × 14	80	No	180 to 255	70
Thinking Cap	$199	18 × 18 × 7	18	No	0 to 200[6]	None
vanEE	$750	49 × 22 × 15	75	No	0 to 200	200

[1] Air Changer also has a "Standard" model for $650.
[2] This unit is not a true air-to-air heat exchanger. A resistance heating element in the unit heats air drawn into the house to replace negative pressure brought about by losses up flues.
[3] Rotary type.
[4] Mitsubishi (Lossnay manufacturer) produces two smaller models and one larger unit for residential application. The smallest exchanger is not an enthalpy unit and is suitable for manually operated, high-humidity areas, such as a bath.
[5] The same model is available for $500 without fans.
[6] Thinking Cap is a thermostatically controlled home venting system that varies airflow by temperature and ceiling vent regulation. Two caps and six ceiling vents in system can move from 0 to 400 c.f.m. (200 c.f.m. per cap).

MANUFACTURERS LIST

Air Changer Co., 334 King St. E., Studio 505, Toronto, Ont. M5A 1K8 (**Air Changer**).
American Energy Products. 603 Fenimore Rd., Mamaroneck, N.Y. 10543 (**Thinking Cap**).
Berner International Corp., 12 Sixth Rd., Woburn, Mass. 01801 (**Econofresher**).
Conservation Energy Systems Inc., Box 8280, Saskatoon, Sask. S7K 6C6 (**vanEE**).
Des Champs Laboratories Inc., Box 440, East Hanover, N.J. 07936 (**E-Z-Vent**).
Enercon of America Inc., 2020 Circle Dr., Box 632, Worthington, Minn. 56187. (**Enercon**).
Memphremagog Group, Box 456, Newport, Vt. 05855 (**Memphremagog**).
Mitsubishi Electric Sales America Inc., 3030 East Victoria St., Compton, Calif. 90221 (**Lossnay**).
Standex Energy Systems, 620 Main St., Detroit Lakes, Minn. 56501 (**Air-X-Changer**).

thermostatic roof vents

Another air exchange system relies on rising hot air for circulation and thermostatic controls in roof vents to minimize heat losses. Called the Thinking Cap, it includes one or more roof vents to remove the stale air and manually controlled ceiling grilles to regulate airflow.

Each cap has a thermostat which opens air flaps when the temperature reaches 80° F. and closes them at 60° F. It has a built-in fuse to close the vanes and keep them closed in case of fire. By opening ceiling vents that feed inside air to the cap, you can keep the house comfortable and the humidity controlled.

With these vents closed in winter, the system is claimed to balance humidity and conserve energy. Fresh air enters the house through open downstairs windows or by natural infiltration if the house is not too tightly sealed. While this system does not heat the incoming air with the outgoing stale air, it requires no power for fans because it works by giving the hot, stale air a place to go when it rises.

air exchanger problems

Three problems remain: how to select the right size unit, how to install it or have it installed, and where to find one.

Sizing depends on the volume of your house. A rough rule of thumb is to specify an air exchanger delivering 75 c.f.m. (cubic feet per minute) per 1,000 square feet of floor space.

You can arrive at a more precise estimation by using the calculations of ASHRAE (American Society of Heating, Refrigeration and Air Conditioning Engineers). They advise 40 c.f.m. for each bath or kitchen and 10 c.f.m. for each occupant. Then multiply the number of cubic feet in your home by the air-infiltration rate to get the air-change rate.

The Big Sucker

Air-infiltration rates were once determined by multiple instruments all over the house, but this expensive piecemeal method has been replaced by a machine which creates a vacuum and then measures how hard it has to work to do it. Called The Big Sucker (what else?), it was developed by a Texas utility about six years ago. Now, you can hire its services through local utilities and some air conditioning contractors. Once The Big Sucker gives you the air-infiltration rate per hour for your home—remember, adding insulation and sealing windows, doors or other air leaks changes it drastically—you can figure your air-change requirement.

In a supertight house, the average number of air changes per hour ranges from 0.2 to 0.3. To find out yours, multiply the air-infiltration rate per hour by the number of cubic feet in the house. Divide that number by 60 to get the number of c.f.m. of air your house changes naturally. Subtract this c.f.m. rate from your calculated need to get the exchanger capacity.

installing an air exchanger

Installation calls for commonly used home-handyman skills and tools. Do not attempt to tie in with any existing ductwork if your house is heated by hot air, but make the air exchanger system separate and independent.

As the outgoing air gives up its heat to warm the fresh air coming in, moisture condenses. The drain line (which can be a plastic tube leading to the floor drain in the basement) gets rid of this water.

You will also have to work with ducting. Most air exchanger makers recommend flexible, insulated ducting with a vapor barrier. It must also fit the air exchanger fittings and should be available from the same source as the air exchanger.

cellar and attic installations

Cellar installations support the air exchanger system on ceiling joists with straps. Attic installations can rest on ceiling joists. Some smaller models can be wall-mounted in a bathroom or kitchen like a sort of super exhaust fan.

Stale air can come from anywhere in the house, but the most effective systems take it from as high up in the room as possible. The area of the air intake should be open to the rest of the rooms. Plan to deliver fresh air to one room or several and exhaust it from another to minimize cross-contamination. There's no advantage in exhausting your fresh air or mixing it more than necessary with the outgoing stale air. Keep the outside air intake and the exhaust vent at least 6 feet apart to avoid cross contamination outside the house.

Air exchanger systems can be found in your classified directory under Conservation, Heat Exchanger, or Heating Equipment. Air-conditioning contractors might be a source, or you can write directly to one or more of the manufacturers listed in the equipment chart. The chart on page 96 compares features. Use it as a guide in determining which exchanger is right for you. (Prices were current at the time this was written.)

Get pure drinking water from the sun

Here is an economical solution for people all over the country who are alarmed by the deteriorating quality of their domestic water. The sun supplies the energy

By GEORGE CAMPBELL

■ THIS SOLAR STILL, operating on the simple principles of evaporation and condensation, will remove *all* impurities from about one gallon of water a day.

Build the still box first. It should face south and receive full sun. If it's necessary to mount the unit on the sloped surface of the roof, cut the back end (CC) 21 in. high and the front (BB) 6 in. high, plus whatever is required so that the pan supports will be level.

Bore holes for the supply and return lines in the plywood bottom (AA). Also bore two 1-in.-dia. weep holes, one at each end. Screen these to keep out insects.

frame comes next

Next, build the frame for the still's lid and a platform for the supply tank. Prime all wood components with top-quality wood primer, then apply two coats of high-quality exterior latex enamel.

Give the evaporation pans two coats of rust-resistant paint—such as Versaflex or Rust-O-Crylic enamels. These are nontoxic and adhere to galvanized surfaces. Plumb the system as shown

in the drawings. A handsaw can be used to cut the trough in half (after assembly).

With help, take the unit up on the roof and position it where it will receive full sun, then make final connections.

If it's installed on a roof slope, attach a 2x4 cleat to the roof at the lower end of the still. Use lagscrews in the rafters and apply ample sealant at the holes. Run braided guy wires from the sides of the still to the eave. These will anchor the still. Install turnbuckles, but do not tighten the turnbuckles yet.

Run the supply-line tubing to a convenient water supply and connect through a valve. The output line should not be connected to the storage tank at this time.

spread aquarium gravel

Lay a small piece of screen over the openings in the evaporation pans, then spread a layer of black aquarium gravel over the surface of the pans. Since the evaporation of the water will deposit light-colored minerals in the pans, stir the black gravel periodically.

To prevent the growth of microorganisms in

the tank and pans, put a quarter pound of copper sulfate crystals in the supply tank.

When you're ready to activate the system, turn on the water supply. As the water begins to run into the evaporation pans, use shims to attain the final level of the unit. Adjust the water level in the pans by bending the shaft of the float valve (Bobby valve). The float should stop the flow when the water just covers the gravel. At this point, tighten the turnbuckles on the braided anchor wires.

weatherstrip the cleats

Next, apply weatherstripping to the bottom of the glass-support cleats (PP and QQ). Put the lid with glass in place on the box and attach with wood screws. Water will begin to condense on the glass and drip off the silicone bead into the trough.

Let the still run for three days before collecting the distilled water for use. During this time, find a convenient location for the insulated picnic cooler that serves as a storage tank and install an overflow tube in it. Seal the points where the tubing passes through the walls of the cooler with clear silicone.

set the timer

Run plastic tubing from the air pump, through the lid of the cooler, to the air stone and seal with silicone once again. Set the timer so that the air pump runs for about three hours in the evening.

Once the still has run for three days, pass the output line through the lid of the cooler; use silicone to seal the joint. Before use, let the cooler fill a day or two to provide a buffer supply of water.

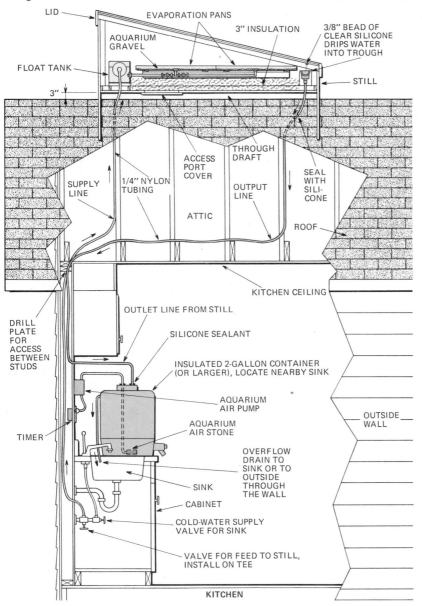

MAKE BOX for still of exterior-grade plywood. Use resorcinol glue at joints. Cut V-notch to suit roof pitch.

USE ½-in. PVC pipe to make feeder lines from the supply tank to the black evaporation pans. Use brass drains.

SUPPLY TANK, with float valve (Bobby Valve), controls water level in the still and is connected to cold-water supply.

continued on next page

MATERIALS LIST—SOLAR STILL

Key	No.	Size and description (use)
A	1	Robert Bobby valve (float valve) with ¼" tubing fitting
B	1	2"-dia. float (for Bobby valve)
C	5	Brass evaporative cooler drains
D	5	Brass evaporative cooler-drain locks
E	5	Evaporative cooler-drain rubber washers
F	9	½ × ½" PVC male pipe-thread adapters
G	1	½" × length to suit PVC pipe (feeder line)
H	1	½" PVC cross fitting
I	9	½" PVC nipples
J	2	½" galvanized unions
K	1	½" PVC tee
L	4	½" PVC elbows
M	2	2" PVC caps (collecting-trough ends)
N	1	2" PVC tee (collecting-trough drain)
O	1	2×36" PVC pipe (collecting trough)
P	1	½ × 2" PVC female pipe-thread reducer
Q	1	Compression fitting
R	*	¼" nylon or soft copper tubing (supply and output tubing)
S	*	Glazier's points
T	*	No. 6×1" Phillips-head screws
U	*	3d galvanized box nails
V	4	¼"-dia. screw eyes or eyebolts with washers and nuts
W	2	Turnbuckles
X	1	5×6×12" plastic ice-cube storage tray (float tank)
Y	4	1×17½×23½" galvanized automotive drip pan (evaporation pans)
Z	1	20 lbs. aquarium gravel
AA	1	½×37×63" exterior plywood (bottom)
BB	1	½ × 37" × height to suit (overall) exterior plywood (front support)
CC	1	½ × 37" × height to suit (overall) exterior plywood (back support)
DD	2	½ ×21×64" (overall) exterior plywood (sides)
EE	1	½ ×12×13" exterior plywood (access port cover)
FF	2	¾ × 3½ × 66" pine (sides of top)
GG	2	¾ × 3½ × 38½" pine (front, back of top)
HH	2	¾ × 1½ × 63" pine (cleats)
II	2	¾ × 1½ × 19" (overall) pine (back cleats)
JJ	2	¾ × 1½ × 35½" pine (front and back bottom cleats)
KK	2	¾ × 1½ × 4" pine (front supports)
LL	2	¾ × 1½ × 2⅝" pine (filler block)
MM	2	¾ × 3½ × 4" pine (collecting-trough supports)
NN	2	¾ × 1½ × 44" pine (evaporation-pan supports)
OO	4	¾ × 1½ × 37" pine (evaporation-pan supports)
PP	2	¾ × 1½ × 63" pine (glass supports)
QQ	2	¾ × 1½ × 38½" pine (glass supports)
RR	1	⅛ × 38⅜ × 64⅜" double-strength glass
SS	8	2" corner braces
TT	1	½" × ¾" × 18' adhesive-backed foam weather-stripping
UU	2	¾ × 1½ × 12" pine (float-tank supports)
VV	2	¾ × 1½ × 3¾" pine (float-tank supports)
WW	1	¾ × 5¼ × 12" pine (float-tank platform)

Misc.: ⅛" braided galvanized guy wire as reqd., 3" fiberglass batt insulation, silicone sealant, insulated 2-gal. container, timer, aquarium air pump, aquarium air stone, in-line valve.
*As required.

SHOPPING INFORMATION

The ice-cube tray (part X) is from Rubbermaid. It's model No. 2862 and is available at houseware stores that carry the Rubbermaid line.

The Robert Bobby Valve (part A) is Model RM-64 and is available at most True Value hardware stores and many other hardware outlets. If you have a problem locating one, write to Robert Manufacturing Co., Drawer A, 10667 Jersey Blvd., Cucamonga, Calif. 91730, for the nearest dealer. The automotive drip pans can be found at auto supply outlets.

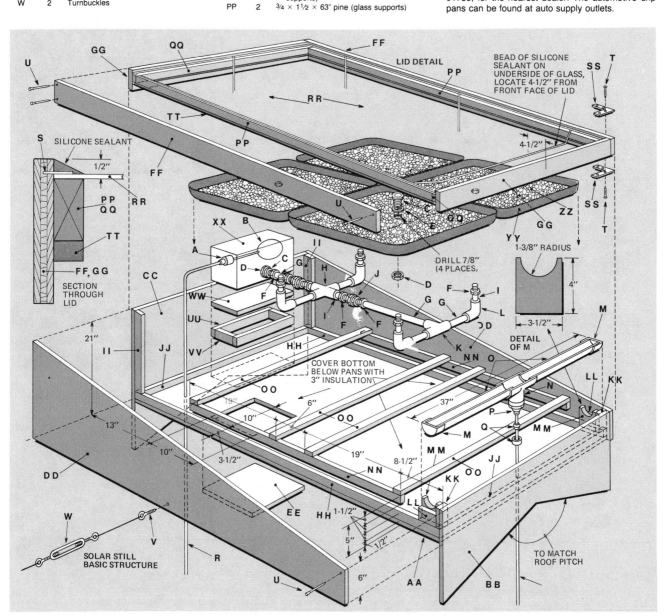

Caulk: the fuel saver in a tube

By JOHN INGERSOLL

■ GET OUT YOUR keyhole saw. Cut a hole the size of a basketball in the north side of your house and let the cold wind whistle in. Nutty? Right. Yet an equivalent amount of air leaks through minute cracks and crevices in an average house.

Cold air infiltration remains the No. 1 heat robber and energy waster, even though fewer houses suffer from winter chills than a decade ago. In summer, the same cracks leak out cooled inside air and let in hot outside air. Homeowners are learning: Among the energy conservation steps they take most often—after insulating—is caulking those energy-dumping slits.

Though it takes time and a little practice, caulking isn't difficult. Few do-it-yourself home energy improvements pay back more, sooner, or for less outlay.

Costs, based on a standard 11-oz. cartridge, depend on the type of caulk, the size of the bead it takes to fill the crack, and the number of feet to be sealed. In the case of a house with severe cracks, or a new, unsealed house, the cost of applying a ⅜-in.-wide bead of caulk to 500 linear ft. of cracks would require 28 cartridges of caulk, each covering about 18 linear ft. of cracks; at $6 a cartridge, total cost would run $168. However, the cost of tightening an average house might run under $100. Here's why:

• You don't have to buy the highest priced caulk. Materials at $3 to $4 a cartridge could serve you admirably.

• Whatever the age of your home, it would be odd if some caulk didn't already pack the cracks around the windows, doors and other joints.

• A ⅜-in.-wide opening at seams is big. Most cracks are narrower. Figure a ¼-in. bead as average for the job.

• The coverage estimate of 18 linear ft. per cartridge in the example is conservative. Depending on crack depth and spreading technique, you will actually be able to cover from 18 to 27 linear ft. with a ⅜-in.-wide bead, with one single cartridge.

Added up, these four price-reducers put your actual cost for caulk more in the range of $20 to $50.

buying the right caulk

In store racks, you'll find a number of different basic qualities of caulk. Here's a rundown on each, listed by its approximate price, starting with the cheapest.

Oil-base caulks are used by contractors because they're cheap. Homeowners shouldn't use them. That's a statement by a lab technician for a company that makes oil-base caulks, along with a full line of acrylics, butyls and others.

Consider yourself lucky if you get two years' performance from an oil-base sealer before cracking and shrinkage begin to appear. Some of these products won't survive one year. Oil caulk doesn't gun as easily as acrylic latex, requires a prime coat in the crack before application on new work, shouldn't be applied unless ambient temperature is 60° F. or above, and is paintable—in fact, should be painted to stretch its durability. Cost: $1 to $2 per 11-oz. cartridge.

Butyl caulk is a rubber-base material that lasts for many more years than oil-base because of its elasticity. Available in some colors, as well as white, butyl doesn't require a primer, and can be painted after approximately 12 hours of curing.

You'll find it is somewhat more difficult to gun than acrylic. Don't apply butyl when temperature is below 50° F. Cost: $2 to $3 per 11-oz cartridge.

Acrylic latex caulk is a favorite of many pros. One homeowner, with a house in Pennsylvania's Pocono Mountains, gunned acrylic into the house cracks 15 years ago, and hasn't touched it since. Acrylic flows from the cartridge more easily than any other material, yet doesn't sag, especially those brands reinforced with a small amount of silicone.

Acrylic can even be applied over a surface that's slightly damp, but not when temperatures are below 50° F. The bead is paintable when the surface forms a skin and isn't sticky to your touch. That takes 24 to 36 hours of curing in temperatures above 50° F. Available in colors, clear and white, it costs the same as butyl: $2 to $3 per 11-oz. cartridge.

Acrylic copolymers are the new guys in town.

CAULK wherever unlike materials meet, even if you cannot feel an air leak or spot water seepage. In this photo, a wooden door jamb meets brickwork.

METAL FRAME for sliding window should be caulked by pushing gun (from left to right as shown here) to force caulk into crack.

SEALING a vertical joint where brick chimney meets board-and-batten siding keeps out driving rain. Push the gun up at an angle to drive caulk deep.

Pros say their performance is every bit as good as that of still higher-priced stuff, maybe better. Makers claim acrylic copolymers adhere more tightly to a wider variety of materials than do the silicones.

Available in white, clear and some colors, these materials don't need a primer before application and can be painted once the solvent has evaporated, a process that takes about seven days. As with acrylics and butyls, caulk only when temperatures are above 50° F. These caulks gun easily, don't sag and stick to themselves when you make two runs in wide crack. Cost: $3 to $4.50 per 11-oz. cartridge.

Hypalon caulk is a high-quality elastomeric available in white and colors. It can be applied in

HOW TO CHOOSE THE RIGHT CAULKING

	Price	Color	Paintable?	Applications	Advantages	Disadvantages
Oil base	$1 to $2	White	Must be painted	Around windows, doors; not for outside use	Inexpensive; paintable	Short life; usable only above 60° F.; guns less easily than acrylic; needs painting; cracks
Butyl	$2 to $3	White and some other colors	Yes, when cured	Around windows, doors; joints, foundations, flashing	Inexpensive; long-lasting elastic	Short life; usable only above 50° F.; guns less easily than acrylic
Acrylic latex	$2 to $3	Clear, white, gray, brown, red, black, some others	Yes, when cured	Same as for butyl	Inexpensive; long-lasting elastic; guns easily; many colors available	Usable only above 50° F.; takes 1½ to 2 days to cure
Acrylic copolymer	$3 to $5	Clear, white, some colors	Yes, when cured	Same as for butyl	Moderately priced; durable; long-lasting elastic; guns easily	Usable only above 50° F.
Hypalon	$3 to $6	White, some colors	Yes	Same as for butyl	Durable; long-lasting elastic; usable at temperatures as low as 40° F.	Guns somewhat slowly; difficult to buy at retail; expensive in quantity
Silicone	$5 to $7	Clear, white, gray, brown, some other colors	Specially formulated silicone only	Same as for butyl	Durable; long-lasting elastic; usable at temperatures below freezing	Guns slowly in cold weather; expensive in quantity
Foamed urethane	$7 to $9	White	Yes, when cured	Same as for butyl; also good for filling holes	Moderately priced; easy to foam; insulative	Usable only above 75° F.; as combustible as wood framing

All materials are packaged in 11-ounce cartridges, except for foamed urethane, which comes in a 14-ounce spray can.

SUPPLIERS—CAULKING

Bostick Consumer Div., USM Corp, Muhlenberg Industrial Mall, 4408 Pottsville Pike, Reading, Pa. 19605.
Dap' Inc., Box 277, Dayton, Ohio 45401.
Darworth Co., Box K, Avon, Conn. 06001.
Dow Corning Corp., Elastomer Business, Midland, Mich. 48640.
H.B. Fuller Co., 315 South Hicks Rd., Palatine, Ill. 60067.
General Electric Co., Silicone Products Div., Waterford, N.Y. 12188.
Geocel Ltd., Box 653, Elkhart, Ind. 46515.
Gibson-Homans, 1755 Enterprise Pkwy., Twinsburg, Ohio 44087.
Gulf Adhesives & Resins, Box 2900, Shawnee Mission, Kan. 66201.
Insta-Foam Products Inc., 1500 Cedarwood Dr., Joliet, Ill. 60435.
Macco Adhesives, SCM Corp., 900 Union Commerce Bldg., Cleveland, Ohio 44115.
Red Devil Inc., 2400 Vauxhall Rd., Union, N.J. 07083.
Tremco Mfg. Co., 10701 Shaker Blvd., Cleveland, Ohio 44104.
United Gilsonite Laboratories (UGL), Box 70, Scranton, Pa. 18501.
Weldwood Products, Roberts Consolidated Industries, 600 North Baldwin Park Blvd., City of Industry, Calif. 91749.
Woodhill Permatex, Box 7183, Cleveland, Ohio 44128.

ALUMINUM-SHEATHED soffit meets brick wall and air escapes. Use dark caulk, match soffit color or use clear caulk which looks like adjacent surfaces.

FOAMED URETHANE insulation from aerosol tube can seal larger gaps, like this rough opening around hose bib in brick foundation. Apply several thin coats.

OUTSIDE CORNER where sidewalls meet can be caulked with clear acrylic copolymer. Be sure to drive caulk deep and completely fill the joint.

BLACK CAULK is inconspicuous where chimney flashing tucks under shingles.

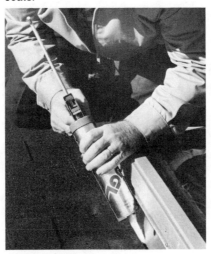

PUSH CAULK into joints where skylight meets roofing, and over flashing.

CLEAR CAULK seals joint between acrylic bubble and skylight frame.

temperatures down to 40°F. You can paint this caulk, it doesn't require a primer and makers claim a 20-year life for the material. It doesn't gun as easily as acrylic or acrylic copolymer caulk. Some producers distribute it in a cartridge with an oversized tip for that reason. One problem: You may not find it stocked at your favorite building-supply outlet. Cost; $3 to $5 per 11-oz. cartridge.

Silicone caulks were king until the acrylic copolymers came along. Silicones are still excellent—in fact, they've been improved since makers now offer three types: a plain silicone for most outside jobs, a masonry caulk formulated to adhere to masonry better, and a door-and-window caulk that now, for the first time, is paintable. All three are priced almost the same.

Silicone caulks can be applied in just about

any weather—even below freezing. They don't gun as easily as acrylics, and are tougher to use in icy temperatures. Durability is certainly as long as competing materials and, in many cases, longer. Most of the silicones do require a primer before application. Check the label. Cost: $5 to $6 per 11-oz. cartridge.

Neoprene, moisture-cured urethane and polysulfide caulks are used mostly in commercial construction, where substantial movement in the building requires a highly elastic sealer. They cost about the same as silicones, or a bit more.

Foamed urethane caulk is a relatively new workhorse that not only seals a joint, but insulates, as well. Use it alone, or apply a bead in a deep crevice to fill the space before sealing it in with a standard caulk. The foam applies and cures fastest at 75°F.

Tips to save energy

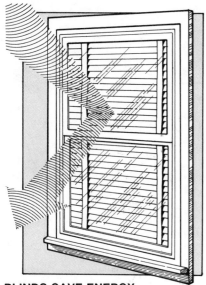

BLINDS SAVE ENERGY

Blinds help keep out undesirable solar radiation in summer, yet let in cool breezes. In winter, they can let in solar radiation and diffuse sunlight to give natural lighting.—*Louise Lavelle, Lodi, NJ*

SEALED MAIL FLAP

Make certain that your mail slot flap closes tightly after mail has been delivered. Weatherstrip around the flap if necessary, to keep cooled air from escaping in summer, and cold gusts from entering in the winter.—*Marsha Hallahan, East Lynn, MA*

WEATHERSTRIPPING

FREEZING NEWSPAPERS

As you empty your freezer, or when you buy a new one, fill the empty sections with newspapers. The paper displaces airspace with solid, cold-retaining material, so your freezer won't run as often. In a power outage, a filled freezer keeps food frozen longer than a half-filled one.—*Sherrine Whalley, Springbrook, WI*

PREHEATING WATER

To reduce the cost of heating water, I wrapped 25 ft. of flexible copper tubing around the exhaust flue of my furnace. (I prevented contact of dissimilar metals by separating them with high-temperature insulating strips.) Then I hooked one end of the tubing to the water source, and ran the other end into my water heater. I covered the copper with 1,200° F. fiberglass insulation. In this way, water going into the heater is preheated by the furnace.—*Kevin Callahan, Scranton, PA*

INSULATING WATER LINE

Water from our water heater must travel a long distance, dissipating heat en route to the opposite side of the house. I realized that for the water to reach our sink and dishwasher at the proper temperature (at least 140° F.), it had to leave the hot-water tank at a slightly higher temperature. However, I was able to turn down the water-heater thermostat after I blanketed the hot-water line with an inexpensive foam tape covered with aluminum foil. Not only do we save money, but we expect that our den, through which the line runs, will stay slightly cooler this summer.—*John D. Bowman, Birmingham, AL*

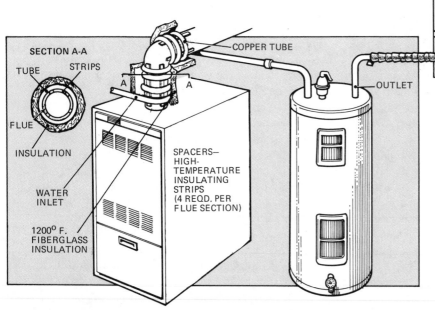

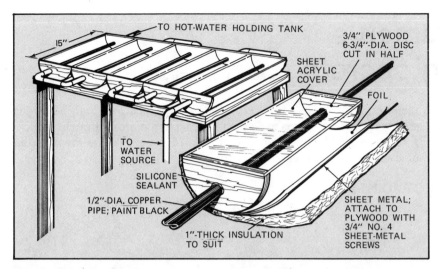

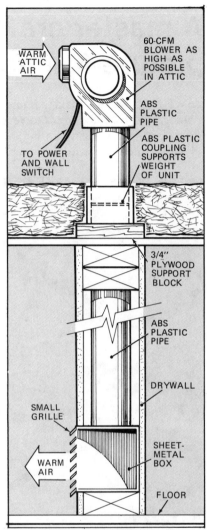

SOLAR WATER HEATER

I have a solar water-heater trough that boils water in 30 minutes when the outside temperature is 70° F. You can combine several troughs, or use a single unit on camping trips. To build it, cut a 6¾-in.-dia. disc of ¾-in. plywood; cut it in half. Use sheet-metal screws to fasten the wood at both ends of a 15-in.-long piece of sheet metal, cut to proper width.

Mark the center of both plywood pieces and bore holes for ½-in.-dia. copper pipe. Glue heavy-duty aluminum foil inside the trough. Insert copper pipe painted black into the two holes, then seal them. Place acrylic cover on trough and glue insulation on back. Hook up one pipe end to a water source, the other to a holding tank.—*Enoch E. Welch, San Antonio, TX*

FOILING THE SUN

I live in a trailer house which gets no natural shade and is quite warm in summer. Several years ago, I covered my windows with aluminum foil. It reflects the sun away from the trailer so that my home is much cooler. I've used this idea for several summers now, to my great relief.—*Ann Williams, Lake Village, AR*

COOLING THE KITCHEN

In order to cool the kitchen/family room of my house without airconditioning, I installed a used, hot-air furnace blower on the basement floor with the discharge facing upward. A duct discharges the cooled air through a kitchen cabinet. I've removed the cabinet floor and subflooring under the cabinet. The blower operates from a switch inside the cabinet. I leave the doors open when the blower is on. I've placed return air grilles in the floor of my family room which opens onto the kitchen; these grilles return warmed air to the basement to be cooled again. Since the basement area is about one-third larger than the area cooled, the upstairs is cooled comfortably at minimal cost.—*Thomas Freemes, Chapel Hill, NC*

WEATHERSTRIP SAVER

To protect pile weatherstripping on sliding patio doors from wearing out and letting in cold air, lubricate it with silicone spray. First, vacuum all of the grit from the weatherstripping and tracks; then use a silicone spray with a tube applicator (or trade tops with another compatible can with a tube applicator). This will make the door slide more easily, as well. Also, file any rough metal edges that may rub against the weatherstripping and tear it. Repeat this procedure each summer.—*Tim Verschuyl, Palo Alto, CA*

SPREADING THE HEAT

Since our Northwest home is extremely well insulated, warmth from the sun cannot penetrate on many spring and autumn days, even when the sun is bright. Yet, operating the electric furnace to take off the chill would be overkill. On these days, the attic (under dark shingles) stays quite toasty. I've captured this heat by installing plastic pipe ducts at each end of the house in a centrally located partition. I topped these ducts with 60-cfm blowers in the attic, which feed to small grilles in a sheet-metal box that I pop-riveted together at floor level of the floor below. Each blower is controlled independently by a manual wall switch. When we need heat and the sun's been shining an hour or more, these gadgets do the job, almost for free.—*Ken Brooks, Vashon, WA*

A master craftsman's picture-framing secrets   By ADOLPH J. MAIER JR.

■ WHEN I BEGAN making frames for the prints and photographs collected over the years, I used very few tools: a 10-in. table saw, a 4-in. jointer, a shaper with about 30 cutters, a vacuum cleaner and some small ac-cessories. Gradually, I designed and built additional items to do the job faster and more accurately. Following are useful aids that have evolved as my work has progressed.

MITER JIG HELPS MAKE PERFECT JOINTS

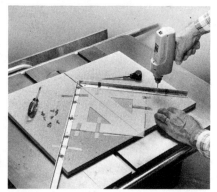

MITER JIG (left) aids in mitering frame molding accurately. Jig's spring clamp applies tension to sliding holding block to secure molding. To position jig's aluminum angle guides (above), abut the long edges of two accurate 45°/90° triangles over centerline. Tape them firmly in place; then tape guides as shown. Saw guard is removed for photo.

■ THE FIRST ITEM that I built was a miter jig. This aid ensures that frame members are mitered accurately on a table saw, so they will come together in a perfect joint. The jig consists of a base, two aluminum angle guides carefully positioned at 45° angles from the saw blade, and two clamping mechanisms that hold the molding being cut against the aluminum angles. This method of securing the molding as it passes through the saw blade eliminates stock drift and ensures its receiving an accurate 45° miter cut.

Each of the identical clamping mechanisms for the aluminum angle guides consists of a clamping block that applies even pressure to hold the molding against the aluminum angle, a spring tension clamp which works with a lever action to apply tension on the clamping block, and a clamp slide on which one end of a spring from the spring tension clamp is fastened.

To build the miter jig, first cut the ⅝-in. plywood or particleboard base. Two guides of flat bar stock or hardwood, which are attached to the base, should fit snugly in the miter gauge grooves of the table saw. They should slide without binding.

Before locating the aluminum angle guides, make a 5-in. saw cut centered on the base. Then turn off the saw. With a carpenter's square placed flat against the blade but not in line with the (set) teeth, use a sharp, 4H pencil to draw a line from the end of the cut to the back of the base. Butt the long edges of two 45°/90° triangles over the centerline (see photo) and tape them firmly in place. Then, tape the aluminum angle against the short edges of the triangles. Bore pilot holes and fasten the angles in place with screws.

Use metal shears to cut out the 26-ga. steel slide hold; a hacksaw will cut ⅛-in. bar stock for the clamp slide and spring tension clamp. Cut the wood parts.

You can bend the slide hold to shape with it clamped between two hardwood blocks (of the same size) held in a machinist's vise. One ¾x4x5-in. block should have a ¼x1⅛-in.-wide center groove. On the second block, center and temporarily tape in place the ¼x¾-in. flat stock used in the clamp slide.

Bend the angles that hold the spring tension clamp to the base by clamping the stock vertically in the vise—shorter leg of the angle in the vise—up to the bend point. Apply pressure with a wood block to make the bend.

Assemble the spring tension clamps as well as the clamp slides and wood blocks. Locate the components on the jig base. Secure the clamp slide with the slide hold. Secure the spring tension clamp. Install the screen door spring.

To cut moldings, I have found it best to cut the frame molding to approximate length before making the miter cuts.

I make the first miter cut on the right (short aluminum angle) side. I measure and make the second cut on the left side.

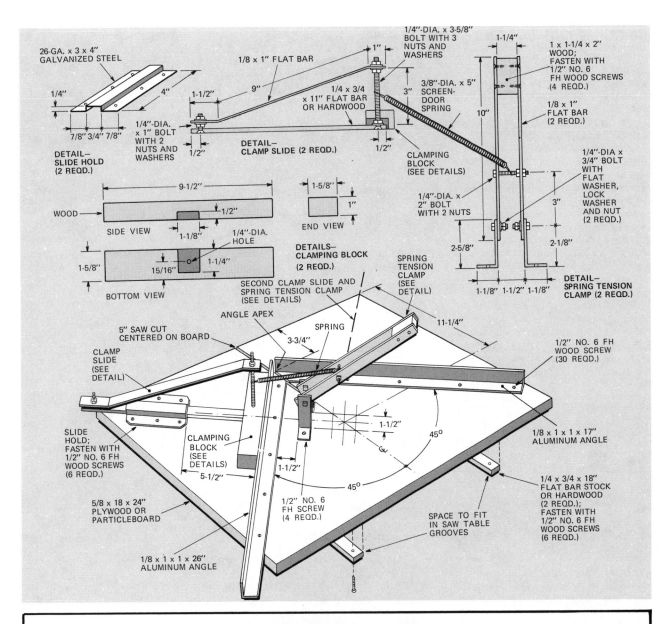

MAKING FRAMES FROM SCRAP MOLDING

■ YOU CAN EASILY turn salvaged mold-ing remnants into useful picture frames.

Simply cut a rabbet along the length of one edge, and you have picture frame mold-ing that's ready to be cut to length. Most of the time, you'll want to rabbet the thicker portion of the molding, so the frame tapers outward (see top drawing at right).

In situations where you want to position the thicker portion of the molding outward, and the other edge isn't thick enough for a rabbet, you can form a rabbet by gluing to the back of the molding a ¼-in.-thick strip of matching wood, set back ¼-in. from the in-side edge (see bottom drawing). The outer edge of this strip can be either flush with the molding or project beyond it if you want to add an extra dimension.

PHOTO FRAMED *with base molding shows rabbet being cut on circular saw. Final feed with pusher stick.*

Even purchasing new molding of suitable size and shape and converting it to picture molding will help to reduce frame cost.

—Walter E. Burton

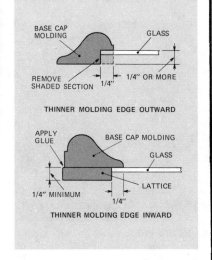

RIP GUIDE AIDS CUTTING

■ THIS GUIDE lets you rip several pieces of stock to exactly the same width on a table saw. Molding from one piece can be used with molding that is made from another.

The guide is made of a wood block that fits snugly into the miter-gauge groove; a movable, dimensioned cross-piece with a guide pad of plastic-laminate-faced hardboard abuts the work, while hardwood blocks on both sides of the crosspiece guide it.

You can set the crosspiece to the width of the molding desired and lock it in place by tightening the wingnut. After securing the guide from the bottom with a steel bar, carefully apply an epoxy adhesive fillet to the wingnut's bolt to lock it.

To make a cut, place the side of the board against the guide pad. Then move the fence firmly against the other side of the board. Back the fence away very slightly with the micro adjusting knob, so the board moves freely, and lock the fence in place.

SET THE RIP guide to produce a molding of the desired width. Adjust the rip fence so the work butts against the laminated guide pad, yet still is able to move freely.

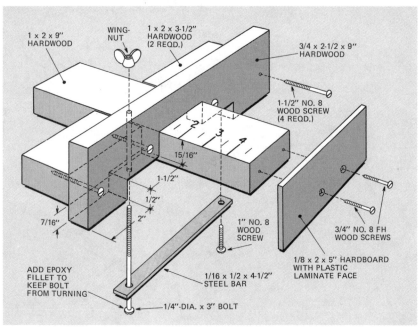

1 x 2 x 9" HARDWOOD
WING-NUT
1 x 2 x 3-1/2" HARDWOOD (2 REQD.)
3/4 x 2-1/2 x 9" HARDWOOD
1-1/2" NO. 8 WOOD SCREW (4 REQD.)
15/16"
1-1/2"
1/2"
7/16"
2"
1" NO. 8 WOOD SCREW
3/4" NO. 8 FH WOOD SCREWS
1/8 x 2 x 5" HARDBOARD WITH PLASTIC LAMINATE FACE
ADD EPOXY FILLET TO KEEP BOLT FROM TURNING
1/16 x 1/2 x 4-1/2" STEEL BAR
1/4"-DIA. x 3" BOLT

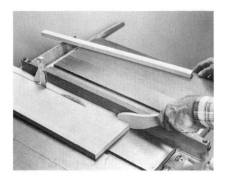

STANDARD METHOD of ripping multiple pieces to the same width requires push stick and antikickback-finger.

SHAPER HOLD-DOWNS INCREASE SAFETY

USING SPRING tension, hold-down and hold-in secure a frame strip in place for safe cutting on a shaper.

■ THIS HOLD-DOWN and hold-in, both on rubber casters, keep wood strips in place while they're being cut on the shaper. The hold-in rests flat on the shaper table and is held in place with clamps. Attach the hold-down to two 4x4-in. slotted angles with bolts and wingnuts. In turn, fasten the angles to the shaper fence with the bolts that came with the tool; or use 1-in.-long screws.

The slots in the brackets of the hold-down let you adjust it horizontally or vertically. To raise the hold-in, add a shim under it.

The holders are blocks of hardwood with rubber caster wheels. The wheels are cold-riveted to steel plates which are mortised into the wood block. A spring installed in the block at a 7½° angle and

attached to the casters causes them to press against the work as it passes through the shaper. After you have bored holes for the springs, a straightened paper clip with a small hook shaped at one end can grasp the spring and guide it in place through the hole. The free end of the spring is secured by a steel angle installed in the wood block.

To use the holders, position them so the wood strip being cut stretches the springs about ½-in. Push the work past the cutter, using a push stick. When the end of the strip arrives at the rubber wheels, move to the opposite side of the shaper and pull the strip completely through, exerting pressure in the direction of the fence to keep the strip from moving away and distorting the cut.

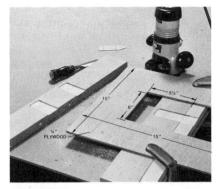

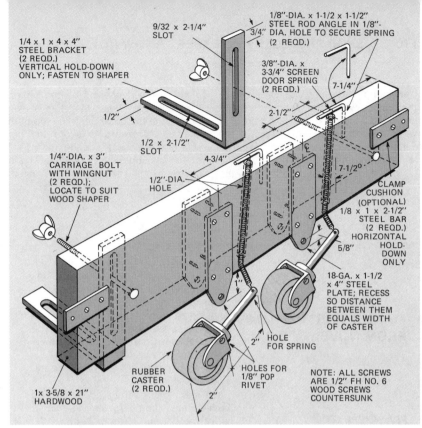

JIG GUIDES router with 5-in.-dia. base and ½-in.-dia. mortise cutter as it plows mortises for caster plates. Alter dimensions to fit router shoe.

Usually, the last few inches are distorted a bit. Allow for this by working with slightly overlength pieces and planning to cut them off when you make miter cuts.

FASTER GLASS CUTTING

■ THIS GLASS-CUTTING setup rivals the commercial rigs on the market. The cutter runs in a guide channel that is attached to a plywood cutting board. The guide channel lets you make a clean stroke with the cutter.

The base of the cutter is an oak block with a 1x2¾-in. center opening. The cutter rides on two pairs of ball bearings, each pair located on an axle installed in an axle block. The ball bearings I used were taken from old hand tools, such as screw guns and drills. The tool handle is made of flat bar stock bent in a metalworking vise and fastened over the rear axle block; an oak grip secured with contact cement then fits within the handle.

An angle secured over the front axle block contains an eyebolt and wingnut. The eyebolt is connected to the center

PLACE GLASS on cutting board and under guide channel. Cutter is moved from top to bottom in one clean stroke.

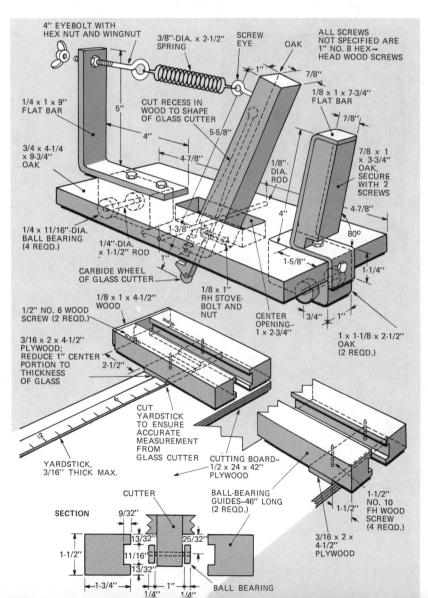

by a spring. The spring applies tension to the cutter when the eyebolt is connected. The glass cutter is bolted to a vertical wood block cut to receive the cutter. The block pivots on a rod secured to the cutter base.

To use the jig, align the left side of the glass to the dimension on the board's yardstick that you want the finished glass. Run the cutter from the top of the channel downward to score the right side of the glass. Place the scored side of the glass up on the worktable with the excess hanging over the table. Grasp the edge of the excess firmly, raise the glass slightly and crack it sharply on the table.

Note: If you can't locate ball bearings in your area, a set of four ($\frac{1}{4}$-i.d.x$^{11}/_{16}$-o.d.x$\frac{1}{4}$-in. thick) is about $12 postpaid from Armor Co., Box 290, Deer Park, NY 11729.

MAKE A RUSTIC FRAME FROM NOVELTY SIDING

FRAME CREATED
from drop siding is simple, fine for country scenes.

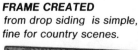

■ THE CONTOUR of novelty (drop) siding used on houses and other buildings can be used to advantage in making rustic picture frames. Often you can find such siding in rural areas or purchase it from house-wrecking companies. The less paint on it and the more weather-beaten its appearance, the more handsome your frames will be, providing the wood is still sound.

To make frames from siding, first rip both edges of the board, leaving about 2 in. of the flat surface and ¾-in. of the curved portion. You may wish to vary these dimensions according to the over-all size of the frame you're working with.

Second, cut a ¼-in.-deep x ½-in.-wide rabbet in the frame back so the art can be mounted in place. You can cut the rabbet with a table saw, a radial saw or a router.

Third, cut mitered frame members to size. Assemble them with glue and two finishing nails per joint. Start one nail on each frame member of the joint. A miter clamp helps make good frame joints.

You can paint the newly cut edges to match the weathered surface. Usually, black, white and brown pigments are suitable.

—Ralph S. Wilkes

PAINT fresh-cut edge to match frame's aged surface as closely as possible.

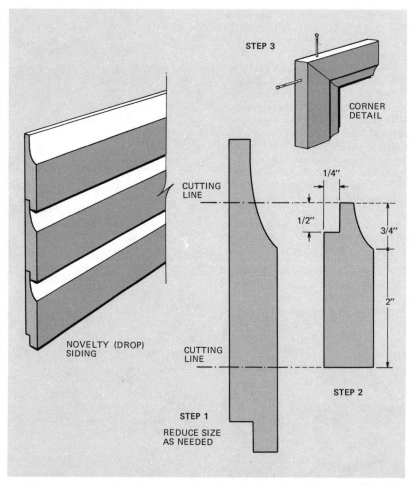

STEP 3

CORNER DETAIL

CUTTING LINE

1/4"

1/2"

3/4"

2"

NOVELTY (DROP) SIDING

CUTTING LINE

STEP 1

REDUCE SIZE AS NEEDED

STEP 2

SPRAY PAINTER'S 'THIRD HAND'

■ THE ACCESSORY that pleases me most is the holder I use to paint picture frames. I devised it one day after a freshly painted frame—hanging precariously on a coat hanger—crashed to the floor.

The major parts of the holder are two pieces of wood held together by a carriage bolt, external tooth washer, flat washer and wingnut. The accessory hangs by a screw eye in the end of the shorter wood member. The longer member holds the picture frame impaled at the top and bottom of its rabbet on 4d finishing nails, their heads cut off.

The nails are installed in a pair of wood blocks. A drill press and sloping jig help bore holes for these nails to uniform depth. One of the wood blocks is stationary. The other block is secured in a sheetmetal slide positioned so the nails can secure the frame. Once the block is in position, you can apply tension to it by stretching a spring fastened to one end. The spring is covered by a rectangular aluminum tube to protect it from paint.

Begin painting the vertical frame members with both wood pieces of the jig positioned vertically. Swivel the jig to paint all sides of the vertical frame members. Next, loosen the wingnut and rotate the longer wood member so it is in a horizontal position. Then paint the remaining frame members.

I've built several of these jigs. After one frame is painted, I return the jig to the original position and hang it on a nearby nail until the frame is dry.

My paint booth consists of a 16-in., direct-drive fan with explosion-proof motor installed in the end wall of my shop. Two curtains on rods are attached to the ceiling joists. The leading edges of the curtains have vertical steel rods in the hem. When I am ready to paint, I extend the curtains and secure them with ties at the lower corners.

Selecting the right type of paint is sometimes a problem. However, if you're painting several frames in different colors, it's convenient to use spray paints. I've had luck antiquing frames using a solid blue with black glazing. A coat of solid gold, followed by a light spray of either red, black or light green paint also works well.

One last tip: Although it is difficult for me to buy mats or other framing supplies locally, an economical mail order source is: Herbert A. Japs, 126 Seventh Ave. N., Hopkins, MN 55343.

FAST AND EFFICIENT way to spray-paint a frame is to impale it securely on the frame holder. The horizontal wood piece is then rotated vertically to paint the edges.

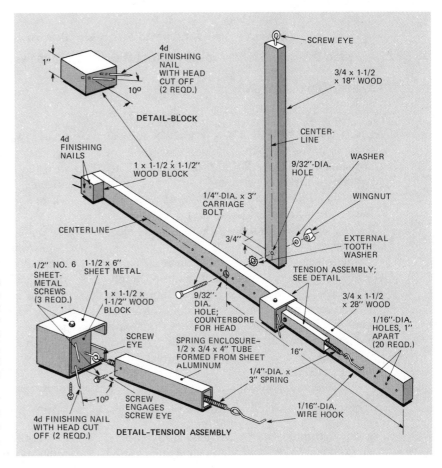

A RANDOM SAMPLING of available solvents illustrates why picking one isn't always easy.

The right way to choose and use solvents

The correct solvent simplifies a job; the wrong one can ruin it or even
lead to injury. Here's how to select the best one for your needs

By BERNARD GLADSTONE

■ CHANCES ARE that hardly a day goes by at home or in your shop that you don't use a solvent of some kind, even if it's water—one of the oldest and most widely used solvents.

By definition, a solvent is a liquid that dissolves things to create a solution. For most of us, it's also a thinner (although there are technical differences).

The solvents that are sold in your local paint, hardware, auto accessory and marine supply stores are almost always organic compounds derived from petroleum or by-products of petroleum-based compounds. Many have long and strange-sounding names that would probably mean nothing to a store clerk if you asked for them by chemical name.

However, the most widely available and most useful of these solvents have generic or "common" names that *are* familiar to most of us. The so-called common names are not always accurate, and don't always mean the same thing to ev-

eryone who buys, sells, and uses solvents. To avoid misunderstanding, it pays to be familiar with the most widely available and most useful solvents, and to know something about when, where and how to use each.

safety first

Since many of these substances are highly flammable and emit toxic fumes, observe strict safety habits when working with *any* solvents.
• Work in a well-ventilated room.
• Wear gloves and respiratory protection if required.
• *Always* read the manufacturer's instructions before you open the can.

turpentine

One of the few common solvents not derived from petroleum (it's distilled from the sap of certain coniferous trees), turpentine is used principally for thinning oil- or alkyd-base paints.

Contrary to popular opinion, turpentine (turps) is never actually used by manufacturers in formulating paint. One reason is that turpentine is more expensive than the other available solvents.

Another popular misconception is that turpentine is better than the less expensive, petroleum-based thinners for thinning paint. It is true that turpentine is a more powerful solvent; that is, it has more solvency than other paint thinners. But this can be a drawback. You have to be much more careful about the amount you use. If you add a little too much turpentine, paint can be overthinned, causing it to run or drip when it is applied.

This ability to thin or dissolve paint more effectively does have one advantage: Turpentine is more effective at cleaning brushes and rollers than most other types of paint thinner (although it is still not as good as a solvent that is made specifically for cleaning brushes). However, turpentine won't soften hardened paint; it only dissolves paint that is still soft and not fully cured.

mineral spirits and varnolene

Also called "white spirits" or "subturps" in some areas, mineral spirits is the solvent used in most brands of paint thinner sold over the counter in local paint and hardware stores. Odorless paint thinner is much the same, except that it is treated to remove or mask the odor. These solvents have less of an odor than turpentine.

Mineral spirits and varnolene are refined petroleum distillates with a low aromatic hydrocarbon content and a higher flash point (less flammable) than naphtha and similar solvents that are sometimes used for thinning paint. It also is less volatile, so it doesn't evaporate as fast. This helps improve working qualities by making it easier to spread on the paint or varnish without leaving lap marks.

Like turpentine, mineral spirits can be used for cleaning brushes and rollers, but only if used immediately after you stop painting. Turpentine will soften a brush that is partially hardened if you soak it first, but mineral spirits generally won't; it only dissolves paint that is still liquid.

These petroleum distillate solvents can also be used as a cleaning and degreasing solvent to remove or dissolve grease and oil when cleaning metal, masonry and similar surfaces.

ALTHOUGH MANY makers of wood fillers recommend thinning the compound with their own brand of solvent, lacquer thinner can sometimes be used.

YOU CAN USE odor-free, commercial paint thinner to thin oil or alkyd-base paints. Mineral spirits is the solvent in this product that thins the paint.

USE 1,1,1-trichloroethane to clean and degrease metal. Use it to clean typewriter type and machine parts. It also dissolves tar, oil and adhesive.

SEMIPASTE paint and varnish remover dissolves stain and varnish on desk drawer for removal by scraping. Then surface is neutralized with water.

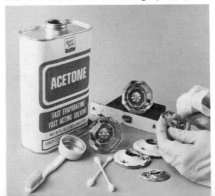

WHEN YOU can't scrape paint off with a razor, it can be removed from glass and metal with acetone. It evaporates fast and is best for removing spatters.

SPOT REMOVER sprays on clear, then dries to a white powder to lift spots in clothing and upholstery. Cap is a brush to remove the powder.

naphtha

Very often, this is sold under the name of VMP maphtha (stands for "Varnish Makers' and Painters' " naphtha) or benzine. Naphtha can be used for thinning many oil-base paints, but its most popular use is to clean and degrease. As a general rule, it is better to use mineral spirits for thinning paint unless the label on the paint can specifically says that naphtha or VMP naphtha can be used.

Naphtha is more volatile than mineral spirits and turpentine, so it tends to make paint dry faster. It also has a higher solvency rating, so it will thin paint more than the same amount of other thinners, though it's more flammable. Wear gloves and a respiratory mask when you work with naphtha.

lacquer thinner

This substance is actually a blend of various solvents, such as acetone, toluene, ketone and others. There is no standardization of formulas, so not all brands are the same. However, as the name implies, the main use for lacquer thinner is to thin lacquer and lacquer-based synthetic finishes, as well as to clean brushes used in lacquer. It is also useful for thinning fast-drying wood plastic patching compounds.

Lacquer thinner is also a pretty good all-around brush cleaner. It will soften or break up most paints, as well as lacquer, even after they have hardened.

You can also use lacquer thinner to clean off excess adhesive when working with cements and adhesives that have a solvent baste. As it will atack many plastics, be careful where and how you use it. It is much more flammable than regular paint thinners or turpentine, and evaporates much faster when left in an open container.

alcohol

The type of alcohol we are talking about here is denatured alcohol (not medicinal or rubbing alcohol). It is used for thinning shellac and shellac-base sealers, and for cleaning brushes and tools that have been used in shellac.

SOLVENTS made for cleaning hands don't remove needed body oils. This one wipes off to remove grime, grease and stains.

STORE SOLVENTS in a lockable metal cabinet out of a child's reach. Flammable solvents should be kept in a metal cabinet, preferably out of the house.

SOLVENTS—USES AND LIMITATIONS

Solvent	Flammable	Principal uses	Drawbacks
Turpentine	Yes	Thinning oil, alkyd paint and varnish; cleaning brushes and rollers	Strong odor; expensive
Mineral Spirits or Varnoline	Yes	Thinning oil, alkyd paint and varnish; cleaning brushes and rollers	Won't soften brushes that have started to harden
Naphtha (Benzine)	Very	Spot removal; degreasing; thinning paint	Highly volatile; very strong odor; wear gloves and face mask
Lacquer Thinner	Very	Thinning lacquer and some patching compounds; brush cleaning; grease removal	Evaporates very rapidly; attacks some plastics and many finishes
Denatured Alcohol	Very	Thinning shellac; cleaning shellac brushes	Softens shellac; affects some finishes
Acetone	Very	Thinning resins used with fiberglass; cleaning tools used with resins and some adhesive cements	Very volatile; attacks all finishes and most plastics; attacks nylon brushes; strong odor
Methylene Chloride	No	Removing paint and varnish	Tough on skin; attacks all finishes and plastics
Perchloro-ethylene	No	Cleaning; degreasing; spot removal	Fumes can be mildly toxic in confined quarters
1,1,1-Trichloro-ethane	No	Cleaning; degreasing; spot removal; dry cleaning	Fumes can be mildly toxic in confined quarters
Kerosene	Yes	Thinning asphalt paints for slower drying times	Strong odor; can irritate skin; leaves oily film

Unlike some types of thinners, alcohol will soften dried shellac, no matter how old it is. It will soften a brush that has been used in shellac. It is also useful for removing light pencil marks from raw wood.

other useful solvents

Acetone. One of the main ingredients in most lacquer thinners, and in many paintbrush cleaners, acetone is a very strong solvent and one of the most volatile. Although it can be used to thin lacquer and some synthetic finishes, it generally does not make a good thinner because it evaporates too fast.

You can use acetone as a remover on small jobs. But it evaporates so fast that it is not effective except for removing spots.

Acetone, similar to lacquer thinner, is highly flammable. Its main use around the shop is when working with polyester resins and fiberglass. It is often recommended as a thinner for these products, and it is normally the best solvent for cleaning off tools and equipment when working with these materials. It is also an effective solvent for removing excess plastic cement. It is almost the only solvent you can use to soften and remove one-drop or instant-type glues (the cyanoacrylates).

Acetone will dissolve many plastics and synthetic fabrics, so you have to use it carefully. It will soften and sometimes attack nylon. Therefore, you shouldn't use a nylon brush to apply any material that has acetone in it, or that uses acetone as a thinner. You can use it on natural bristle brushes, or those made of polyester filaments.

Methylene chloride. If you go into your local paint or hardware store and ask for this by name, you'll almost certainly get a blank stare. However, this is the principal ingredient in most modern paint and varnish removers.

It is a very powerful solvent that will soften most old paints and finishes. But it is almost always combined with other ingredients such as acetone, isopropyl alcohol, ethyl alcohol and one or two other solvents in order to improve working qualities, or to make it more effective on some hard-to-remove finishes such as epoxy.

Perchloroethylene. Here's another useful solvent that you really can't ask for by chemical name. However, you will find it listed as the principal ingredient on the label of many cleaning and degreasing solvents. Often labeled as a cleaning fluid for general use on fabrics and other materials around the home, it is the product that

has taken over as a replacement for carbon tetrachloride since that dangerous solvent was removed from the market.

While still marginally toxic, the fumes given off by perchloroethylene are not nearly as dangerous or as toxic as carbon tet. It isn't flammable. It is an excellent "dry cleaning" and spot-removing fluid, which also works well as a degreaser for cleaning off metal parts or machinery. Although it is sometimes used alone, very often it is mixed with 1,1,1-trichloroethane and sold as a combination spot remover, cleaning agent and degreaser.

1,1,1-Trichloroethane. This solvent's name is seldom given as part of the brand name, but several products include the "1,1,1-" as part of their name. Like perchloroethylene, 1,1,1- is a nonflammable degreasing and cleaning solvent that is widely used in place of carbon tetrachloride these days.

Kerosene. Used primarily as a fuel, kerosene also removes grease and oil from machinery and metal parts, though it leaves an oily film. It has limited use for removing or softening tar and asphalt patching materials, but can be used to thin roof cement.

Chemically similar to mineral spirits, kerosene is much less volatile, doesn't evaporate as fast and is oilier.

storing and using solvents

Although they vary in degree, almost all solvents are toxic if taken internally. Most of them also give off fumes that are at least mildly toxic if inhaled to any degree. Therefore, it is wise to follow these safety procedures:

• Store these products where children can't get at them.

• Avoid using solvents in confined places that are not well ventilated. It helps to use an exhaust fan.

• Not all solvents are flammable, but those that are should be stored in tightly closed containers *outside* the living quarters of the house, or at least kept in the garage in a metal cabinet.

• Avoid keeping large containers of solvents if you don't often use them.

• Periodically check containers for leakage.

• Never store or use solvents near a furnace or other source of heat, such as a stove, outdoor barbecue or in front of a window that gets direct sunlight.

• If you use solvents above eye level or in a situation where solvent may splash, wear safety goggles.

Expert solutions for nitty-gritty little problems

Have you ever painted yourself into a corner or tried to build a full-size boat in your basement? Here are 11 typical aggravations you might have in your home workshop—and how the experts solve them

By JOHN INGERSOLL

■ BEGINNERS DO IT. Journeyman carpenters do it. Even mastercraftsmen do it. No one who tackles home repairs or has a workshop is immune to an occasional workworking snafu. The professional falls back upon his experience— time-proven steps and methods that will get him out of trouble with comparative ease. You can, too.

On these pages, we have collected 11 of the most common workshop problems, and the solutions for extricating yourself from them. The answers come from a number of professional woodscraftsmen who were happy to share the techniques they use to get their jobs back on the track again.

1 EMBEDDED SCREW   *WHEN YOU BACK OUT A SCREW, ITS HEAD BREAKS OFF.*

IF SURFACE damage is no problem, bore holes around shank of screw.

GRAB SCREW with square or needle-nose pliers and twist counterclockwise.

With a ⅛-in. bit, bore holes straight down all around the screw shaft. In softwood, puncture with a thin finishing nail. A little digging may be needed to get needle-nose or locking pliers around the top of the shaft. Twist and pull.

If you can't mar the wood, drill a hole in the center of the shank, about one-third the shank's diameter. Pick a screw extractor to fit the hole; set extractor head in a socket or tap wrench; insert head and turn wrench counterclockwise. Reverse threads on the extractor bite into the inside of the screw shaft, forcing it to turn. This also works on a shorn bolt in an engine head.

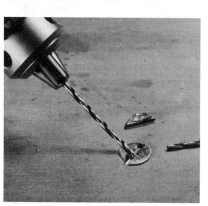

TO AVOID damaging surface around screw, drill hole in shank. Start at angle if surface is uneven.

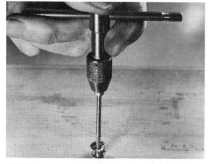

INTO screw-shank hole, insert screw extractor set in tap wrench. Twist counterclockwise. Sets are about $1 from Brookstone Co., Vose Farm Rd., Peterborough, NH 03458.

2 BROKEN DRILL BIT   *IN THE MIDDLE OF A DRILLING JOB, YOUR ONLY DRILL BIT BREAKS.*

The first thing to do is to file away the burrs on the protruding tip of whatever is left of the broken bit. Then, you can rechuck this piece and continue the drilling procedure, if possible.

If this doesn't work, there's another solution to the problem. File a spade tip on a nail of the same diameter as the broken bit. Then, cut off the nailhead, insert the revised bit (the nail) in your drill chuck, tighten securely and resume the drilling.

3 END SPLITS

WHEN YOU DRIVE IN A NAIL, YOU SPLIT THE END OF A BOARD.

STRAIGHTEN protruding shank and set it well below surface with nailset. Fill hole and sand smooth.

EXTRACT NAIL; wipe away glue. After it's dry, bore pilot hole.

Force a thin line of carpenter's glue in the crack; remove the nail. Wood tends to return to its original form, so it will press sides of the crack together. When glue sets, bore a hole slightly less than the diameter of the nail and renail through this hole.

Predrill holes for all fastening near the edge of a wood member.

4 STUCK DRAWERS

HUMIDITY SWELLS DRAWERS, FORCING THEM TO STICK.

Locate a retail outlet that sells desiccants (chemical drying agents) such as silica gel or calcium chloride. Well-stocked hardware stores often carry them.

If you can't find any, write to Lionel Industries Inc., 2035 Burlington Rd., Akron, OH 44313. This company makes a desiccant called Hum-i-dry in 12-ounce packages for about $2.

Now, buy a plastic trash bag large enough to enclose the chest, or make your own sealed cover with a polyethylene dropcloth and tape. Put the pack of humidity-absorbing chemical in a saucer on the chest. Cover everything with the plastic and seal tightly with tape. Wait about 48 hours. Unseal the bag. The chemicals should have absorbed enough moisture—the culprit that makes drawers stick—to loosen them.

If this doesn't work, examine each one of the drawers. Use a piece of 220-grit abrasive to sand scuffed areas where drawers bind. Sand scuffed areas in the cabinet also.

Once the drawers slide out as they did in the drier weather, put a coat of clear, glossy polyurethane varnish over the drawer interiors.

5 CRUSHED THREADS

NUT WON'T THREAD OR BACK OFF BECAUSE THREADS ARE CRUSHED.

A hand-operated thread restorer from Brookstone (around $33), does the job. It slips over the bolt at a point where good threads remain. Claws are tightened until the cutting edge is inside a groove. You rotate the tool over the damaged part and the cutter restores the threads to let the nut pass.

Where enough threads are exposed, a standard thread-cutting die of the correct size may also be used.

USE THREAD restorer for job. With one of these tools, you'll be able to make quick repairs. It sells for about $33 from the Brookstone Co., Peterborough, NH 03458.

6 MISCUT MITER   *AFTER YOU CUT TWO MEMBERS OF A WOOD FRAME TO SIZE, YOU DISCOVER THAT THE MITER JOINT DOESN'T MATCH.*

If you have plenty of frame stock, simply cut another length. If not, carefully measure the width and angle of the joint undercut area. From any leftover scraps,

cut a slightly oversize section to fit the gap.

This may sound easy, but it isn't, according to master woodscraftsman John Harra, the president of John Harra Wood Supply Co., New York. "Cutting that tight an angle takes a lot more skill than most people have. It would probably be easier to use plumber's epoxy and mold the stuff into the joint," he suggests. This is meant for wood frames that you plan to paint.

POSITION members with square. Measure gap. From same framing stock, cut piece slightly oversize to fill gap.

7 LOST NAILHEAD

A NAILHEAD BREAKS OR BECOMES MANGLED AS YOU PULL IT OUT.

There are several solutions. You can set the shank below the surface with a nailset and fill the hole with wood putty. If the nail must be removed, start driving the shaft down with a nailset, then force it through the other side of the wood member with a nail of the same diameter, the tip of which you've clipped off with a hacksaw. Then pull out the shank from the other side.

If the shank juts above the surface, grip it with locking pliers and rock the pliers back on the outer curve of the jaws. This produces the same action as a hammer's claw.

If you run into this problem often, you might want to get a tool that's specifically designed to yank out headless nails. The Brookstone Co. makes one—it's called a ''nail outener''—for under $16.

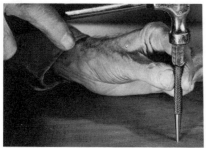

STRAIGHTEN protruding shank and set it well below surface with nailset. Fill hole and sand smooth.

IF NAIL must be removed, cut tip off nail of same size or file tip flat. Use nail to drive embedded nail through far enough on other side to pull it out.

8 SPLINTERED CUTS

IN SAWING PLYWOOD, HOW DO YOU AVOID SPLINTERED WOOD PARTICLES ON THE UNDERSIDE?

Using a backup board is the usual way to minimize splintered edges. But for this to work, the boards must be clamped together tightly. Since clamps are often unavailable at the job site, you can make do with masking tape. Press the tape securely to the plywood on the back side of the cut. The cut won't be absolutely clean, but it will be better than without tape.

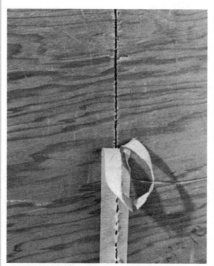

TAPE PEELED away reveals cleaner cut made with this technique.

9 LIMITED SPACE

YOU WANT TO TIGHTEN A NUT IN CLOSE QUARTERS, BUT EVEN A RIGHT-ANGLE WRENCH WON'T FIT IN THE SPACE.

This is a tough one. If the job doesn't require that the nut be tightened to the maximum, chances are you can reach in and push the nut finger-tight. But, if it must be absolutely secure, you can try holding it with an adjustable-grip or needlenose pliers while you turn the machine screw or bolt with the appropriate tool. To keep the plier jaws from slipping off the nut, wrap a turn or two of masking or friction tape over the serrated jaw surfaces.

For those jobs where this stunt won't work, you should consider adding a specialty tool (that Brookstone offers) to your toolbox. Called Starwheel Ratchet Drive, the tool is only 1⁹/₁₆ in. high. With this tool, you can tighten a nut with your hand on the wheel at all times; the ratchet allows you to turn the handle without removing your hand from the tool. Brookstone sells it for approximately $14.

CUTAWAY shows tight spot that is ideal for Starwheel Ratchet Drive.

10 MISCUT MORTISE

*YOU MISTAKENLY CHISEL A HINGE
MORTISE IN THE WRONG PLACE.*

Start by marking the correct measurement for the
hinge. Score the marked lines and mortise the piece
with a sharp chisel. Position the hinge and install the
leaf. Then measure the portion of the mortise to be
filled. Cut the wood patch (called a Dutchman in the
trades) of the same type of wood as the door, if possible. Check it for fit. Apply carpenter's glue sparingly
to both surfaces and install the Dutchman. If the wood is
pine, secure it with ⅝-in. brads set below the surface. If
it's hardwood, prebore lead holes so you don't split the
patch. Wipe off all glue squeeze-out. After the glue
dries, fill the joints, set nails with filler and sand
smooth.

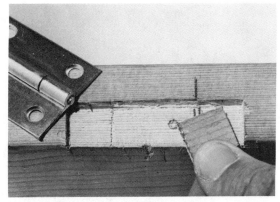

EXTEND MORTISE to receive the hinge in the cor-
rected position. Cut a wood patch called a Dutchman
to fill the excess portion of the mortise.

CHECK DUTCHMAN for proper fit. Then hold it in position with carpenter's glue.

11 CRACKED HANDLE

*WHILE WORKING WITH YOUR HAMMER, THE HANDLE BREAKS, AND
YOU NEED A TEMPORARY REPAIR.*

Wrap the handle with electrical tape. Be
sure to use strong tape and wrap it
tightly. This is not intended to be a permanent solution to your dilemma; it's
only a temporary measure to keep you
going until you can purchase a new handle.

Henry Lanz of Garrett Wade Tools in
New York recommends that you saturate
the split or broken portion of the handle
with an epoxy glue mixed with sawdust.
"Of course, that's going to take 24 hours
to dry," he says.

For those of you who are a little more
ambitious, Lanz also suggests that you
whittle a new handle from scrap hardwood in your shop or from a larger handle that's intended for a bigger tool. An
ax handle, for example, can be chiseled
down until it is just the size necessary for
your hammerhead.

WRAP HANDLE with electrical or other
strong tape and proceed with caution.

AN AX, or other oversize handle, may
be chiseled down to fit hammerhead.
This may only be a temporary solution.

VERSATILE ROUTER is a must-own tool for serious woodworkers. Here, V-groove is routed using tacked-on straightedge. Strip against which router shoe rides must project past workpiece to prevent mishap.

A craftsman's secrets for using a router

Though it screeches like a banshee as it turns at incredible speed, it's the tool you're sure to turn to as your woodworking skills increase from beginner to craftsman

By HARRY WICKS

■ THE ROUTER is a high-speed tool that performs similarly to the stationary shaper except that it is taken to the workpiece instead of the other way around. It can be used for certain other tasks such as trimming high-pressure plastic laminates, mortising for door hinges and making dovetails.

Routers come with speeds from 20,000 to 28,000 rpm. The reason for the high speed is that many shaped edges will not allow hand sanding; they must be smooth enough to finish as soon as they are made. Thus, if you buy a router with a speed of 25,000 rpm you'll get 50,000 blade passes a minute when you use a two-flute bit. That's impressive.

Make it your habit from the start to disconnect the tool from power whenever changing bits. Insert the desired bit into the collet until it bottoms, then back it out 1/16 to 1/8 in. This procedure is to protect the collet from breaking due to heat expansion.

Make absolutely certain that the collet is *fully tightened* before restoring power to your router. Failure to correctly install a bit and tighten the collet could result in a bit hurtling about the room like a piece of shrapnel.

Next, reassemble the motor into the base (on my model I just have to loosen a wingnut on the base). Slide the motor fully into the base and tighten the wingnut.

GENERAL INFORMATION

TYPICAL home router consists of two basic parts: motor which holds bit, and base section for holding and guiding the working half of the tool.

TO CHANGE cutters, start by loosening device holding motor in base. Here, there's thumbnut and slotted screw.

QUICKEST way to change bits is to separate motor and base. Bit can be changed with unit intact, if preferred.

MANUFACTURER supplies wrenches for loosening split collet. Pressure is exerted in opposite directions.

INSERT the bit all the way, then withdraw about 1/16 in. for expansion.

WHEN SHANK is at the desired position, retighten collet with wrenches.

TO SET cutter depth, use a scaled ring supplied on many routers or simply check the bit with a ruler. Here, rabbet cutter is set to 3/8 in. depth.

EASY METHOD is to hold installed cutter against marked workpiece. Waste is marked with X to prevent miscut.

FINISHED rabbeted edge is cut using bit set as shown in preceding photos. The cut is right on the mark.

Installing and removing a bit from a router varies slightly from one brand to another but, basically, the how-to procedure is quite similar. The router, in fact, grips a bit by its shank, somewhat like a drill grips a drill bit. The difference is that instead of three jaws closing around the shank, most routers have a split-nut collet which closes tightly as a second nut is tightened.

Read the instruction book packed with your tool for the correct how-to.

To use the micrometer ring on a router to set bit depth, follow these steps:

1. Place the router on a flat surface.

2. Loosen the wingnut and slide the motor down until the bit barely touches the surface.

3. Retighten the wingnut.

4. Rotate the depth adjustment ring until it hits the base. Now the bit is set for 0 in. depth of cut.

5. Note the position of the graduations on the depth-adjusting ring in relation to the index on the router base (usually a point, or arrow).

6. Rotate the ring in the appropriate direction to achieve the desired depth of cut. On my router the depth is changed by 1/64 in. for every three graduation lines; thus the depth is changed 1/32 in. for every six graduation lines.

7. Loosen the wingnut and slide the motor as far into the base as the depth-adjusting ring permits. Retighten the wingnut and you can put the router to work.

Pro trick: Certain cutters are used more often than others in the type of woodworking most of

CUTTERS TO HAVE IN YOUR ACCESSORY BOX

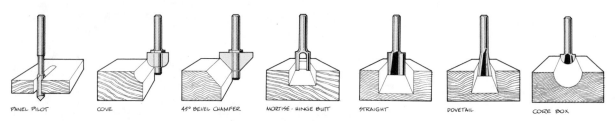

PANEL PILOT   COVE   45° BEVEL CHAMFER   MORTISE - HINGE BUTT   STRAIGHT   DOVETAIL   CORE BOX

THE V-GROOVE and bead bits which are presented on the preceding pages as well as those pictured above and on the opposite page are available in many sizes. Methods of using the bits are described in text.

GUIDING YOUR ROUTER

WITH THE ASSISTANCE of an edge guide, it's even possible to rout a circle.

ALL MAKERS produce edge guides for their routers. Guide shown is for the author's Model 150 Rockwell.

AS ALSO SEEN in the photo on page 120, projecting guide strip gets cutter into the workpiece without mishap. The work, in turn, is clamped to the workbench (clamp not visible).

us do. This includes the rabbet and straight (mortise) cutters. Thus, I made up a board with both of these cuts plowed to exactly ¼- and ⅜-in. depths—the usual depths for working with ¾-in.-thick boards. Each time I need to set a ⅜-in. rabbet cutter ⅜-in. deep, I don't have to fiddle with rulers; I simply and quickly set the bit using the precut board.

There are five ways to guide a router:
1. With a pilot on the bit.
2. With an edge guide.
3. Freehand.
4. Against an edge.
5. With a templet guide.

Methods are listed in the order that I think a beginner should tackle them—the easiest is first.

guiding with a bit

Almost all decorative edging done with a router is with a bit that has a self-contained pilot. The pilot rides the edge of the material during the cut, so it is important that the edge be in perfect shape. For example, when putting an edge on a piece of plywood the pilot will enter any voids in the plywood, causing the decorative edging to indent, too.

When using a piloted bit make the cuts sequentially as shown on page 124. Always start the router with the cutter standing away from the wood, then feed the spinning bit into the workpiece. Since the router bit spins in a clockwise direction, when viewed from above, an outside edge is always routed from left to right. Feed the tool in about ¼ in. or so from the left end of the

ROUNDING-OVER bit might well be first one you will purchase. This shape is available in at least four radii.

ROMAN OGEE is also a good bit to own; shape gives an attractive edge to plaques and the like. By using lower portion only, you create a small cove.

Router bits fall into two major classifications—one-piece bits and three-piece screw-type bits. All are of high-quality steel that has been heat-treated for hardness (so the cutting edges will be retained over fairly long periods of use). Steel bits are priced from about $8 to $20 with the three-piecers at the upper limit.

If you plan on doing a lot of woodworking you should consider purchasing carbide-tipped bits on those shapes you'll use most often. These start at about $18.

EDGE GUIDE on this router is installed into two holes in router base.

THUMBSCREWS are finger-tightened so that rods are secure, but movable. Next, router is turned over and guide set the desired distance from bit.

THUMBSCREWS are securely tightened; you might damage workpiece if edge guide should shift. To rout, lower spinning cutter into work.

If you buy your router in a kit form, which generally means it comes with a carrying case, the chances are the manufacturer will include a router-edge guide. If not, be sure to buy one.

The router (except when you do freehand routing) must be guided to create the professional-looking finishing touches you want. Thus, when you work with a straight (nonpiloted) bit you'll often need an edge guide.

The guide used to control the router is also handy for cutting along the edge of

a board. It is particularly useful for routing decorative grooves parallel to the edge of a board and for cutting grooves on long pieces of lumber. It is frequently used in mortise and dovetail work.

The edge-guide installation may vary from that shown. Here, the two rods are installed in holes provided on the base. They are held by tightening the machine screws already in the base. The guide is then installed on the rods and slid in or out until the correct distance from bit to guide is obtained. Thumbscrews are

then tightened.

Though some craftsmen measure from bit center to edge guide, I work with dimensions from bit edge to guide.

To start shaping, butt the guide against board edge, tilt-elevate the router to clear the cutter from wood and start the motor. Then lower the cutter into the workpiece.

The router will do far more than simply make decorative edges on boards. Try rigging a setup for cutting dovetail-shaped "tongue and grooves" on boards to be edge-joined.

board, push right for a couple of inches then bring the tool all the way to the left and off the board. If you are routing just the one edge, don't allow the pilot to turn the board corner or you will edge-shape the end of the board as well. If necessary, you can tack a guide to the workpiece in order to prevent this.

several rules:

■ Always rout the edge grains first as shown in the drawing on page 124. You will learn that as the router bit exits an end grain on the far end it is not uncommon to have some splintering. If this is your last pass, it means that the finished adjacent edge may be splintered. But, done correctly, end grain first, the following pass—with the grain—will remove the splintered wood.

■ A constant rate of feed is important for achieving a smooth cut. The point is to work your tool so that the router is working at its highest possible rpm. This will vary, depending upon the material being worked, depth of cut, sharpness of cutter and so on.

■ As soon as the cut is completed, release the trigger to turn off the power to the router. Do not put the tool down until the cutter stops spinning.

using an edge guide

An edge guide should probably be the first accessory that you buy for your router. As can be seen in the photos it is particularly useful for cutting blind mortises and the like, such as for the hidden-spline miter joint.

OTHER STUNTS YOU SHOULD KNOW

WHEN face-routing a board it is often impossible to use clamps. Instead, nail-fasten cleat along bottom for gripping in vise. Caution: Make certain nails are not in cutter's path.

YOU CAN CUT dovetails to join boards with assistance of an edge guide and two pieces of scrap which are clamped on to support the router shoe. In this instance, it is particularly important for you to locate the edge guide accurately.

MORTISE SHAPE in mating edge is cut using same technique, but cutter is set to leave center (tenon) intact.

MAKING AN EDGE CUT

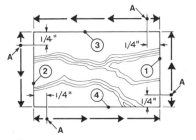

CORRECT WAY to shape an edge using a cutter with pilot bearing: Start cut about ¼ in. from left end and push router into wood until bearing makes full contact with edge. Then move router right.

Since a router bit revolves clockwise as you look down on it from above, feed the router in a counterclockwise direction when shaping an outside edge. Con-

CORRECT sequence for edge shaping is shown at right. When this work is handled properly, the router cuts a neat edge, as shown above.

versely, if routing an inner edge—that is, a cutout—feed the router in a clockwise manner. The point is to feed the cutter to the work so the cutting edges can do

THIS IS the sequence to use when routing all four edges. Always shape end grains (1 and 2) first, then finish up by making with-the-grain passes (3 and 4). Points A are starting points for all four of the edges as shown in the diagram above.

their job. When shaping all four edges use the sequence shown. If you rout just one edge, be sure the pilot doesn't turn the corner.

freehand work

Freehand routing is plain fun, even when you're just showing off. More often than not when routing freehand you will probably be making a sign or plaque.

There are two basic freehand techniques:

The letters or pattern can be cut directly into the wood.

You can rout out the background, leaving the letters raised from the surface.

To do freehand routing you must first put the pattern directly on the workpiece, using either a pencil or felt tip marker. Next, select the appropriate bit. Bits generally used for freehand work include the core box, straight (mortise type) for large areas and the veining bit for more delicate work.

WHEN ROUTING freehand, work slowly and always push router so that cutter bites the wood as you go: Since the cutter spins clockwise—as you look down on it from above—push from left to right whenever possible. To make an S, for example, start at the bottom and work up.

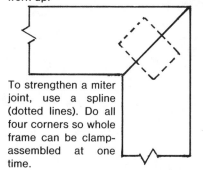

To strengthen a miter joint, use a spline (dotted lines). Do all four corners so whole frame can be clamp-assembled at one time.

YOU CAN strengthen otherwise weak miter joints by using splines. To create hidden splines, use your router. Clamp scrap stock on both sides of workpiece to keep router from wobbling, then grip setup in the bench vise. It's best to use edge guide to ensure accuracy.

The more you use a router, the greater your mastery of the tool will become. Once you are fully comfortable with it, you can try some of the more exotic router tasks such as cutting mortises for hidden splines and freehand routing.

Whenever you rout the narrow edge of a board you should increase the surface that the router shoe will ride on by clamping stock alongside as shown in the photos. The idea is to make certain that the router will not wobble as you

CUT SPLINE mortises in both work-pieces, then fashion the splines to suit openings they will fill. Here, in 5/4-in. stock, ½-in. splines will be glued into mortise.

make your cut. If it does, damage to the workpiece is almost guaranteed.

Freehand routing is done with a core box or other straight bit. It requires full control by the operator; otherwise the stock will be wasted. The big trick is to work slowly—that is, push the router at a very slow feed rate.

No matter what new technique you try with a router it makes sense to perfect your skills first by practicing with scrap stock.

In general, you should not rout more than ¼ in. deep. The deeper the cut, the more difficult it will be to follow a pattern. Ordinarily, you should make the first depth setting equal to about 25 percent of the desired finish cut. The initial cut then acts as a guide for the final, full depth cutting.

guiding against an edge

The fourth method for guiding a router is to keep the base against an edge of material. The edge can be straight, such as for plowing long grooves or dadoes, or it might be curved or scalloped to suit a custom task.

Clamp the board (or templet) securely to the top surface of the material being routed and guide the router in a counterclockwise rotation (left to right, as in edge shaping). Be sure to *keep the shoe in contact with the guide at all times.*

A typical application of such cutting would be the plowing of dadoes to receive let-in shelves, (on opposite vertical panels in a bookcase). Once the panels are laid out, they can be clamped or tacknailed together (side by side) so the grooves (dadoes) can be made across both boards at the same time.

templet guides

Templet guides are accessories available for the router. Since these elevate the user into the world of advanced wood craftsmanship, some of the simpler do-it-yourself router models are not designed to accept templet guides.

The guides are locked in the router subbase using various means, depending upon the maker: Some are held with screws, others with locking nuts. In place, the guide's collar projects down from the shoe. The collar, in turn, rides a pattern edge, such a a dovetail templet or a templet for butt routing (routing the mortises for door hinges).

about bits

Over the long haul, you'll come out ahead if you purchase carbide-tipped bits to begin with. But this is true only for those who use a router fairly regularly. Here's my reasoning: Steel router bits, depending upon style, are priced from $8. The average person cannot sharpen his own bits; thus each time the bit is sharpened professionally you'll pay another $3 to $5. Cutting edges on a carbide bit will outlast those on a steel bit many times. Even with an initial outlay that may be three times as much ($18 to $25) you'll save money after only three or four projects.

Build a professional woodworking center

By HARRY WICKS

■ EARLY IN HIS woodworking pursuits, every craftsman realizes that he needs an assembly bench. The bench shown here—created by four experienced craftsmen—provides the ultimate in furniture assembly and tool storage. The assembly bench is built lower to save your back. Its grid top provides plenty of biting surface for clamps and, because it's on wheels it can be rolled aside for storage. The portable tool center also rolls on wheels.

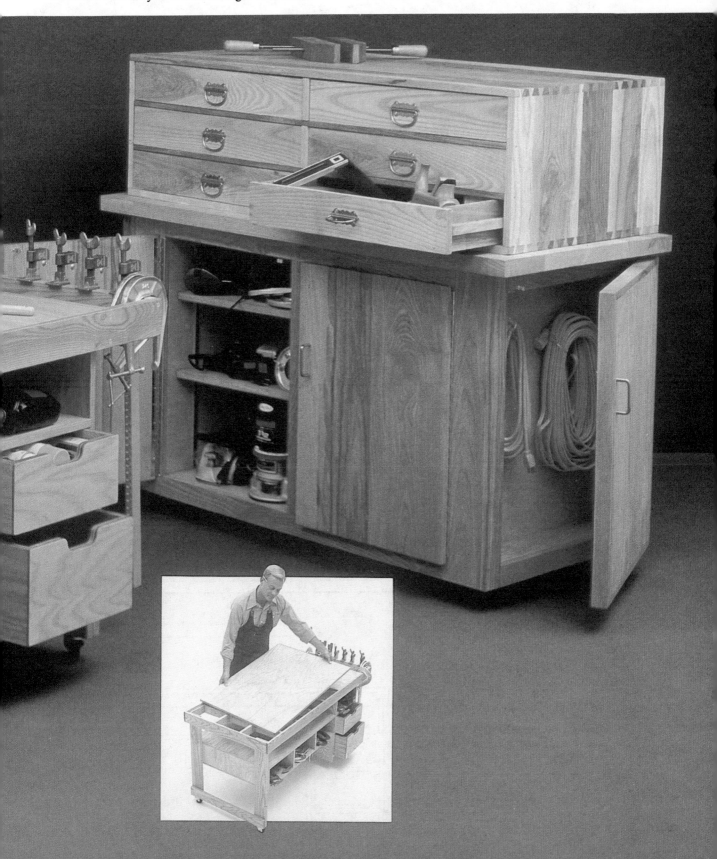

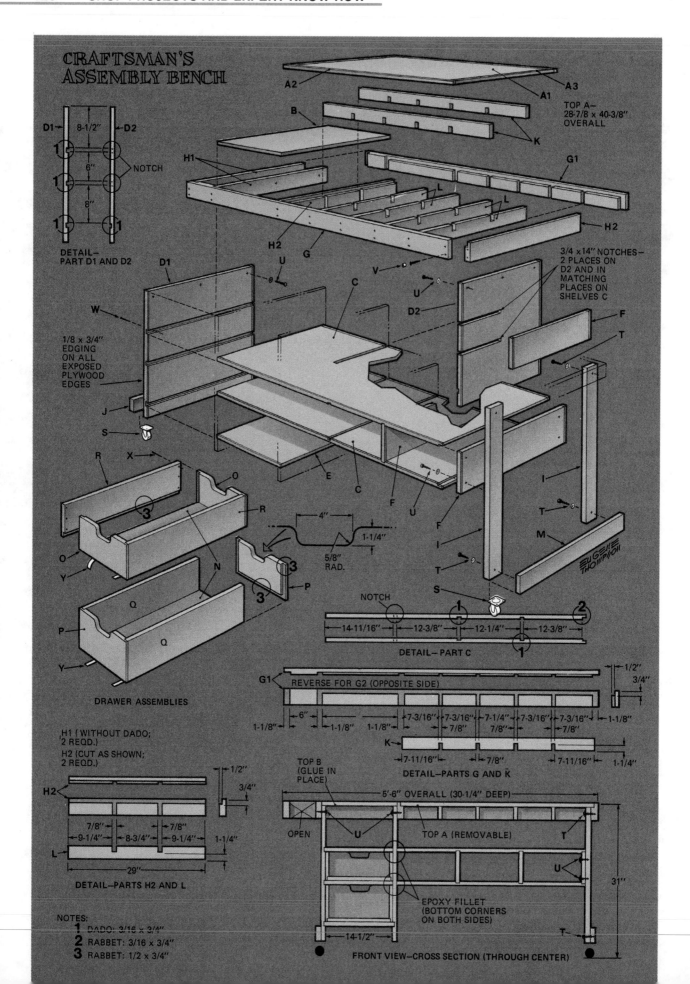

CRAFTSMAN'S
ASSEMBLY BENCH

TOP A—
28-7/8 x 40-3/8''
OVERALL

8-1/2''

6''

8''

NOTCH

DETAIL—
PART D1 AND D2

3/4 x 14'' NOTCHES—
2 PLACES ON
D2 AND IN
MATCHING
PLACES ON
SHELVES C

1/8 x 3/4''
EDGING
ON ALL
EXPOSED
PLYWOOD
EDGES

4''

1-1/4''

5/8''
RAD.

DRAWER ASSEMBLIES

NOTCH

14-11/16''   12-3/8''   12-1/4''   12-3/8''

DETAIL—PART C

1/2''

3/4''

G1   REVERSE FOR G2 (OPPOSITE SIDE)

6''   7-3/16'' 7-3/16'' 7-1/4'' 7-3/16'' 7-3/16'' 1-1/8''

1-1/8''   1-1/8'' 1-1/8'' 7/8'' 7/8'' 7/8'' 7/8''

K   7-11/16''   7/8''   7-11/16''   1-1/4''

DETAIL—PARTS G AND K

H1 (WITHOUT DADO;
2 REQD.)

H2 (CUT AS SHOWN;
2 REQD.)

TOP B
(GLUE IN
PLACE)

5'-6'' OVERALL (30-1/4'' DEEP)

1/2''

3/4''

OPEN

TOP A (REMOVABLE)

H2

7/8''   7/8''

9-1/4''   8-3/4''   9-1/4''

1-1/4''

L

29''

DETAIL—PARTS H2 AND L

EPOXY FILLET
(BOTTOM CORNERS
ON BOTH SIDES)

31''

14-1/2''

FRONT VIEW—CROSS SECTION (THROUGH CENTER)

NOTES:
1 DADO: 3/16 x 3/4''
2 RABBET: 3/16 x 3/4''
3 RABBET: 1/2 x 3/4''

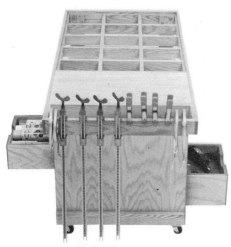

COMPLETED BENCH, top removed, reveals grid which is great aid for clamping. At near end are clamp racks.

MATERIALS LIST—ASSEMBLY BENCH

Key	No.	Size and description (use)
A1	1	$\frac{3}{4} \times 28\frac{1}{8} \times 39\frac{5}{8}$″ plywood (removable top)
A2	2	$\frac{3}{8} \times \frac{3}{4} \times 40\frac{3}{8}$″ solid stock (edging)
A3	2	$\frac{3}{8} \times \frac{3}{4} \times 28\frac{1}{8}$″ solid stock (edging)
B	1	$\frac{3}{4} \times 16 \times 29$″ plywood (stationary top)
C	2	$\frac{3}{4} \times 28 \times 54\frac{15}{16}$″ plywood* (shelf)
D1	1	$\frac{3}{4} \times 27\frac{3}{4} \times 28$″ plywood* (left side—drawer case)
D2	1	$\frac{3}{4} \times 27\frac{3}{4} \times 28$″ plywood* (right side—drawer case)
E	1	$\frac{3}{4} \times 14\frac{7}{8} \times 28$ plywood* (bottom—drawer case)
F	3	$\frac{3}{4} \times 6\frac{3}{8} \times 28$″ plywood* (divider)
G1	1	$1\frac{1}{8} \times 3\frac{1}{4} \times 66$″ ash (long rail—right hand)
G2	1	$1\frac{1}{8} \times 3\frac{1}{4} \times 66$″ ash (long rail—left hand)
H1	2	$1\frac{1}{8} \times 3\frac{1}{4} \times 29$″ ash (short rail—square)
H2	2	$1\frac{1}{8} \times 3\frac{1}{4} \times 29$″ ash (short rail—rabeted)
I	2	$1\frac{1}{8} \times 4 \times 27\frac{3}{4}$″ ash (leg)
J	1	$1\frac{1}{8} \times 3 \times 28$″ ash (side stretcher)
K	2	$\frac{7}{8} \times 2\frac{1}{2} \times 40\frac{1}{2}$″ ash (long grid stretcher)
L	4	$\frac{7}{8} \times 2\frac{1}{2} \times 29$″ ash (short grid stretcher)
M	1	$\frac{7}{8} \times 3 \times 28$″ ash (leg stretcher)
N	2	$\frac{3}{4} \times 13\frac{3}{4} \times 27\frac{1}{2}$″ plywood (drawer bottom)
O	2	$\frac{3}{4} \times 5\frac{3}{4} \times 14\frac{1}{4}$″ plywood (small drawer end)
P	2	$\frac{3}{4} \times 7\frac{3}{4} \times 14\frac{1}{4}$″ plywood (large drawer end)
Q	2	$\frac{3}{4} \times 7\frac{3}{4} \times 27\frac{1}{2}$″ plywood (large drawer side)
R	2	$\frac{3}{4} \times 5\frac{3}{4} \times 27\frac{1}{2}$″ plywood (small drawer side)
S	4	Heavy-duty 2″ rubber wheel, swivel plate caster
T	4	$\frac{5}{16} \times 2$″ lagscrew, washer (for legs)
U	10	$\frac{5}{16} \times 1\frac{1}{2}$″ lagscrew (6 for sides D, 4 for end F)
V	32	$1\frac{1}{2}$″ No. 10 fh screw

Misc.: 4d and 6d finish nails, dowel plugs, sandpaper, Nyl-o-tape No. IP572 (self-adhering sliding tape), glue, wood filler.
*Overall dimensions for part are given. Allow for $\frac{1}{8}$″-thick edge-banding on exposed edges when cutting plywood to size. Note: White ash used throughout.

TAPE PAIRED members together to mark and cut dadoes and rabbets.

IF BOARDS don't lie flat, notches will be too deep. Avoid this by clamping.

PENCIL STUB is more accurate marking tool for reaching undersides.

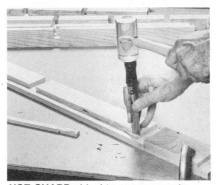

USE SHARP chisel to remove waste and to square corner of stopped rabbet.

CUT NOTCH into a new fence to simplify alignment of marked workpieces.

MARK EDGE half-laps for grid with parts in place to prevent errors.

OVERLAPPING kerf cuts form notches. Cut two taped pieces at once.

CLAMP assembled grid to bore the screw body holes into cross members.

assembly bench, continued ➤

CUT PLUGS of matching stock if you have plug cutter, or use dowels.

FLUSH trimming cutter in router trims overhang flush with plywood.

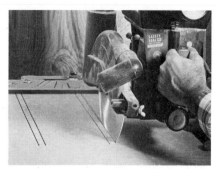

PARALLEL cuts halfway through panel form deep edge half-lap notches.

ROUTER with simple guide ensures accurate dado cuts in the panels.

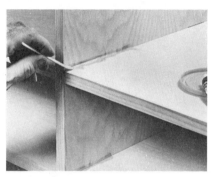

QUICK-SETTING epoxy fillets lock the free ends of panels in position.

RIGHT-ANGLE drive is used to bore lag-screw holes in tight spot.

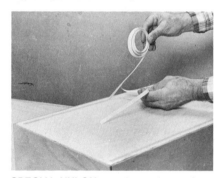

SPECIAL NYLON tape is used to make drawers slide with ease.

DEFTCO'S Danish oil finish is very easy to apply; simply saturate wood.

NOTE DETAILS: edge band around tabletop, screw-hole plugs, base banding.

A CRAFTSMAN'S ASSEMBLY BENCH

■ THE ASSEMBLY BENCH shown here features a removable top which exposes an open grid surface to permit easy vertical placement of clamps. The shelf below the grid can be covered with newspapers to catch glue drippings. The long shelf compartments below are great for storing clamps during assembly and they permit access from both sides.

The drawers are constructed so they can be opened from both sides, too. And the bench rides on rubber-wheeled swivel plate casters.

We used ¼- and ⁵⁄₄-in. white ash and ¾-in. plywood to build this bench and its companion piece, the portable tool center. Except for the drawers, all exposed plywood edges are banded

(edged) with ⅛-in. solid stock (see drawing). Notice that the drawings indicate the overall sizes of the plywood parts. When you lay out the cutting lines, make sure you compensate for the banding by reducing the dimensions by ⅛ in. or ¼ in. where applicable. For strength, edge the removable top with ⅜-in.-thick stock.

Begin with the bench top frame by cutting ⁵⁄₄-in. stock to length and width. This includes the two sides and the four cross members. Tape paired members together so they can be marked and cut at the same time (see photographs). Use a dado head on either a table or radial-arm saw to make the cuts. If you own both, the radial-arm saw's better.

Ash is a very hard wood, so set up the dado head at less than full-width capacity (about ⅜-in. maximum width) and make the cuts in several passes. If you move a clean section of fence into the cutting path on the radial-arm saw and make a cut into it, visual alignment for the cuts in the work will be quick, easy and accurate.

When the frame members have been notched, assemble them to mark the edge half-lap joints for the grid members. The grid is made of ¼-in. stock. Lay the four short members into place and check for square with a framing square. Place the two long members on top and mark the top edges of the short cross members for the notch cuts. Then, using a short pencil stub, trace against the cross members to mark the bottom edges of the long members for the mating notch cuts.

Unless you have an oversize dado head, the motor housing on the radial-arm saw will interfere and prevent cutting the notches to the required 1¼-in. depth. Therefore, cut the notches by making repeated (overlapping) kerf cuts with a conventional saw blade. If you make a fresh cut in the fence, it will simplify visual alignment of the initial outside cuts for the notches.

You'll need a stopped rabbet on the top edges of the two side members. The rabbet can be cut with the dado head, but it's quicker to make two right-angle saw cuts into the edge and side. We used a chisel to sever the remaining waste and to square the inside corner.

the top

Assemble the top with screws and glue. To bore the screw holes, drill ½-in.-dia. holes for the wood plugs ⅛ in. deep, using the drill press. Follow up by boring $\frac{5}{32}$-in. through holes (body size for No. 10 screw). Assemble the grid and frame temporarily on a flat work surface and use bar clamps to hold it all together and square. Chuck the $\frac{5}{32}$-in. bit in a portable drill and continue the screw body holes into the ends of the cross members. Disassemble the unit and bore $\frac{3}{16}$-in.-dia. screw shank clearance holes in side parts.

All sanding must be done before assembly. To minimize sanding, use a cabinet scraper first. Now glue-assemble the top using two 1½-in. No. 10 screws at each joint. Glue in wood plugs to conceal the screwheads.

To cut the parts for the base section, you'll need three 4x8-ft. plywood panels. You'll wind up with three good-sized cutoffs for other projects.

Cut the plywood to size, then add the edge banding. Since a considerable amount of edging is involved, you may find it more convenient to use tape, rather than clamps when gluing the strips in place. Cut the banding from ¾-in. stock, then partly drive two thin brads at opposite ends to prevent sliding after glue is applied. Allow the banding to overhang all around and use strips of duct tape to force the wood into good contact. After the glue has set, remove the tape and alignment brads and use a router with a flush trimming cutter to trim the overhangs flush to the plywood surface.

The shelf and upright members are joined with a combination of dadoes and deep edge half-lap notches. Make two parallel kerf cuts halfway through the one upright and the two shelf members. Then clear out the waste with a chisel or sabre saw. The easiest way to cut the long dadoes is with a router chucked with a mortising cutter. This simple jig on page 130 will ensure accuracy and speedy setup. The two parallel strips are spaced so a pass against each side will leave a ¾-in.-wide groove. If you have a ¾-in.-dia. cutter, a single pass will do it. The spacing of the guide strips varies according to the diameter of your router base and the cutter used. For example, the spacing in the jig shown is 5¼ in.; the router base is 5-in. dia.; cutter is ½-in. dia.

assembling the base

Begin assembly of the base section by interlocking the edge half-laps. Instead of glue, apply a fillet of quick-setting epoxy to the corners of the undersides of these joints. (See photo, page 130.) Use glue and 2-in. finishing nails to assemble the dado joints. Set the nails and fill the holes.

The two legs are secured with $\frac{5}{16}$-in. lagscrews inserted from inside the frame and the end shelf compartment. Because of space limitations, you can't bore the lagscrew holes from straight on. But you can use an accessory right-angle drive in a portable drill.

The drawers are assembled with simple rabbet joints, glue and finishing nails. The ¾-in. plywood stock used for the sides and bottom results in a strong drawer. For friction-free sliding, apply two strips of Nyl-O-Tape. This is a self-adhesive, nylon band, available at hardware stores and home centers.

Finish is optional, but a deep-penetrating, tung oil/urethane resin finish, such as Deftco Danish Oil Finish from Deft Inc. is ideal. Wipe on two liberal coats as directed on the label. For color accent, we mixed 25 parts Deftco with one part walnut stain.

—Rosario Capotosto

MOBILE CENTER FOR PORTABLE POWER TOOLS

MOBILE tool center is designed to corral portable tools and accessories, which are used on many shop projects. Craftsman David J. Warren built it.

MATERIALS LIST—TOOL CENTER

Key	No.	Size and description (use)
		BASE CABINET
A	1	1½ × 26 × 56″ ash, edge-joined (top)
B	2	¾ × 20 × 26¾″ ash, edge-joined (door)
C	2	¾ × 4 × 29¾″ ash (end stile)
D	2	¾ × 2 × 41½″ ash (rail)
E	1	¾ × 2 × 27¾″ ash (center stile)
F	4	¾ × 2 × 29¾″ ash (side stiles)
G	4	¾ × 2 × 22″ ash (side rails)
H	4	¾ × 1½ × 28¾″ ash (door side frame)
I	4	¾ × 1½ × 23″ ash (door top/bottom frame)
J	1	¾ × 22¾ × 47½″ ash, edge-joined (bottom)
K	1	½ × 28½ × 47½″ A/C plywood with ash veneer (bottom)
L1	3	½ × 22¾ × 27¾″ A/C plywood with ash veneer (partition)
L2	2	½ × 22⅝ × 19″ A/C plywood with ash veneer (shelf)
M	2	½ × 21½ × 27¼″ A/C plywood with ash veneer (side-door panels)
N	14	¼″-dia. × ⅞″ dowel pins
01	2	1½″ (open) × 28½″ piano hinge
02	2	1½″ (open) × 26½″ piano hinge
P1	2	3″-dia. swivel caster with brake
P2	2	3″-dia. rigid caster
Q	4	3″ brass wire pull
Q2	4	roller catch
R	8	27¾″-long shelf support strip
		CHEST
S	2	¾ × 24 × 52″ ash, edge-joined (top/bottom)
T	2	¾ × 15 × 24″ ash, edge-joined (side)
U	1	¾ × 13⅜ × 23½″ ash, edge-joined (partition)
V	24	⅝ × 1 × 22½″ ash (drawer guide)
W	2	½ × 1½ × 50½″ ash (drawer spacer)
X	1	½ × 14⅛ × 51¼″ A/C plywood with ash veneer (back)
Y	72	1″ No. 10 fh screw (48 in chest, 24 in drawers)
Z	6	¾ × 4 × 24¾″ ash (drawer face)
AA	12	⁹⁄₁₆ × 4 × 21⅝″ ash (drawer sides)
BB	6	⁹⁄₁₆ × 3½ × 22¼″ ash (drawer back)
CC	6	¼ × 21½ × 22¾″ A/C plywood with ash veneer (drawer bottoms)
DD	12	¹¹⁄₁₆ × ⅞ × 21¼″ ash (slide)
EE	6	brass bail pull

Misc.: Carpenter's glue, 10d finish nails, 16¾″ No. 12 rh screws (16, for casters), 16 ½″ No. 6 fh screws (16, for shelf support strip), filler, sandpaper, Deftco Danish Oil finish, walnut stain.
Note: Use white ash and northern brown ash.

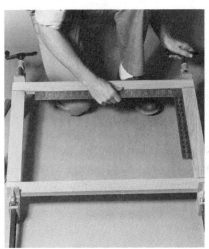

MORTISE the facing stock with a mortising chisel; use clamp as a stop to avoid measuring. Mortise left then right edges; clean out center.

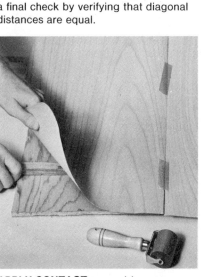

MAKE SURE facings are square. Make a final check by verifying that diagonal distances are equal.

USE A tenoning jig to cut the ends of members on a table saw. This method allows you to get accurate and square tenons quickly and safely.

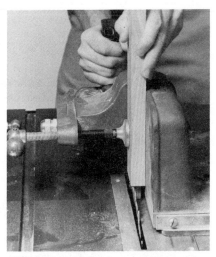

AFTER facing has dried, bore ¼-in.-dia. hole. Glue and pound in a ¼x⅞-in. dowel. Sand the assembly.

APPLY CONTACT cement to veneer and plywood. Spacer prevents veneer from sticking until it's aligned.

TO ATTACH facing, bore pilot holes to prevent splitting and to keep nails from bending.

TO CREATE 9/16-in. lumber for sides, author planed down ¾-in. stock. Or resaw it on a band saw.

CUT SLIDING dovetails on drawer sides, using a tenoning jig, saw blade at 22°. Thicker stock is spacer.

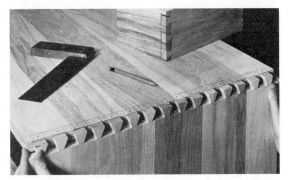

A PRACTICE dovetail joint was made as an exercise. Dovetails are cut first and used as a pattern for pins. Dots indicate wood to be removed.

CLEAR OUT dovetail socket in the drawer front with a ¼-in. chisel. The groove at bottom of drawer front accepts the drawer bottom.

■ IN MOST HOME workshops, portable power tools are stashed away wherever there's room. This usually means many trips back and forth across the shop when building a project.

But with our portable tool center, you can store all your portable tools and many of their accessories in a handsome roll-about cabinet. The tools, including extension cords, are all close at hand when you're working.

Like its mate, the assembly bench, the tool center is built of two highly compatible types of ash: white ash, with a little brown streaking, and northern brown ash, with some white streaking.

The tool center has two parts, a base with roomy adjustable shelves and side storage panels, and a slightly smaller upper chest with six drawers. If you use ash, remember that it's a hard wood, requiring bored pilot holes for all nails used in construction.

Start construction by gluing and clamping boards to make the base cabinet doors, partitions, bottom and top. Use ¾-in. stock for the front

doors, the center partition and the bottom, and 1½-in. stock for the top. You can glue up long lengths, then cut two or more parts from each. To save time, you can have a millwork shop plane and sand your glued-up boards.

While your boards are clamped and drying, make the facing framework for the front and sides of the base cabinet. Cut the stock to length. Then, cut mortises in the ends of the horizontal stiles. Cut tenons in the vertical rails. The front center rails get a mortise to match a tenon cut at the center of the front top and bottom stiles. Glue and clamp the facing assemblies and place them on a flat surface overnight. Be sure that each unit is square. When dry, bore holes for ¼x⅞-in. dowel pins, using a 15/64-in. drill bit to assure a tight fit.

We used ½-in. A/C plywood to fabricate the doors on each side of the cabinet, the side panels and the back. Cut the plywood to size, as per the drawing, then top it with ash veneer, applying contact cement to both surfaces. Place sticks or

MOBILE TOOL CENTER

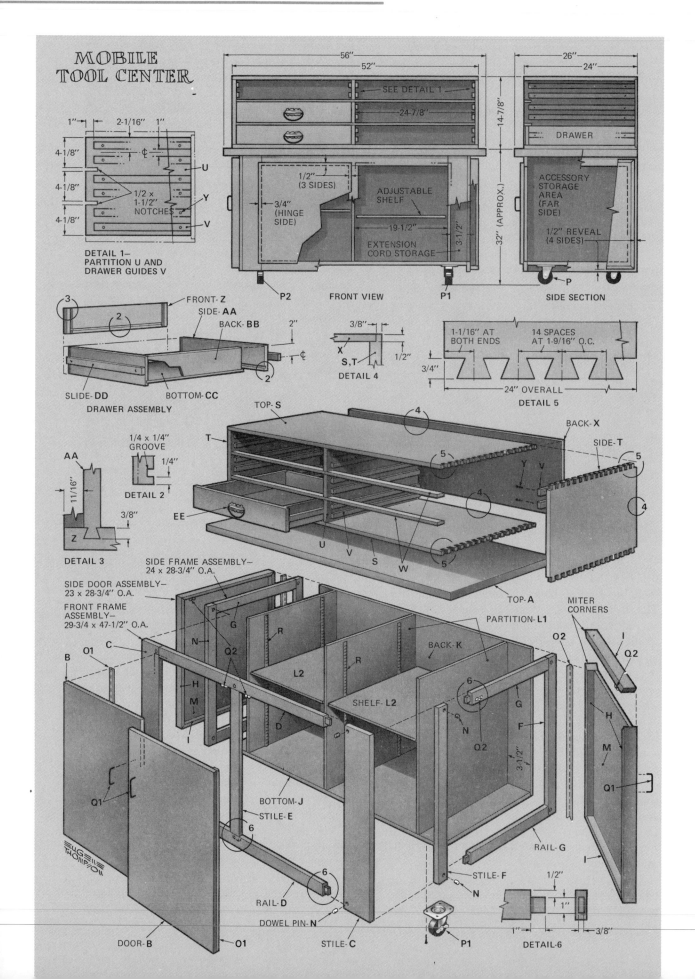

DETAIL 1—
PARTITION U AND
DRAWER GUIDES V

1″ 2-1/16″ 1″
4-1/8″
1/2 x 1-1/2″ NOTCHES
4-1/8″
4-1/8″
U
Y
V

SEE DETAIL 1
24-7/8″
56″
52″
14-7/8″
1/2″ (3 SIDES)
3/4″ (HINGE SIDE)
ADJUSTABLE SHELF
19-1/2″
3-1/2″
EXTENSION CORD STORAGE
32″ (APPROX.)
P2
FRONT VIEW
P1

26″
24″
DRAWER
ACCESSORY STORAGE AREA (FAR SIDE)
1/2″ REVEAL (4 SIDES)
P
SIDE SECTION

FRONT- Z
SIDE- AA
BACK- BB
2″
3
2
2
SLIDE- DD
BOTTOM- CC
DRAWER ASSEMBLY

3/8″
X
S,T
1/2″
DETAIL 4

1-1/16″ AT BOTH ENDS
14 SPACES AT 1-9/16″ O.C.
3/4″
24″ OVERALL
DETAIL 5

AA
11/16″
Z
3/8″
DETAIL 3

1/4 x 1/4″ GROOVE
1/4″
DETAIL 2

TOP- S
4
T
5
BACK- X
SIDE- T
5
Y V
EE
U V S W
5
TOP- A
MITER CORNERS

SIDE FRAME ASSEMBLY—24 x 28-3/4″ O.A.
SIDE DOOR ASSEMBLY—23 x 28-3/4″ O.A.
FRONT FRAME ASSEMBLY—29-3/4 x 47-1/2″ O.A.

PARTITION- L1
BACK- K
O2
O2
I
Q2
Q2
G
H
M
Q1
I
B
O1
C
N
Q2
G
R
R
L2
SHELF- L2
D
H
M
I
N
F
6
N
Q2
3-1/2″
BOTTOM- J
STILE- E
6
RAIL- D
DOWEL PIN- N
DOOR- B
O1
STILE- C
STILE- F
N
P1
RAIL- G
I
1/2″
1″
1″
3/8″
DETAIL-6

dowels between the plywood and the veneer to help position the veneer before the two cemented surfaces come in contact. When the veneer is in place, apply pressure and roll it smooth with a roller, or use a wooden block and hammer.

Next, cut ¾x1½-in. stock to lengths required for the side door frames and miter each end. Glue, nail and clamp to surround the side door panels, fitting the door flush with the exterior edge of the frame.

Your glued-up boards for front doors, bottom and the center partition, as well as the board for the top, should now be surfaced and ready for use. Cut out the components as shown in the drawing and start assembly, using 6d finishing nails and glue. *Remember to bore pilot holes for the nails to avoid splitting your ash stock.*

Nail the partition and the sides to the bottom, then attach the back panel to square the entire assembly. Finally, install the front facing frame, which you have previously glued and clamped square. For now, don't install the top—finishing will be easier with it off.

Like the assembly bench, the tool center was finished with Deftco Danish Oil. The tone on both was obtained by mixing 25 parts natural to one part medium walnut. To this you can add a few drops of McCloskey Mahogany Tung Oil stain for warmth.

To complete the cabinet, install metal shelf support strips on the center partition and sides. Use a 4-in. block to position each strip. You might want to bore a series of holes for shelf clips instead of using metal strips. If so, make a template of your hole pattern and use it to mark the holes for boring.

adding casters

Next, turn the cabinet upside down and apply heavy-duty industrial casters, preferably with wheel locks, to each corner. Use two fixed wheels at one end and two swivel casters at the other end. Then, place the cabinet upright, attach the doors with piano hinges and affix the door catches. Attach the top and use wax stick filler to fill all 10d nail holes.

As a final touch, you can add a fused electrical outlet strip to the face of the cabinet. If you do, keep the cord short, so it doesn't drag on the floor and catch under the wheels.

Your base cabinet is complete and now you're ready to make the chest.

Start by gluing up boards from which the 24-in.-wide top, bottom, sides and center partition will be cut. When these boards have been planed and sanded they should be ¾-in. thick.

When this work is done, cut each of the two sides and the top and bottom to the dimensions shown. Then, make the dovetail template in the drawing on page 134. Our template was made from sheet brass. But for one-time use, you can use heavy cardboard or ⅛-in. hardboard.

Use the template to draw the dovetails on the top and bottom edge of each side piece. When cut, use the sides to outline the pins to be cut on the ends of the top and bottom pieces. Be sure to mark mating edges so that they can be repositioned correctly when the pins have been cut.

When this step is completed, use a router with a rabbeting bit to cut a ⅜x½-in. rabbet at the inside back edge of each side. Then, dry-assemble all components to check for fit. If dovetails and pins project slightly in the final assembly, sand them to make flush joints.

Next, cut and apply drawer guides to the side pieces and the partition as shown in the drawing. These are glued and the screws are countersunk. Use two 1-in. No. 10 wood screws on each. With a backsaw and chisel, cut the two ½x1½-in. slots in the center partition to accept drawer spacers. Then, cut the back panel to fit, making certain all corners are square and true. Clamp the entire assembly, nailing the back in place to square it up.

the drawers

Now you are ready for the drawers. Sides and backs are ⁹/₁₆-in. stock, planed down from ¾ in. The fronts are ¾-in. stock. Cut them to length.

Use a table saw to cut a ⅜-in. sliding dovetail the full height of the front end of each side piece. Then, use the saw to cut a ⅜-in. matching groove on the inside face of the drawer front. With a ¼-in. chisel, cut away the waste the saw couldn't reach, so the groove will accept the dovetail.

Next, cut a ¼-in. groove in each side, back, and front, ¼ in. from the lower edge, to accept a ¼-in. plywood bottom. Finally, attach a ¹¹/₁₆x⅞-in. guide strip to the outside of each side piece. Glue, nail and clamp the assembly and let it stand overnight. Test each drawer by sliding it into place in the chest assembly and sand as needed to assure easy sliding. When in place, the drawer front should recess about ¼ in. into the face of the chest.

To locate the chest on the base, we provided small recesses in the top of the base cabinet. The wood plugs installed on the bottom of the chest fit into these. You can use nonslip pads if you prefer.

—David A. Warren

Four tools to make for your shop

1 HANDSOME EDGE SANDER

■ A ROUGH EDGE is usually left on lumber after it's ripped with a saw. An experienced woodworker might choose to plane the edge, but there is an easier way. This edge sander, when used with care, helps you to do professional-quality work.

Use heavy hardwoods, bolts, rods and brass plates to bring your sander in at a hefty 4½ pounds or more. The heavier weight requires less muscle power for downward contact pressure. If it is necessary to "one-hand" the sander, the curved brass bar on top (besides adding some extra weight) directs some of the downward pressure from the back handgrip toward the front of the tool.

Cut the main body block from a well-seasoned piece of maple. We made the side plates from black phenolic plastic, but since this material is expensive and hard to find, you can also use sheet acrylic or any sheet metal.

Cut the handle and front knob from mahogany. The hold-down bolts in the handle and front

AS YOU HOLD sander firmly by the knob and handle, you'll find its beefy weight helps you do the work. You'll be proud of this handsome tool.

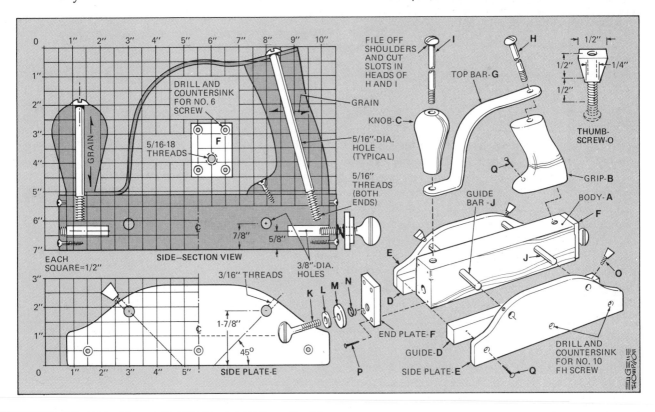

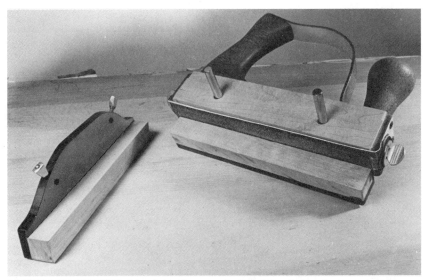

MATERIALS LIST—EDGE SANDER

Key	No.	Size and description (use)
A	1	1¾ × 1⅞ × 9½" maple (body)
B	1	1¼ × 3 × 5" mahogany (grip)
C	1	2"-dia. × 3" mahogany (knob)
D	2	¾ × 1 × 9½" birch (edge guide)
E	2	5⁄16 × 2¾ × 9½" sheet acrylic (side plate)
F	2	¼ × 1½ × 1⅞" brass (end plate)
G	1	⅛ × 1 × 11½" brass (top bar)
H	1	5⁄16"-dia. × 6" carriage bolt
I	1	5⁄16"-dia. × 4" carriage bolt
J	2	⅜"-dia. .× 5" steel (guide bar)
K	2	5⁄16"-dia. × 2" thumbscrew
L	2	⅞"-dia. brass washer
M	2	1¼"-dia. leather washer
N	2	⅜"-dia. compression spring
O	2	¼ × ½ × 1" (thumbscrew)
P	8	1" No. 6 oval-head brass screw
Q	7	1" No. 10 fh steel screw

Misc.: Epoxy, wood finish, metal-buffing materials.

LOOSEN OR REMOVE side plates for easy installation of abrasive paper. Paper must be tightly secured with wingnuts. Any slack will cause paper wear and tear.

knob are carriage bolts with their shoulders filed off to allow flush tightening.

Cut a slot for a screwdriver in the top with a hacksaw. Carriage bolts are preferable because they have a larger head and a lower profile than most machine bolts.

Assemble the side plates and birch edge guides and then clamp them to the main body. Now bore the holes for the ⅜-in.-dia. guide bars. This step assures perfect alignment.

The oval screws in the end plates protrude slightly above the surface. This provides two distinct points for the leather washer to bear against so that it can grip the abrasive strips securely.

Because of the limited finger room when the side guides are brought in close to the body of the sander, the thumbscrews must be narrow, yet strong and easy to operate. Make them from ¼-in.-thick brass bar stock and 3⁄16-in.-dia. bolts.

Scribe the shape of the knobs on the bar stock. Then drill and tap before cutting knobs from the bar.

Use epoxy to glue the 3⁄16-in.-dia. screws into the knobs. Since metal does not have a porous surface to absorb the epoxy, its bond depends on a tough mass that surrounds irregular shapes, and makes them immobile. So, the trick is to create pockets into which the epoxy can run. Grinding or filing irregular notches along the portion of the bolt that is to be threaded into the head creates these epoxy pockets. Polish and buff the knobs and then saw off the heads of the bolts.

Be sure to use brass instead of steel to keep the ⅜-in.-dia. steel guide bars from becoming dimpled. This would allow them to skip out of adjustment and would also cause the travel of the guides to become ragged.

—*Robert F. Bessmer*

2 SHEET STEEL TOOL

■ GROUND FLAT STOCK is sheet steel ground on both sides to produce flatness and a specific thickness such as 0.0625 (1⁄16 in.) Use this stock to make this handy one-piece tool.

This tool consists of a combination of holes, slots and other useful details: It includes a screwdriver, wrenches for small square and hexagon nuts, gauges for checking rods for ⅛-, ¼- and 5⁄16-in. diameters; thread chasers for renewing and cleaning 6-32 and 8-32 threads, slots for bending sheet metal and wire, a modest ruler and an edge

arrangement for checking 45°, 90° and 135° angles.

First, make a pattern drawing of the tool on self-sticking label paper and apply it to the cleaned surface of your steel blank. Shape the blank and make slots with a milling machine or with hand tools. Drill each hex hole to its bolt diameter and scribe a line around the outer nut for the hexagon shape. Then convert the round hole into a six-sided one with a jeweler's saw and file. Provide the threaded holes with clearance to

ATTACH this tool to your key ring and you'll be surprised how handy it is.

USE SMALL hand grinder for smoothing edge at base of screwdriver blade. Finally, remove pattern.

EACH SQ. = 1/4"

SHEET METAL AND WIRE BENDING SLOTS

SCREWDRIVER
ROD GAUGE
THREAD CHASER
WRENCH
ROD GAUGE
KEY HOLE
ANGLE CHECK
ROD GAUGE
WRENCH   RULE   THREAD CHASER

8-32
1/4
6-32
5/16

catch dirt and chips by cutting two opposing notches in each hole with a jeweler's saw.

To make the rule divisions, clamp the blank flat on the compound rest of your lathe and position it to move parallel to the lathe centerline. Then clamp a boring bar in the lathe-headstock collet, with its cutter tip extending downward and pressing lightly against the surface of the tool blank. Space the graduations at 1/16-in. (0.0625 in.) intervals by using the scale on the compound feed screw, and engrave by operating the cross-feed screw.

File all tool edges and sand to make them smooth and bring measuring parts to the correct angles. Round corners for comfort in handling.

To harden the tool, heat uniformly to a "cherry red" and then plunge it edgewise into cool water. Polish a small area on one surface to brightness, and then reheat the piece uniformly, over a gas burner, until a straw color appears on the polished spot.

Remove tool immediately from the heat, let it cool, and then polish all over.

—*Walter E. Burton*

3 ACCESSORY SANDING TABLE

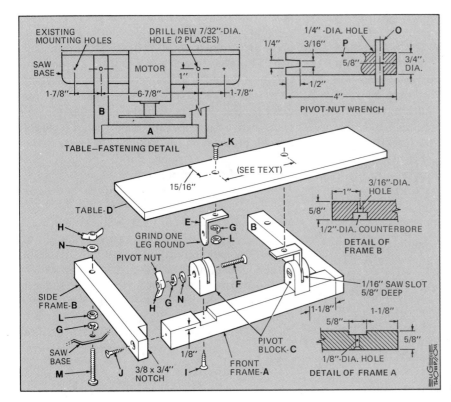

TABLE—FASTENING DETAIL

PIVOT-NUT WRENCH

DETAIL OF FRAME B

DETAIL OF FRAME A

MATERIALS LIST—SANDING TABLE		
Key	No.	Size and description (use)
A	1	5/8 × 3/4 × 67/8″ oak (frame front)
B	2	5/8 × 3/4 × 57/8″ oak (frame side)
C	2	5/8 × 3/4 × 1″ oak (pivot block)
D	1	1/4 × 23/8 × 75/8″ hardwood (table)
E	2	1/2 × 1 × 1″ corner brace
F	2	10-24 × 3/4″ fh machine screw
G	6	10-24 lockwasher
H	2	10-24 wingnut (pivot nut)
I	2	3/4″ No. 6 fh screw
J	2	5/8″ No. 4 fh screw
K	2	10-24 × 1/2″ fh machine screw
L	4	10-24 hex nut
M	2	10-24 × 1″ rh screw
N	4	No. 10 flat washer
O	1	1/4″-dia. × 15/8″ dowel
P	1	3/4″-dia. × 4″ dowel

Misc.: Epoxy.

■ **WHEN YOU SAND** small parts such as doll-house furniture or model fittings, a sanding table is often a necessity for accuracy. The table shown here can be easily made by the hobbyist. Most of the work can be done with the Dremel Moto Shop for which the table is an accessory to the sanding disc.

Use hardwood such as oak and note that all pieces can be cut from a single piece of stock 1x6 x10 in. long. The frame and wood pivots are constructed of pieces 3/4 in. by 5/8 in., and the table is 1/4 in. thick.

Once the pieces are rough-ripped, you can make final cuts with your Moto Shop. Then cut the 3/8x3/4-in. end notches in the frame sides to let in the frame front. The pivot blocks are let into the front frame member in dadoes 1/8 in. deep. Bore holes and cut the slots in the pivot blocks before rounding the tops. Use your corner braces to determine the width of the slot (kerf). The braces should be fairly snug, yet free enough to move within the slot. Attach pivot blocks to front frame member with screws and glue.

Bore the side frame pieces for assembly and counterbore the underneath side to let in the hex nut and lock washer at the saw base. Assemble the frame with screws and glue.

Now, using the dimensions in the drawing, po-

sition and drill one of the holes in the saw base. Attach the frame and use the hole in the other leg to position and bore the second hole. Don't worry if the second hole doesn't fall exactly where it should according to the drawing. Just keep the front frame piece parallel to the sanding disc plane.

Install the corner braces after grinding one leg of each corner brace round. The pivot screws must be locked in place so they won't turn when

ADJUST ANGLE of table with a pivot-nut wrench, as shown here. You make the wrench yourself from a 4-in. length of 3/4-in. dia. dowel. Store it with the table.

the wingnuts are adjusted. You can do this by applying quicksetting epoxy cement over the head of the countersunk screw. To be effective, the holes in the wood pivot blocks should be counterbored sufficiently so the screwhead will be slightly recessed. This will allow the epoxy to grip some wood as well as the screwhead.

Once braces are installed, position and bore the holes in the saw table. If you think that you haven't been too accurate, mount the table frame on the saw base with the sanding disc in place. Then check to be sure you can tilt table as re-

quired without coming into contact with the disc.

To adjust the table's angle, you must make a pivot-nut wrench, as shown in the drawing on page 139. The wrench is made from a ¾-in.-dia. length of dowel 4 in. long, and a short piece of ¼-in.-dia. dowel that acts as a finger grip for extra torque. You may make a similar tool of your own design, but be sure you can apply enough pressure on the wingnuts to fix the table securely in place. A slight shift in the table's position could cause problems.

—*John E. Gaynor*

4 V-BLOCK CLAMP

■ V-BLOCK CLAMPS are simple tools, but they are indispensable for the jobs they do. To make one chuck one end of the stock piece in a lathe and support the other end with a steady rest. Use a conventional cutting-off tool bit to cut a ring from the pipe; make it ⅝ in. long. Then, make a C-segment by cutting a section from the ring to form a gap a few thousandths of an inch wider than the V-block width between its side grooves. Next, mill or file 90° notches at the ends of the C-segment.

At the mid-point of the C-segment, drill a hole

with a No. 7 bit and tap for a ¼-20 carriage bolt.

Use a 2-in. carriage bolt threaded its entire length. For ease in turning, drill a ⅛-in.-dia. hole in the square part of the bolt head and fit it with a 2⅛-in. length of steel rod. Cap the ends of the rod with sections cut from 3/16-in. aluminum rivets. Drill rivets so they can be press-fitted.

—*Walter E. Burton*

V-BLOCK CLAMPS are indispensable for metal-working projects on tubes and rods. This clamp can be made in a short time and duplicated in various sizes.

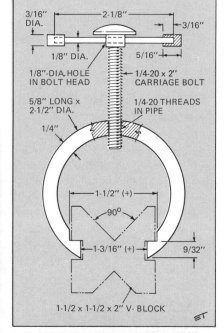

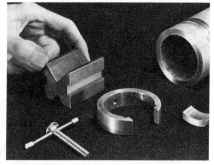

ORDINARY V-block is shown with parts of simple clamp. After ring section is cut from pipe, C-segment is made.

How to use corrugated nails

By HARRY WICKS

■ FREQUENTLY referred to as "wiggle" nails, steel corrugated fasteners are a perfectly valid woodworker's tool—when used for the proper job. You wouldn't turn to them to close the joints on a fine walnut Pembroke table, of course, but you certainly should consider them for out-of-sight applications within the strength limits of the nails.

The nails are available in widths of ¼, ½, ⅝ and 1 in. This dimension refers to the width shown (as A) in the photo in the middle, below. Many hardware stores stock the type with one edge filed to a sawtooth configuration. These are for use in softwoods such as pine. If you plan to use corrugated fasteners in hardwoods, you will have to lay in a supply of the plain, non-sawtooth-edge nails. If you are an active woodworker, you should have both on hand.

Corrugated fasteners are made in two styles: One has the ridges running parallel; the other has two sets of ridges running at a very slight angle to each other.

The nails with the angled ridges are designed to compress the joint because the ridges are closer together at the top than at the base (teeth). Thus, it is obvious that as the nail is driven, it will help to draw the two members toward each other.

There is a small tool available that makes driving these nails especially easy. It is an oblong-shaped device with a sliding, free piece of steel inside. The sleeve is placed over (around) the corrugated fastener and the loose bar is struck with a hammer to drive and set the nail. All hardware stores may not stock this handy gadget, but the one that I own is made by Stanley Tools.

Another type of connector that you should be at least familiar with is the Skotch Connector shown in the photo at the lower right. This type has eight very pointy nails—four on either side of the wasp-shaped bar, which straddles the joint.

STEEL corrugated nails are used by furniture manufacturers when two surfaces in the same plane are edge-joined.

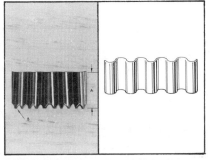

DESIGNATED size of nail, ⅝ in. left, pertains to nail width (A, in photo). This one has sawtooth edge. Nails with plain edge (right) are for hardwoods.

HOLD BUTT-JOINTED boards securely, with clamps if necessary, while you drive wiggle nails. Author prefers to start one end in one board, as shown.

THE OTHER END is tapped into the second board and the nail is driven home. Use straight blows to avoid bending the nail when driving.

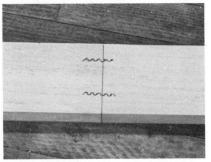

THOUGH STEEL corrugated nails can be used to butt-join two boards, end-to-end, this is a weak joint unless it is beefed up with a backing board.

TYPICAL USE for wiggle nails: A, to strengthen a miter joint. Fastener in B is called Skotch Connector and works like a charm. Use glue with both types.

Two basement water alarms

Nothing is worse than going down into your basement and discovering an unexpected flood. Whether through sump pump failure or backed-up drains, the result is always the same—property damage and a mess to clean up. Here are two alarms that you can build yourself to warn you before it's too late

■ SUMP-PUMP failure is a worry for all homeowners who depend on their pumps to prevent basement flooding. And since sump pumps are located, by necessity, in damp areas, where rust always takes its toll, failures are common. There are commercial alarms, starting at about $17, which you can buy. But you may enjoy making your own and saving the money.

This inexpensive alarm can be assembled easily by referring to the drawing. Aluminum may be substituted for the Plexiglas sheet and an ordinary carriage bolt could be used in place of the hinge pin. The critical consideration is that the bottle-float shaft move freely within the stationary "sleeve." Sleeves like the one shown are available at electrical-supply stores, but an ex-

SUMP-PUMP ALARM

POSITION YOUR alarm so that its activating position is just above the sump-pump float activating position. This will be nearly impossible to do by eye alone, so manipulate the sump-pump float by hand, turning the pump on momentarily.

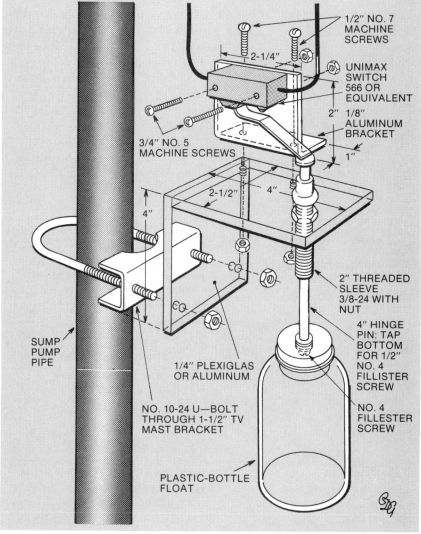

1/2" NO. 7 MACHINE SCREWS

2-1/4"

UNIMAX SWITCH 566 OR EQUIVALENT

2" 1/8" ALUMINUM BRACKET

1"

3/4" NO. 5 MACHINE SCREWS

2-1/2"   4"

4"

4"

2" THREADED SLEEVE 3/8-24 WITH NUT

4" HINGE PIN: TAP BOTTOM FOR 1/2" NO. 4 FILLISTER SCREW

NO. 4 FILLESTER SCREW

SUMP PUMP PIPE

1/4" PLEXIGLAS OR ALUMINUM

NO. 10-24 U—BOLT THROUGH 1-1/2" TV MAST BRACKET

PLASTIC-BOTTLE FLOAT

terior threaded tube and two nuts could be used.

Place the alarm where it will be heard from the living quarters.

Use a 6-v.d.c. lantern battery to power the alarm bell; test it about every six months. If you're tempted to use a discarded car battery, be aware that it can generate hundreds of amps. To avoid any hazard of melted wires or fire, put a fuse in your circuit between the positive battery pole and the alarm.

We suggest the Unimax switch (available at Radio Shack), because it allows flexibility in the power source you use. The other switch consideration is the pressure needed to trip the switch. Some model No. 556-type switches have lever arms that multiply the force; others don't. If your switch does, you can use a relatively small float.

Place the alarm device with the float slightly above the pump float activating position. This will probably require some trial and error work, as sizes of floats and the pressure in triggering mechanisms will always vary. You can do this by hand, but don't leave the sump pump running for long without any water to pump.—*George Ten-Elshof*

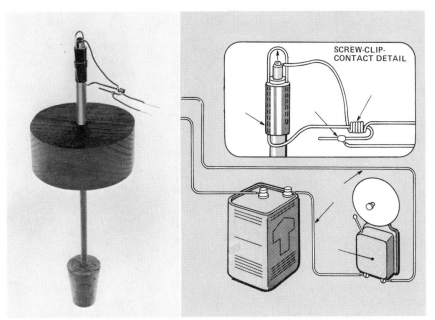

SCREW-CLIP-CONTACT DETAIL

BASEMENT DRAIN ALARM

WHEN HEAVY rains threaten, remove drain cover and place alarm in position.

■ SERIOUS FLOODING may not be a major concern of yours, but sometimes, a sudden, heavy rain causes water to back up in basement drains. This condition can lead to minor flooding that could damage belongings on the floor. If this has happened to you, this gadget should interest you.

Keep the alarm close to the drain. Then, if you suspect a storm or shower may cause flooding, plop the device into the drain hole. If rising water causes the alarm to sound, you'll have ample time to take steps to protect your property.

The alarm is a simple device, easily made from common household articles. But make sure the disc fits evenly inside the lip of the drain hole, so the dowel will hang perpendicular and not bind anywhere inside the aluminum tube. Check the diameter of your drain and adjust any measurements so the disc will rest level, just inside the drain hole.

The wire attached to the roundhead screw in the top of the dowel acts as a stop, keeping the dowel in its rest position. If you decide you need a heavy float and relatively long dowel, insert a small brad through the dowel just below the screw shank. This will act as a stop and not interfere with the operation.

Only use a 6-v.d.c. dry-cell battery for this alarm. Because you may be handling the device when it is wet, *you must use a perfectly safe power source.*—*Jorma Hyypia*

THIS 15-TON splitter is a Sears Craftsman. It's powered by an 8-hp gasoline engine.

How to pick a log splitter

■ FOR MANY cost-conscious homeowners, wood-burning stoves and energy-efficient fireplaces inserts offer a cozy alternative to ever-rising fuel bills. With renewed interest in wood as an economy fuel, several manufacturers are now offering improved log-splitting equipment.

We tested nine of the best-known splitters on the market ranging in power and sophistication from a hand-pumped model to a gas-powered behemoth delivering 15½ tons of ram pressure.

The nine splitters we tested offer different wedge and frame designs and varying degrees of power, sturdiness, portability and speed. We tested horizontal and vertical splitters with prices ranging from $260 to more than $1,600. (All prices were current at the time this was written).

the SolidAx

The most economical and compact unit we looked at was the SolidAx from Cleanweld Turner. It's equipped with a hand-operated hydraulic pump that delivers eight tons of splitting force.

The complete assembly is 44 in. long and weighs just 80 pounds. Mounted on two small rubber wheels, it can be moved by hand easily.

WITH THE Flowtron DS-26, you can split wood coming and going. With wedges at both ends of main beam and a double action ram, this electric unit splits one log while the next is set up.

RAM PRESSURE builds up as the handle on the SolidAx is pumped by hand. With enough power to split seasoned logs easily, the SolidAx is lightweight and easy to store.

WOODMATE I shown below is a powerful and highly portable electric splitter. It's designed for vertical splitting. This makes it much easier on the back because there is less stooping and lifting.

MODEL 1160 from Northern Hydraulics can be set up to split logs vertically or horizontally. The horizontal position is usually easier on your back.

ALL AMERICAN, a gas-powered horizontal splitter with a 10-ton rating, is shown here. It's classy-looking, with a yellow frame and glossy red fenders.

THERE'S AN advantage to the low design of Didier's C26A—the user doesn't have to lift heavy logs very high to get them up onto the main beam.

The pump and ram are mounted on a heavy steel plate that slides along the main steel T-beam so the space between ram and wedge can be adjusted to each log's length.

The SolidAx operates horizontally. A log is placed on the beam with one end against the wedge. The ram is then butted against the opposite end of the log and the plate locked in position with a pin system. The ram is activated by pumping a long handle. As pressure builds, the log is forced against the wedge until the grain snaps. The ram remains extended after the split. To retract it, you must remove the handle from operating position and use its keyed end to turn a valve on the pump. As the pump pressure is released, two coil springs retract the ram.

The SolidAx is a lightweight but sturdy tool, highly portable, easy to store, and, with its broad wedge, very reliable for splitting seasoned logs. Because of its relatively low power, green logs may prove difficult.

The system for ram retraction makes the SolidAx relatively slow. It would be more efficient if the release valve were fitted with a handle of its own.

Flowtron DS-26

Among the motorized units we tested was an 11-amp. electric splitter from Flowtron with

RELATIVE RATINGS OF SEASONED FIREWOOD

HARDWOOD	HEAT EFFICIENCY	SPLITTING EFFORT	SMOKINESS	SPARKING	OVERALL RATING
Apple, ash, beech, birch, dogwood, hard maple, hickory, locust, mesquite, oak, pecan, Pacific madrone	High	Moderate	Little	High when poked	Excellent
Alder, cherry, soft maple, walnut	Medium	Low	Little	Low	Good
Elm, gum, sycamore	Medium	High	Moderate	Low	Fair
Aspen, basswood, cottonwood, yellow poplar	Low	Low	Moderate	Low	Fair, good kindling
SOFTWOOD					
Douglas fir, southern yellow pine	Medium	Low	Heavy	Low	Good
Cypress, redwood	Low	Low	Moderate	Low	Fair
Eastern red cedar, western red cedar, white cedar	Low	Low	Moderate	High	Fair, excellent kindling
Eastern white pine, ponderosa pine, sugar pine, western white pine, true firs	Low	Low	Moderate	Low	Fair, good kindling
Larch, tamarack	Medium	Low	Heavy	High	Fair
Spruce	Low	Low	Moderate	High	Fair, good kindling when dry

Source: U.S. Forest Preserve

Here are factors to consider when you select firewood. Keep several types of wood on hand: Burn the more efficient hardwoods for heat; use softwoods for kindling. Pleasantly scented fruitwoods can add "atmosphere" to your fires.

For safety, avoid unseasoned wood and types that give off heavy smoke and sparks. Smoky fires cause a build-up of resins that can lead to chimney fires.
■ Plan ahead for your firewood needs: Split green logs take 8 to 10 months to dry.
■ If you don't own a wood lot, you may be able to get burnable logs nearby at no cost.

Most national forests permit clearing of dead wood. Call a ranger for local policy.
■ Check your local electric company: When clearing for power lines, it is often necessary to cut down or top off trees. Other possible sources include new construction sites and road-widening operations. Look for storm damage on private wood lots and orchards. Owners may be eager to have you clear broken limbs and damaged trees. Your local town dump may even prove a good occasional source for burnable wood. Important point: Always obtain owner's permission before removing any logs.

If you don't plan to prepare your own wood with chain saw and log splitter, check classified ads in your newspaper or look in the classified directory under "Firewood." Prices for cord wood vary according to species, moisture content and geographic area. Seasoned logs cost more than green wood.

Familiarity with a few terms is useful when ordering firewood. It is usually sold by the *cord*, which represents a stack of logs piled 4 × 4 × 8 ft. A *face cord*, sometimes called a *tier* or *fireplace cord*, is a stack of logs 16 to 24 in. long, 4 ft. high and 8 ft. deep.

THE DESIGN of the High Profile model is yet another approach to solving the back-strain problem. The main beam is positioned higher from the ground than those on most other horizontal splitters. Here, the operator is able to work the splitter standing almost straight up.

PM'S SHOP EDITOR TRIES THE HEATH LOG SPLITTER

I have just spent a most pleasant afternoon splitting logs. Before you think I've lost all my marbles, I'll quickly add that the cutting was done with Heath's Model GU-1810 Hydraulic Splitter. The tool comes in a kit—with very well-written instructions for putting it together. In order to give the kit a fair test (since I've got a lifetime of assembly experience), I asked my 21-year-old son, Jim, to do the assembling; I didn't even look over his shoulder. He did the job easily.

If you have ever assembled any Heath kit you know how complete the instructions are; that quality is maintained in the log-splitter instructions. The result is that putting the tool together "wasn't a job, it was fun," Jim reported. To this I'll add that using it is fun, too. Though the ram seems to travel slowly, I was amazed at the quantity of logs that the two of us split in less than two hours. In fact, we couldn't keep up with the tool. With one man splitting and the other hauling logs to the splitter, we had to stop every 15 minutes or so to clear away the pile.—Harry Wicks, Home and Shop Editor.

seven tons of force. The DS-26 is a horizontal, 150-pound design mounted on two small rubber wheels for portability.

A good feature is its two-wedge design—one at either end of the tubular steel main beam. The double-action ram can exert force in either direction along its path. While splitting one log, you can set up another on the main beam. When the first log is split, the ram direction can be reversed with the control lever to begin work on the second log. This speeds splitting greatly.

Wedges on the DS-26 are relatively narrow. This feature improves performance with green logs since thin wedges cut the tougher fibers in addition to exerting splitting action. The ram will travel to within 3 in. of either wedge. If a log fails to split and jams on a wedge, you can back off the ram, insert a log crosswise for a shim, and run the jammed log through.

While we found Flowtron's offering comparable to other splitters in its class, we also noticed some design problems. As with many horizontal splitters, the low main beam forces the operator to bend continually during operation. Also, there is a breaker switch mounted at the back of the motor housing that's likely to be tripped by an accidental bump.

Woodmate I

McCulloch's Woodmate I is a powerful, upright electric splitter. The vertical design eases back strain associated with horizontal splitters.

The Woodmate's ram and wedge are positioned between two, tubular-steel uprights. Its hydraulic pump and 9-amp motor are mounted on a welded-steel base. A slightly curved bar is mounted on top of the ram to serve as a log rest. Its action is guided by the uprights. The broad wedge, shaped like a flattened cone, locks in place with a slipper-gripper mechanism. Released by a clutch, the wedge can be adjusted to the log length.

While holding a log in place on the bar, the operator activates the ram with a foot switch. A foot-operated lever retracts the ram.

We think the Woodmate I is a fine tool for the average homeowner. It is highly portable and comfortable to use. A fine built-in safety feature releases pump pressure should a log slip from point-to-point contact during use.

We were concerned, however, about the footswitch position on Woodmate I. Since it's at the base of the machine, there's a good chance a piece of split log could fall on the operator's foot.

All American

Piqua Engineering invented the hydraulic splitter for industrial use in 1957. Now, it has developed the All American for homeowners. A horizontal splitter with a gas engine and two-stage pump, the All American musters 10 tons of splitting force.

The wedge on the All American is the largest of any machine we tested and its ram cycle is the fastest. Controlled by a single lever, the ram is guided by Teflon shoes and a special wear plate. The main beam is heavy tubular steel and the entire assembly is mounted on large rubber tires. It can be towed by car or tractor with a suitable hitch and stored vertically when not in use.

Didier Model C26A

With its narrow wedge design and 12½-ton pressure rating, the Didier C26A is well suited for tough, unseasoned logs. A gas-powered, horizontal splitter, it has a two-stage hydraulic pump.

The C26A has three quality features not found on other machines we tested: replaceable solid brass ram guide bars, heavy steel tubing linking the cylinder to the hydraulic control valve, and a handsomely cast control lever.

Sears' 'Best' Craftsman

Sears' top-of-the-line model is a gas-powered, horizontal splitter with a 15-ton rating. The main frame is a 4-in. steel I-beam mounted on large tires for road towing.

The Craftsman offers good features for safety and convenience. The control lever must be held forward for splitting. When released, it shifts automatically to neutral. Pushing back on the lever locks it into ram-return position until the ram is completely retracted.

Sears offers two splitter accessories we really liked: a folding hitch stand to keep the tool level during operation and a "log cradle" that's 14½ in. wide to eliminate the need to hand-balance logs on the main beam. Sears also supplies a breatherless cap that allows you to store the tool vertically without draining the hydraulic oil.

High Profile Model 1130

To answer the most common complaint about horizontal splitters—namely, that they require too much bending—the High Profile model is designed with its tubular steel main beam a comfortable 29 in. from the ground. With a mild-steel ram guide, underlayed with hard brass, and a 15½-ton rating, the High Profile is among the most rugged tools we tested.

Standard equipment for the High Profile is a 5-hp Briggs and Stratton engine, but the maker offers an 8-hp Tecumseh motor which it claims cuts the ram cycle from 16 to 11.7 seconds. Another accessory is a quartering wedge that slips over the permanent wedge to divide a log into four parts.

Our test proved the higher design to be a mixed blessing. While there was less bending during operation, lifting heavy logs up to the beam required more effort. Using the quartering wedge caused some flexing of the main beam and we also noticed some leakage of hydraulic oil and gas caused by engine vibration.

Model 1160

The maker of the High Profile unit offers another splitter—the Model 1160—one of our favorites. While identical to the High Profile in power and available options, the 1160 has some important design differences.

It can be operated either vertically or horizontally. Upright, it can be moved easily like a hand truck. Or, it can be towed by car or tractor. The Model 1160 is the only splitter we tested with the wedge mounted directly on the ram. A heavy steel plate backs up the log and serves as a base in vertical operating position.

The ease of operating the Model 1160 vertically was unmatched by any other tool. Heavy logs need not be lifted at all; they can be rolled up and tilted on end for splitting. We also liked the steel fingers on the frame which push off logs jammed on the wedge.

SPECIFICATIONS OF LOG SPLITTERS TESTED

MODEL	MANUFACTURER	OPERATING POSITION	POWER	DRIVE	MAX. LOG LENGTH	WEDGE (width × length × ht.)	SPLIT FORCE	CYCLE (Seconds)	MFR. PRICE[2]
SolidAx	Cleanweld Turner	Horizontal	Manual	Hydraulic	24½"	5 × 5 × 6"	8 tons	NA[3]	$ 260
DS-26	Flowtron	Horizontal	11-amp. electric	Screw	26	½ × 9 × 9½"	7+ tons	40[4]	400
Woodmate I	McCulloch	Vertical	9-amp. elec. B&D[5]	Hydraulic	28	7¼ × 6½ × 13½"	10 tons	18	450
All American	Piqua Engineering	Horizontal	5-hp B&S[6]	Hydraulic	26	4½ × 9 × 9"	10 tons	15	995
Heath Model GU-1810	Heath Co.	Horizontal	5 hp	Hydraulic	21	¾ × 4 × 6"	10 tons	24	550
C26A	Didier	Horizontal	5-hp B&S[6]	Hydraulic	26	1¼ × 6 × 7"	12½ tons	16	1,340
Sears Best Craftsman	Sears, Roebuck and Co.	Horizontal	8-hp B&S[6]	Hydraulic	26	2½ × 6¼ × 8½"	15 tons	16	1,650
Model 1130	Northern Hydraulics	Horizontal	5-hp B&S[6]	Hydraulic	25	1 × 6 × 8"	15½ tons	16	855
Model 1160	Northern Hydraulics	Either	5 hp	Hydraulic	25	4 × 6½ × 8¼"	15½ tons	16	1,190

[2] Many log splitters are unassembled—there may be charges for assembly, freight and handling; [3]Not applicable; [4]One way, splits in both directions; [5]Black & Decker; [6]Briggs & Stratton

A no-frills band saw

By AL SITTNER and HARRY WICKS

RUGGEDLY BUILT saw comes with bare minimum of extras, but is long on quality and important features. Throat capacity is 24½ in. and tool will cut 9-inch thickness. The locking device (near left) isn't fancy, but it does the job. Like studs on the rip fence, this has a 90° bend which makes for effortless turning either direction.

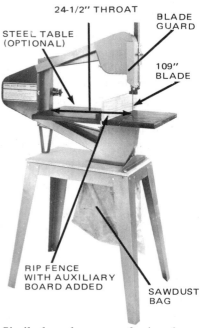

24-1/2" THROAT
BLADE GUARD
STEEL TABLE (OPTIONAL)
109" BLADE
RIP FENCE WITH AUXILIARY BOARD ADDED
SAWDUST BAG

■ THIS NO-NONSENSE band saw manufactured by Dupli-Carver, represents an interesting approach to tool design. The designer started by asking professional cabinetmakers what features they do—and don't—use on a band saw. His findings showed that most band-saw users don't use many of the "extras" commonly found on a band saw.

His findings coincide with our own experience. For example, this isn't the tool we use to make accurate cutoffs. Similarly, when a professional makes a bevel cut on a band saw, he rarely relies on the tool-affixed gauge, he generally uses a bevel T-square or a jig to set the angle.

Based on these findings, Dupli-Carver has produced a saw that is a good buy at about $500. You can purchase an optional steel table, or work with the particleboard top that comes with the tool. A rip-fence—which doesn't ride on scribed rails—also comes with the tool.

SAWDUST IS coaxed into bag below by tiny fins (arrow) added.

RIP FENCE locks positively and quickly, using two 90° studs and wingnuts.

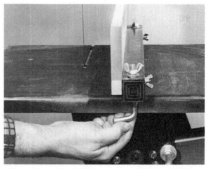

TO LOCK FENCE, you simply swing the L-shaped studs under table.

NEXT, TIGHTEN wingnuts on top. Hardware's grip on table is absolute.

THIS HEFTY piece of walnut was quickly and accurately resawn.

SPECIFICATIONS—BAND SAW

Model: B-245
Throat capacity: 24½ in.
Blade length: 109 in.
Blade tooth speed: 3,600 saw ft. per minute
Cutting capacity: 9 in.
Price: $499
Accessories (at above price): Stand, built-in dust collector, ½-hp capacitor-start motor, scroll saw table, rip fence, ⅜-in. blade.
Manufacturer: Dupli-Carver, 4004 West 10th St., Indianapolis, Ind. 46222. For brochure and dealer information, send $1 to manufacturer.

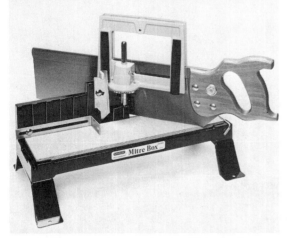

THE STANLEY miterbox with a 4 x 18-in. backsaw.

A low-cost miterbox

■ THE NEW Stanley Workmaster Mitre Box offers top quality at a reasonable price, a winning combination for woodworkers who must be able to cut consistently accurate miters and right angles.

Constructed of cast aluminum, the unit comes with a 4x18-in. backsaw. The vertical travel of this saw permits cutting a 2x4.

In tests the box cut four-, five- and six-sided figures. The results were equal to those obtained with a radial-arm saw. The unit has several fine features: A spring-loaded wedge arrangement for quick, easy angle setting; an adjustable board stop for repeat cuts; and a board clamp for holding the workpiece against the back plate.

The box costs about $57 with the backsaw, $42 without it, from Stanley Tools, Dept. PID, Box 1800, New Britain, CT 06050.

TOUGH, free-floating plastic guides hold the saw in accurate alignment while the cut is made.

SPRING-LOADED WEDGE is pulled back to disengage the saw guide so it can be swung to a new position.

AN ADJUSTABLE board stop can be quickly set to obtain multiple, same-length cuts.

A WINGNUT is turned to clamp the work to the back plate. The clamp and stop can be mounted on either end.

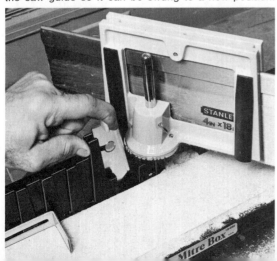

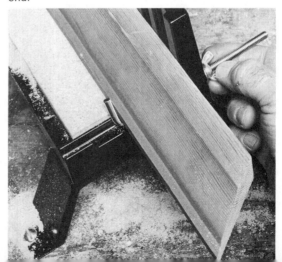

A tough little reciprocating saw

■ THE TIME comes for every serious do-it-yourselfer when he needs a reciprocating saw, such as the one shown at right. This one, a relative newcomer on the market, is from Wells Manufacturing. Priced at $216 or $242, depending on size, the tool is a good value. (These prices were current at the time this was written). We used it to cut several rough openings in a 150-year-old building (right). This meant cutting through sections of 6x8 posts, as shown. The saw performed well.

SPECIFICATIONS—WELLSAW

Blades: 8 available
Motor: 115 v.a.c., 50 or 60 Hz., single phase (or 115 v.d.c.)
Weight: Approximately 8 lbs.
Blade capacity: 8 and 16 in.
Blade stroke length: 1⅛ in.
Blade speed: 8,000 strokes per minute
Price: $216 (8-in. model); $242 (16-in.-model)
Manufacturer: Wells Manufacturing Corp., 407 Jefferson St., Three Rivers, Mich. 49093

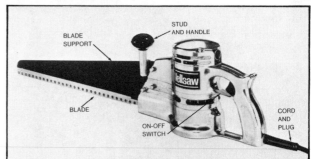

THIS LITTLE beauty of a saw chewed its way through the framing in this old building with bulldog tenacity. Because its blade cuts in both directions, there is practically no kick or pull. The extra handle over the blade is for support.

A new grinding-carving tool

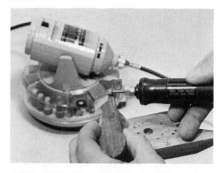

GRINDING and carving tool has a swivel base and a 36-in.-long flexible shaft.

TOOL HAS enough power for light-duty metal and ceramic work and for hardwoods.

■ BLACK AND DECKER'S new 9416 Rotary Hobby Shop is the first of the combination grinding/carving tools to feature a tray for accessory bits that's incorporated into the tool's base. This convenient tray has a clear acrylic cover which rotates independently of the base and an opening for easy bit removal.

The entire base also swivels, allowing the power head to follow the 36-in.-long, permanently lubricated flexible shaft. This reduces the chance of the shaft binding and being damaged.

This tool's 1.8-amp., 0-to-1,900 rpm, double-insulated motor has a sliding, variable-speed switch and produced more than enough power to cut the walnut fish carving shown. It worked equally well for grinding the cutting edge on pruning shears and—using the proper bits—it excelled at drilling, cutting and deburring ceramics, steel and soft metals.

Thirty-five different bits, including sanding drums and polishing wheels, come with the tool. The handpiece's universal collet accepts all ⅛-in.-dia. shank bits.

The manufacturer recommends attaching the base directly to the workbench when using the tool. Holes are drilled in the base for this purpose. Or, if you plan to use the tool infrequently, attach it to a piece of plywood which can then be clamped to the bench or a table when needed.

The complete package is available at hardware stores and hobby shops and retails for about $80. If you can't locate it, write to Black and Decker, Customer Service, 3012 Highwoods Blvd., Raleigh, NC 27625.

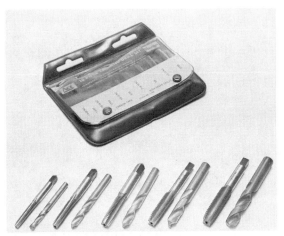

MATCHED TAP AND DRILL sets for the home handyman store neatly in plastic pouches.

HANDY TAP AND DRILL SET

This 10-piece, heavy-duty tap and drill set comes in a handy vinyl pouch for easy, safe storage on a pegboard.

Shown here is the NC set which includes ¼-20, 5/16-18, ⅜-16, 7/16-14 and ½-13 carbon taps and matching high-speed steel drills. NF taps are also available in the same sizes. Industrial quality sets come in the same sizes and feature precision-rolled, high-speed steel taps with high-speed steel drills. Available at hardware stores and home centers, prices range from $29 to $49. From Henry L. Hanson Inc., 220 Brooks St., Worcester, MA 01606.

GLASS CUTTER MAGIC

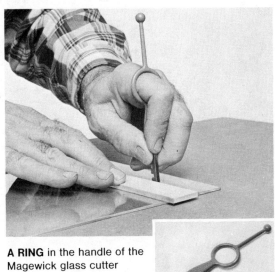

A RING in the handle of the Magewick glass cutter makes it easy to hold perpendicular while pressing down to score the glass.

Cutting glass is relatively easy if you hold the tool perfectly perpendicular, while pressing straight

New for your shop

Prices shown below were in effect when this was written.

down—easier said than done. The hard part is gripping the slender shaft of the conventional glass cutter tightly enough to apply the straight downward pressure required while holding it like a pencil.

Now you can cut glass like a pro on your first attempt with the newly patented Magewick glass cutter. It has a circle in the handle so your index finger becomes part of the same axis as the cutter. This allows effortless downward pressure and makes it easy to keep the cutter perpendicular.

The Magewick Comfort Grip glass cutter comes with steel or carbide wheels from Pro Glass Cutter Co. Inc., 13910 Creekside Dr., Matthews, NC 28105. Cost with carbide wheel is $9.50, steel wheel $4.50, postpaid.

THREE-WAY SCREWDRIVER

Three-sided, angle-tip screwdrivers work from directly above or from an angle for increased leverage. Angle driving increases torque, reduces effort and makes it easier to reach into corners.

Three-tool ScrewTriver kits in ¼-, 5/16-, and ⅜-in. sizes are available from hardware stores or by mail from Rodan Tools Inc., 17200 Libby Rd., Maple Heights, OH 44137 for $12.95 plus $1.50 for handling.

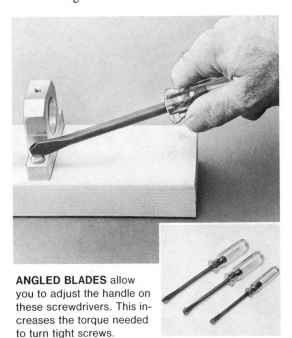

ANGLED BLADES allow you to adjust the handle on these screwdrivers. This increases the torque needed to turn tight screws.

How to pick a perfect knife

By JIM WOODS

Kershaw Camp and Field Model 1030, from Kershaw Knives, Lake Oswego, OR, one of an extensive line, comes with a fitted leather sheath.

Schrade Old Timer Sharpfinger is by Schrade Cutlery, Ellenville, NY, makers of Uncle Henry, Scrimshaw, and limited edition collector lines, as well.

Puma Hunter's Pal, Model 6397, a handmade imported by Gutmann Cutlery, Mount Vernon, NY, is from extensive line.

American Blade boot knife, new from American Blade Cutlery, Chattanooga, TN, has a 3½-inch blade with concave back and buffalo horn handles.

Utica Kutmaster Stockmen's Model 3256, by Utica Cutlery, Utica, NY, is a classic pocketknife with clip, sheepsfoot and spey blades.

Ibberson Extending Ruler folding knife of Sheffield steel, imported by Garrett Wade, New York, NY, shows scale size of knives above.

■ UNTIL RECENTLY, only a few personal-knife types were popular. There was the pocketknife that could be used for whittling and the multiblade camper's knife of the Boy Scout type. The hunter's sheath knife was related to the Army and Marine fighting and survival knives of several years ago. These, in turn, were modified varieties of Bowie knives, with century-old heavy blade and clip-point designs.

Today's knives are different, and the finest are much more expensive. Models shown here range from under $20 for the classic Utica

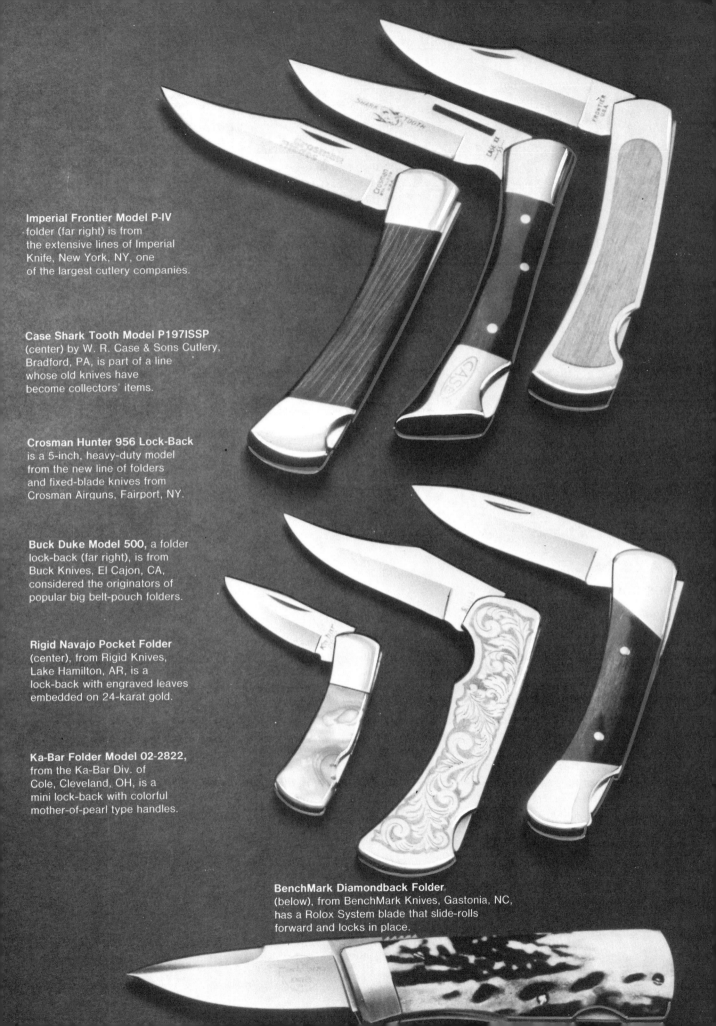

Imperial Frontier Model P-IV folder (far right) is from the extensive lines of Imperial Knife, New York, NY, one of the largest cutlery companies.

Case Shark Tooth Model P197ISSP (center) by W. R. Case & Sons Cutlery, Bradford, PA, is part of a line whose old knives have become collectors' items.

Crosman Hunter 956 Lock-Back is a 5-inch, heavy-duty model from the new line of folders and fixed-blade knives from Crosman Airguns, Fairport, NY.

Buck Duke Model 500, a folder lock-back (far right), is from Buck Knives, El Cajon, CA, considered the originators of popular big belt-pouch folders.

Rigid Navajo Pocket Folder (center), from Rigid Knives, Lake Hamilton, AR, is a lock-back with engraved leaves embedded on 24-karat gold.

Ka-Bar Folder Model 02-2822, from the Ka-Bar Div. of Cole, Cleveland, OH, is a mini lock-back with colorful mother-of-pearl type handles.

BenchMark Diamondback Folder (below), from BenchMark Knives, Gastonia, NC, has a Rolox System blade that slide-rolls forward and locks in place.

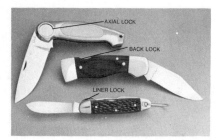

LOCKING folders are popular. Axial Lile-Lock (top) is about $200; Western's Lockback S-534, $40; Utica (bottom), $15.

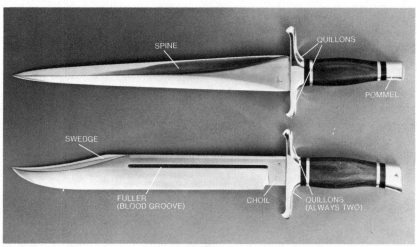

DOUBLE-EDGE Arkansas Bowie (top) and Classic Bowie knife (bottom) are both from Charles Hipp's Bone Knife Co., located in Lubbock, TX.

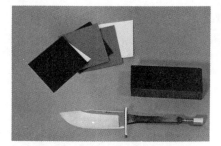

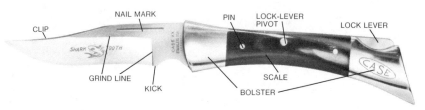

SHARK TOOTH Model P197 L SSP, from W.R. Case & Sons, attracts collectors.

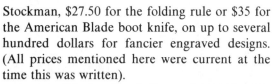

MORSETH custom $50 kit (top) from A. G. Russell and $25 Rigid Knives kit (bottom) are ready for home finishing.

Stockman, $27.50 for the folding rule or $35 for the American Blade boot knife, on up to several hundred dollars for fancier engraved designs. (All prices mentioned here were current at the time this was written).

A material that has influenced considerable change is stainless steel. No longer is it a metal with unpredictable qualities that appeared shortly after World War II. Now, an increasing number of quality knives made worldwide are stainless. Generally, U.S. factory-made blades use 440 stainless, while the several hundred custom knifemakers employ 440C or 154CM.

plastics for handles

The plastics of modern technology have also had considerable influence on knife construction. Natural handle materials—horn, bone and ivory—are still in demand for some expensive knives, but for various reasons are in short supply. To meet a growing demand, plastics such as

Lexan, Delrin and Micarta are the answer. None of these are new. Lexan is the practically bullet-proof material that is sometimes used for cashiers' cages. Delrin has been cast and machined into high-strength aircraft components for years. Micarta, a phenolic resin developed by Westinghouse, has been in use for electric insulators since the 1930s. All of these machine relatively easily, take a smooth finish, are warm to the touch, and will outlast the steel in the blades. Almost any knife you buy today will have a plastic handle—and it probably will be a good one.

better locks

Perhaps the biggest design improvement has been the blade lock for the folders. It has put new safety into folding knives, and has helped personal knives become socially acceptable. This wasn't the case at the start. The first lock-back folders, generally considered to be the product of Buck Knives in California, were large knives with husky blades. For several years, "buck knife" was the generic description of a lock-back folder from any manufacturer. The big folders rode in equally big snap-flap pouches, frequently hanging from the belts of some members of our rougher social element. In time, the knives be-

BROWNING South Pass is in presentation box. Cam III assortment (below) has three-bladed belt buckle.

STAGHANDLE No. 3 Hunter is famous Randall.

GERBER'S folder has Bolt-Action lock.

WESTMARK 702 is a fine knife from Western Cutlery.

PRECISE'S Swiss Army knife has lock.

NEW FOLDER is in Camillus Wildlife Series.

came smaller and more finely finished, disappeared into pockets rather than belt pouches, and then emerged in belt pouches once again as they became respectable. Now, a lock-back folding knife in a belt pouch is as common as a wristwatch in the everyday dress of many men, and a few women, in all manner of occupations.

folding blade lock

There are a number of variations in lock locations and advertising names, but the folding-blade lock is usually a lever that runs the length of the handle back. When this lever is depressed, the forward end that engages a notch in the blade tang pivots up and releases the blade.

A simple and less expensive device is the liner lock, a springy brass divider between blades or handle scale and blade, that snaps into place behind the blade tang when the blade is fully extended. To close the blade, the liner is warped aside with the thumb. More complicated and expensive is the axial lock. This is primarily offered by custom knifemakers, but Gerber Blades and Kershaw Cutlery, both in Oregon, have axial lock models. Blade locks are not new, and some antique folders have clever ones.

better shapes

While the latest popular blade designs aren't brand new, one that was rediscovered about 25 years ago and dubbed the "drop point" is a current favorite and a good compromise shape.

Knife blade shapes are identified by point style and location. Hold the knife horizontal with the edge down. If the blade back is straight to the point, the style is "straight point." It's a good skinning and slicing blade, and knives so equipped are classed as skinners, although there are specialized shapes that do a better job.

point types

If the back of the blade curves up, the point is called a "sweeping" or "swept" point. If it angles down to a point below the blade back or is in a curve that resembles a ski jump, the blade has a "clip" or "clipped" point. If the downward curve is like that of a bullet trajectory and the point is more than midway down the blade, it is the "dropped" point. When the blade back and edge have identical curves, it can be a dagger shape if the back and edge are parallel, or a spear if the blade is widest where the point curve starts. There are numerous other blade shapes for your special needs, and variations include sheepsfoot and spey blades that see lots of use in pocket knives.

most patterns are standard

Almost every knife company produces most of the standard patterns. A pocketknife maker will supply a Stockman's knife with clip, sheepsfoot and spey blades. The camper's model will have a large spear and shorter clip blade, along with a can opener, combination cap lifter and screwdriver, and an awl or punch—like those issued to members of the Swiss Army. The commercial versions of the Swiss Army knife go a lot further, and on some you can count a couple of dozen tools and gadgets.

Owners find constant use for such fold-out items as scissors, screwdriver (including a Phillips-head), saw, file, fishhook disgorger, inch and metric rules, can opener, miniature marlinespike and magnifying glass. More elaborate models also have tweezers and toothpick. There are lots of poor-imitation Swiss Army knives, but only two that have been made for over 80 years and are "official": the Victorinox, imported by Swiss Army Knives Inc., and Wenger, from Precise International.

custom models

In spite of all the knives available, a lot of owners want one that's unique. Custom knifemakers fill this need, often at high prices and most of the time with superior quality. If a factory produces a pocketknife for $25, a lock-back for $50 and a straight blade hunter for $75, you usually can multiply those numbers by five or six for the price at custom makers.

You can also create your own custom knife with the help of knife parts suppliers. The do-it-yourself way to get started is to buy preground blades and put most of your effort into the handle. Shaping blades from raw bar stock and then properly hardening, tempering and polishing the steel takes a good deal of metalworking ability and access to advanced shop equipment.

You will learn that there's more to a knife than a blade and handle. A blade may have a back, belly and sometimes a spine. The handle may be comprised of a guard, bolsters or pommel, along with scales. Underneath the handle of a fixed-blade knife is a tang. All these could be held together with solder, epoxy, cyanoacrylate adhesives, pins or cutlers' rivets.

assessing value

You can probably produce an acceptable home-shop knife for about $20 or less, if you are buying supplies in quantity. Your knife is not likely to increase in value, but you will have the satisfaction of a hand-finished project. Nor do store-bought, factory-produced knives often increase in value. In spite of a few that have become collector's pieces, most are headed for useful work rather than glass cabinet. There are companies like W.R. Case and Sons whose knives have a collector following, perhaps because Case is well into its second century of production.

commemorative models

It's common for knife companies to produce commemorative models in limited quantities—instant collectors' pieces. Unfortunately for investors, it may take a couple of lifetimes for such knives to become more valuable. With hundreds of knife styles and millions of knives in annual production, it takes many years for a make or model to disappear so that a few can become rare. A limited edition knife may reach that rarity earlier, but most "limited editions" don't get used at all. If it's a 500-unit edition, there will be 500 around for a long time.

price indicates quality

Knives are competitively priced—the market is too big to be otherwise—so the price of U.S. knives is usually a good indicator of quality in the knife you choose. As with most tools, buy the best you can afford for the job at hand. Look for top workmanship, or the lack of it, in the fit and finish. If an inspection of two similar knives doesn't show the difference, rely on price to indicate some hidden qualities or shortcuts. A high-priced knife *may* be cheaply made, but a cheap knife is *sure* to be.

SUPPLIERS—KITS AND PARTS

Angus-Campbell Inc., 4917 South Soto St., Los Angeles, Calif. 90058. (Bulk materials, Micarta.)

Atlanta Cutlery Corp., Box 839, Conyers, Ga. 30207. (Blades, kits, fittings.)

CAM III, 243 Millbrook Way, Vacaville, Calif. 95688. (Lock-back folder kit.)

Christopher Firearms, State & Ferry Sts., Miamitown, Ohio 45041. (Blades and fittings.)

Dixie Gun Works, Union City, Tenn. 38261. (Finished and raw blades, fittings, handles. Catalog: $3.)

The House of Muzzleloading, Box 6217, Glendale, Calif. 91205. (Modern and old-style blades, fittings, handles.)

Indian Ridge Traders, Box 869, Royal Oak, Mich. 48068. (Modern and old-style blades, fittings, hardware.)

Koval Knives, Box 14130, Columbus, Ohio 43214. (Bulk and unfinished materials, hardware.)

A.G. Russell, 1705 Highway 71, Springdale, Ark. 72764. (Kits and materials.)

Schrimsher's Custom Knifemaker's Supply, Box 308, Emory, Tex. 75440. (Bulk steel and materials. Catalog: $1.)

The best old guns are new

New laws creating muzzleloader hunting seasons and the growth of commemorative military units have helped convert replicas of antique firearms into elegant collectables

By ANGUS LAIDLAW

■ GOOD REPLICA GUNS and modern muzzleloaders are not cheap. But compared with collector originals, they are bargains indeed. What's more, replicas do a better job of demonstrating how the originals handled, and for that matter, how they shot, than the classics could do themselves today.

How can that be? Easy. Most of the original Revolutionary arms are in museums or private collections and are too valuable to risk firing. Those in good shape are too good to play with, and the bad ones are either nonworking, unsafe,

or both. A good modern replica, however, feels like an original, fires like an original, and can give the real sensation of what old-time shooting was like.

An original Whitworth military target rifle, for example, of the type used by some Confederate snipers and English target shooters, might cost $2,000 to $4,000 in good condition today. The Navy Arms replica of the Whitworth lists for about $575 and is gauged by the same gauges that were used to inspect the originals in the 1860s. The new barrels have the identical hexag-

DIXIE GUN WORKS' modern muzzleloader (left) is Tennessee flintlock squirrel rifle. Customized Kentucky flint long rifle, by George Heinemann, replicates 1790 styling. Whitworth hexagonal-bore sniper rifle (center), from Navy Arms, has 1,000-yard range. Percussion Hawken II, by Navy Arms is suitable field rifle for deer hunting. Navy Magnum 12-gauge shotgun (right) is a black powder choice for clay pigeons and waterfowl. Flintlock pistol copies specifications from Williamsburg for British Army 1761 Dragoon.

CASED dueling
pistols would cost
thousands for the 1870
originals. But shooters can
now get Navy Arms copy set for about $700.

onal rifling making one turn in 20 inches that en-
abled the original Whitworths to hit a 30-inch
target at up to 1,000 yards. The replicas not only
look the same, they shoot as well or better using
modern cast lead bullets. Matches for these and
other slug guns—so-called because they shoot a
conical bullet or slug rather than the round ball
of many other muzzleloading rifles—are featured
in numerous black powder matches.

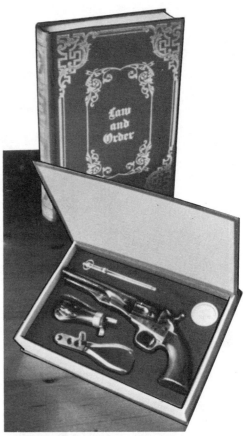

FAVORITE OLD hideaways for pistols were imitation
books. Navy Arms cases 1862 New Police Colt with
accessories.

ETHAN ALLEN model (top left) is a pepperbox.
Mountain Pistol is by Connecticut Valley Arms. Ruger
Old Army revolver is available in stainless steel. Lin-
coln derringer (bottom) is by Navy Arms. Most of
these come either factory-finished or as kits.

1750 TINDERLIGHTER is a neat way to strike light
for the attached candle. Navy Arms: about $70.

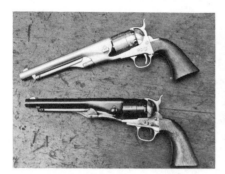

THOMPSON CENTER Cougar Hawken (top) and reissued Colt 1860 Army are in stainless steel.

COLT'S REISSUED 1860 Army .44 is of stainless steel. Connecticut Valley Arms' is a made-in-Italy replica.

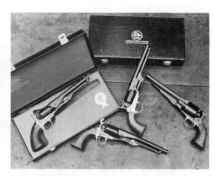

FROM CVA are (left to right) 1861 Colt Navy, 1860 Colt Army, 1851 brass-frame Navy and 1858 Remington .44.

Since 1954, when the first mass-produced muzzleloading rifle and pistol replicas were introduced, more copies of some models like the Walker Colts, have been made than were ever turned out originally. Two developments during the last 25 years have given the black powder sports a major push. Military and civilian organizations and clubs have been formed to duplicate those of a century or so ago, right down to the same uniforms and equipment. And then there have been new laws that make primitive muzzleloader hunting seasons legal in most states.

Military units commemorating the Indian Wars, the Revolution and the Civil War have created a demand for exact replicas of original uniforms, equipment, personal arms and even artillery. To meet the requirements of the Brigade of the American Revolution, for example, no nonperiod items are allowed. No digital watches, cigarette lighters, or zippers, and the barrel on your Brown Bess musket replica must be the correct 42 inches long, with all other features of the arm line-for-line correct when compared with an original. The result now is a quality assortment of authentic modern reproductions of historic muskets, rifles, fowling pieces and pistols.

Hunters have also done much to foster the availability of good quality and reasonably priced replicas. Ten years ago, few states had special seasons for muzzleloaders. Now, nearly all do. Many of the sportsmen attracted by these extra seasons were hunters first and black powder shooters a distant second. While they cared greatly about legal hunting, they gave less than a hoot about historic accuracy. What they wanted was a dependable modern muzzleloader.

From this demand came the Thompson Center Renegade, based on their earlier and more historically correct Hawken. The Renegade has a modern shotgun-style butt plate with no horns to poke you on recoil. It has adjustable sights so that a hunter can develop a load and then zero in his sights without files and a hammer. The Renegade Cougar has stainless fittings and lock parts to make it more durable and to look more like modern stainless models. The wood is quality American walnut.

Besides being used for hunting and reenacting battles from past wars, modern replica arms have rejuvenated a whole field of target and sport shooting. A few old-timers were still shooting originals in competition. But without the inexpensive replicas, there's no way the black powder sport could have achieved its present popularity.

Some stainless-steel muzzleloader revolvers and rifles have been built to modern designs and are intended specifically for competition. Others may become instant collectables. The reissued Colt 1860 Army revolver in blued steel and more expensive stainless only will be in production for a short period. Those who shoot it and care for it well may expect considerable appreciation. A quarter century from now, these few stainless models could be worth more than their original predecessors which fought the Civil War on both sides and helped open the West.

Demands by the buckskinners and others for accurate replicas like the Tennessee Mountain Squirrel Rifle in .32 caliber (Dixie Gun Works) have caused many of these to be mass produced. Both flintlock and percussion cap versions of these are available with extra locks and fittings so that one rifle can be converted to either ignition system. The base price of approximately $300 for the percussion model is a bargain for an accurately styled, straight-shooting long rifle.

Both factory-made and handcrafted Kentucky long rifles are popular. The one shown here is a handmade example by New Jersey hobbyist

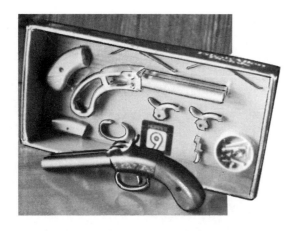

DOUBLE BARREL percussion Ethan Allen pocket pistol is available from Hoppe's for under $100. It comes either as a parts kit or finished.

COMMEMORATIVE military unit, Ronald Plourde's Company of 4th Battalion Royal Artillery, fires cannons such as 3 pounder with South Bend Tube, Ashe carriage.

George Heinemann. Accurately styled modern rifles like this one, made with highest quality locks (LGR), barrels (Bob Paris) and fancy maple stock blanks, can cost upward of $5,000 when created by top-ranking modern muzzleloader gunsmiths like J.S. Brooks or William Buechelle. While this kind of expense can exceed the cost of an original, the buyer gets a safe rifle with a perfect bore capable of fine hunting or competition accuracy. He also gets a gun fitted to him so that it handles as no mass-produced arm ever will.

Besides historical and working replicas, less well-known but interesting arms of the 19th century are being replicated. Finely crafted dueling pistols in both flint and percussion (Navy Arms, Dixie Gun Works and others) can double as target shooters for handgun enthusiasts. Prices range from about $250 per pistol to about $700 for the matched set of LePage duelers with French-style case, brass oiler, powder flask, nipple wrench, turnscrew (the formal term for a screwdriver as pretty as this one) and loading rod with rifling protector.

On a more affordable level, Penguin Industries, makers of Hoppe's No. 9 nitro powder and black powder solvents, have introduced three copies of the early Ethan Allen pistols produced in New England in the 1840s. The pepperbox, so-called because its six rotating barrels looked something like a pepper mill, was one of the early muzzleloading repeaters. It was cheaper than Colt's revolvers at the time, and may also have gotten its name from its tendency to fire all six barrels at once and pepper anything in its path. A simple side-by-side double pistol and a single-

shot target model are also in the Ethan Allen line, selling for less than $100 in home assembly kits or available prefinished.

Time was when a percussion double shotgun cost less than $10 and you could find a good one in almost any antique shop. Those days are gone, but Italian-made replicas, like the 12 Gauge Magnum Percussion Shotgun (Navy Arms) now lists for about $325. That's not expensive, however, when compared to the prices of many modern doubles. What's more, muzzleloader shotguns shoot just as hard as modern breechloaders, and the second barrel of a double can be fired almost as quickly.

Cannon shooters have also gone the replica route. But they can rarely afford to go it alone. This may be a good thing, since it takes teamwork and correct procedures to shoot these monsters safely.

In the past few years, an International Muzzleloading Shooting Program has developed for firing everything from 16th-century Japanese matchlocks—a short length of clothesline ignites the charge—to modern replica percussion revolvers. Information about courses of fire and qualifying dates for future matches is available from Robert Reiber, USIMLC Tryout Chairman, 1505 Spruce Ridge Way, Stone Mountain, GA. 30083.

Those interested in modern black powder shooting can join the National Muzzleloading Rifle Assn., Box 67, Friendship, IN. 47021. Dues are $14 per year and include a subscription to *Muzzle Blasts,* their monthly magazine.

If the black powder sport is booming, and it is, it's because they don't build 'em like they used to. They build 'em better.

New pick-your-power boating

Paddle, power or tack your way across the bay; these new convertibles let you choose

■ THERE AREN'T many vehicles that let you choose a different power if the price of gas goes up, the strength of wind goes down, or you just feel like cruising along in a different way. But a few specialized boats offer that choice. Here are some new examples.

The Multi-Craft 18, from American Multi-Craft Northeast, Box 297, Sparta, NJ 07871, is an 18-foot switch-sailer with trimaran hull, rated for up to 115-hp outboard motors, plus a sloop rig that stores aboard. The three-piece mast, when assembled, mounts 220 square feet of sail. For downwind running, a loose-footed wraparound mainsail can be opened on each side of the mast for wing-and-winging.

Padded seats become four bunks under camper canvas, and the under-8-foot beam is quite suitable for trailering.

With the look of a traditional New

1 Kona Kat's Joy Rider catamaran can be sailed or paddled sitting, and is rigged like a sailboard.

2 Sea Gypsy, with handsome workboat lines, can cruise three hours on a gallon of diesel (below) or sail with a gaff rig (below right).

3 A trihulled 18-footer that switches quickly from power to sail, new Multi-Craft 18 takes outboards to 115 hp or jib and double wraparound main.

4 Almost any sailboat can take an outboard with an adjustable spring-loaded bracket—this one is from OMC—that lowers or lifts the motor.

5 New, steam-powered Morven skiff resembles a classic launch and trailers easily with a five-foot beam.

6 Multiaction Bullfrog, from O'Brien, is a swim and snorkel board or speedy kneeboard for towing tricks.

England lobster boat, the 23-foot Sea Gypsy, from New River Boat Co., 2007 Southwest 11th St., Fort Lauderdale, FL 33312, can cruise along at up to six knots and burn only one quart of fuel per hour with its 10-hp diesel. Yet, if even that seems excessive, you can set the gaff-rigged sail. Options include cuddy or full cabin, center console and wheel steering, bunks, head and galley.

Classic launches that can replace gasoline power with steam are built in England, using the modern wood-epoxy West System, from designs by Glyn Jones.

Now, however, one is available from Rhode Island Marine Services, Box 209, Snug Harbor, RI 02880. The 20-foot Morven Elegance class has a Semple single-cylinder, 5-hp steamer. Jones also has plans for 16- and 24-foot launches

plus a trailerable, paddle-driven, 24-foot side-wheeler.

Kona Corp., Box 878, Oak Hill, FL 32759, builders of the twin-hull Kona Kat sailboard, has a new sit-down two-seater sailboard catamaran with a "joy stick" steering system. The Joy Rider has kick-up rudders and centerboard that let it float in three inches of water, and it can be paddled if the wind goes down. The 150-pound cat can be car-topped or trailered.

High-speed fun without the skills of water skiing is an advantage of kneeboards. The Bullfrog, from O'Brien International, Redmond, WA, doubles as a snorkeling float or planes behind outboards of 10 hp and up.

And to convert sailboats easily to power, up-down transom brackets from OMC Accessories and others are the answer.

Double-duty diving gear

Underwater equipment is surfacing. It is being used for a variety of water sports and even land-based activities

By BILL McKEOWN

■ ANYTHING THAT CAN keep you warmer, safer or better equipped for sport under water is likely to do a good job at water level or above, as well—sometimes, too much so.

The full-length, one-piece wet suit, plus gloves, booties and helmet, keeps you warm while diving. But shorts and a vest of thinner neoprene or a jacket with nylon sleeves may be all that you'll need to ward off cold spray at sea level. These allow much more freedom of motion, and are infinitely easier to put on and take off.

Because underwater accessories are made to survive salt water conditions, their rugged strength is an advantage ashore. What a diving light, for example, gives away in added weight, it makes up for in durability for a camper.

Subsurface electronics are also being adapted for general outdoor use. An underwater range-and-depth finder handheld sonar, from Morrow Electronics, can be used by divers as well as fishermen. Nikon's dive-camera, the Nikonos IV-A, has built-in electric-eye exposure and optional, electronic, self-adjusting flash. Ashore, it can go on shooting through rain or dust storms.

1 WET SUITS for diving have been updated. From Parkway Fabricators, South Amboy, NJ are Reversible Shorties.

2 ALSO FOR cold-weather waterskiing or spray of sailboarding, Parkway has Tempest coverall, a bolero jacket.

3 FOR O'Brien International Bullfrog kneeboard riders and sailboarders, there are waterproof windbreakers and wet suits.

4 The Nikonos IV-A, with automatic exposure and flash, can surface for photography in rain, snow or sand.

5 A WATERPROOF, digital-reading depth/distance finder, Dive Ray from Morrow Electronics, Salem, OR, spots fish.

6 FLASHLIGHTS BY Tekna, Menlo Park, CA, are rated for depths to 2,000 feet and 12,000 candlepower with four AA cells.

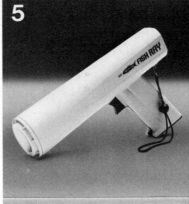

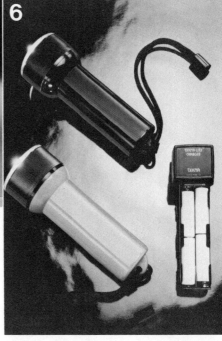

New survival gear for emergencies

The most up-to-date equipment is capable of doing double duty. It's made to be kept stowed in your car, but can serve equally well in a household emergency

■ A HURRICANE, blizzard, power failure or other disaster can take away civilization all of a sudden, even today, and put us in a life-or-death situation. Emergencies often arise with little warning, but fortunately there are a number of new ways to prepare for them in advance. Products developed for everything from backpacking to space exploration are being adapted for household use, as homeowners store away supplies to see them through anything from a blackout to an earthquake.

Basic needs may include food, water, shelter and protection, communication and sanitary facilities. Most modern homes already have some survival gear on hand, although you don't call it that. Bathtubs, buckets and plastic garbage cans can be washed out and used for emergency water storage. Refrigerators and food freezers keep their cool much longer if packed full and kept closed. Add dry ice if you have time and if it's available. Warmth can be supplied with a fireplace, or camp heater. Even candles supply essential light and enough heat to warm some foods when the power goes out.

When it's cold outside, the important consideration is *keeping* warm; it's much easier to retain heat than to try to rewarm a home. The new outdoor sporting equipment—ski clothes, down

NEW HOME-AND-HIGHWAY aids: 1. SOS rescue unit combines 10 tools; one can cut car metal. 2. Pak-Kit contains shelter tent, flare, matches, cord, tape, blade. 3. GE HELP! CB plugs into car cigaret lighter to transmit. 4. Combo strobe/fluorescent light from Yolinda International gives illumination or red-flash warning. All of these items can be stowed in the trunk of your car to keep you prepared for an unexpected emergency on the road.

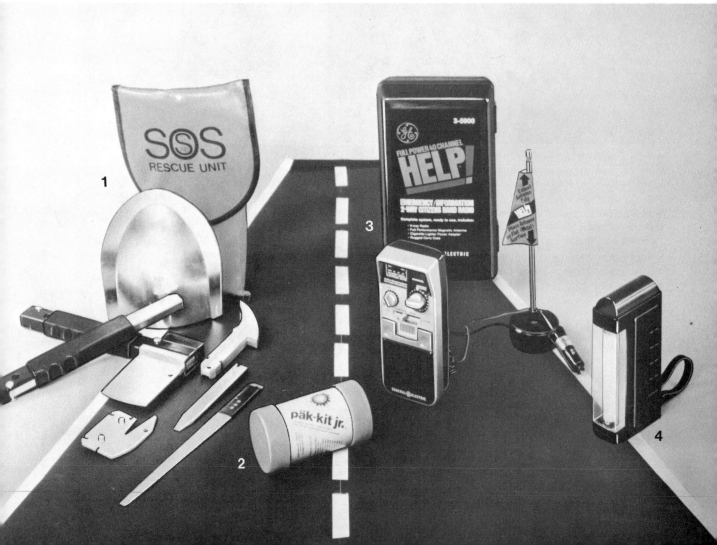

vests, thermal underwear, insulated boots, battery-heated socks and mittens—will all help. Recently developed synthetics such as Thinsulate, PolarGuard and Hollofil insulate clothing to help retain heat, and the metalized space blankets also retard heat loss. An outdoorsman's snow-country clothing makes for welcome indoor wear when the heat goes off.

Don't overlook your car outside, either, when electricity fails at home. As long as it isn't parked in a closed garage and the exhaust isn't blocked, you can sit in your car to warm up with the engine running, and listen to the car radio for disaster information. Better still, you can communicate your problems if you have a CB radio transmitter.

on the road

A well-stocked car trunk normally will have tire and motor-repair tools. In addition, consider the following: a tow cable and a coil of rope plus a lever-type winch, flares, reflectors, flashlight and hand spotlight, jumper cables, small camp stove, mess kit, ice chest with dehydrated food, waterproof matches and candles stowed inside, ground cloth, space blanket and army blanket, duct tape and wire, coveralls and rain gear, work gloves, first-aid kit, hatchet, and possibly, in cold climates, a sleeping bag. This may seem like an extensive list, but all the items should fit into an ice chest and duffle bag. Fortunately, weight isn't the problem it might be for a backpacker. In warm weather, a canteen, water jug, 12-volt portable refrigerator and possibly even a snake-bite kit might be added.

STORAGE SUPPLIES include: 1. Dehydrated bulk foods from Stow-A-Way Industries. 2. BiLan 25, a 12/115/220-volt refrigerator. 3. Canned milk. 4. Packaged meals. 5. Coleman Peak 1 mini-lantern. 6. Coleman backpack stove. 7. Waterproof matches and oversize candles. 8. Super Straw for water purification treatment.

TAKE-DOWN GUNS to store for emergency include: 1. Charter Arms' new Explorer II .22 autoloader pistol with three interchangeable barrels. 2. The Charter AR-7 Explorer carbine .22 (assembled above) comes apart to fit barrel and receiver into waterproof stock. 3. Skatchet is a knife-hammer-hatchet head.

By ANGUS LAIDLAW

Fine new fibers fight the cold

Thinner synthetic filaments are becoming popular in a variety of cold-weather gear.
They hold more trapped air for insulation and are said to be better
than the stuff the birds grow

By BILL McKEOWN

MOUNTAINEERS (above) have tested the Celanese Fortrel PolarGuard in gloves, mittens, jackets, vests, pants and sleeping bags. The continuous-filament polyester fiberfill is from Reliance Products, Oakland, CA. Everest climber John Roskelley (right) was first to field-test Du Pont's new Quallofil polyester fiber.

■ CHICKS AND DUCKS and geese better scurry if they're going to keep up with the latest developments in man-made feather fuzz. The grow-their-own insulation that waterfowl, especially, sprout for foul weather warmth is being imitated and improved on by textile fiber chemists.

Down still fluffs up as the most efficient-for-its-weight insulator—if you're a goose. But once the feather plumules are stuffed between layers of fabric, they lose "loft" (their fluffiness) when they get wet and they scatter into far corners unless they are trapped in place with quilted stitching. Research engineers now are producing extra-thin synthetic filaments that resemble down more closely. These can hold a boundary layer of dead

SLEEPING BAGS filled with polyester fiber, such as Slumberjack above that uses Eastman Kodak's Kodel-brand KodOfill, absorb minimum moisture. Woolrich Mountain Parka (left) has 3M's Thinsulate for warmth.

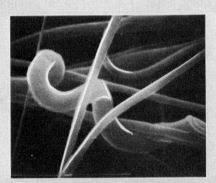

UNDER ELECTRON microscope, Thinsulate shows fiber mix that traps air.

AT SAME magnification, part of a down plumule displays similar surfaces.

ENLARGED even more, DuPont's Quallofil reveals four tubes per strand.

air and keep body warmth from escaping, yet reduce somewhat the balloon look of current cold-weather clothes, and at much less cost than goose and duck feathers.

Basic insulation fillers for clothing can be divided into down, which by law must have a high percentage of goose and duck down; "down-type" fillers, which often are adulterated with feathers and fibers; synthetic fiberfill, usually made of polyester and olefin compounds; and various foams and organic compounds. No product can match all the features of down, but some of the newest synthetics surpass it in notable ways.

Man-made fibers, for example, at about $1 a pound compare favorably with $40-a-pound down, although roughly 15 percent more weight in synthetics is required to equal the warmth-retention properties of down. The weight difference starts to even out, however, when extensive stitching must be added to quilt the down into pockets so that it does not settle out of place. Fabric to enclose the down must also be of a tight weave or treated to prevent "percolation," the name used to describe the way down can work out through cloth and escape. Some forms of chopped staple also require quilting, but others, with long continuous filaments, do not.

down loses insulating ability

Down, unfortunately, loses its loft and insulating ability rapidly when it gets wet, and then takes a long time to dry out. The new synthetics, in contrast, absorb only about one percent of their weight when wet, and dry many times faster than down. They can take machine washing with ease, and sometimes dry cleaning, lose little of their loft when wet, do not cause allergies, and resist moths and mildew.

In theory—and in dry regions and high mountains where it's too cold to rain and snow just dusts off your clothing—wetness should not be a problem.

drying clothes in a sleeping bag

However, Everest climber John Roskelley tells about a week of zero temperatures at high altitude when clothing was soaked with sweat from climbing. While testing sleeping bags using Quallofil, Du Pont's latest polyester fiberfill, Roskelley found clothing could be dried with body heat inside the sleeping bags every night without the Quallofil insulation absorbing the moisture or losing its loft or warmth.

First, to produce fibers only one or two microns (millionths of an inch) thick compared to regular 25-micron polyester fiberfills, 3M found the ultrathins had special insulating properties and introduced Thinsulate several years ago. Because surface friction seems to hold air layers around the tiny filaments, less loft is needed and body warmth can be retained without the usual puffy look of down insulation. (Geese and ducks apparently keep up a comfortable core temperature and streamlined look without excessive fluffing up.) Thinsulate has made possible less bulky ski clothes and, because the material maintains warmth retention while under compression, it is now being used in gloves and boots, as well. The 3M product, unlike most synthetic insulators made from polyester, uses the olefin

WARMTH WITHOUT BULK is from 3M Thinsulate. Examples (left) in leather are Robert Comstock parka and pants. Trim and light insulation in Wilderness Experience vest (right) is Eastman KodOlite.

compounds of polypropylene for a compression-resistant Thinsulate and the addition of polythylene where the insulation is less likely to be compacted.

filaments become tubes

Du Pont's developments to keep us warm have been approached in a different way. To get more insulating air into the batting layer, they turned the solid polyester filaments into tubes that lighten the weight of the fiber while increasing its air-holding ability. Hollofil is the name of the product. Du Pont's micro-thin fiber is called Sontique and is designed for insulation in thin-silhouette clothing such as ski wear. Fashion designers will applaud.

One of the Dacron fiberfills from Du Pont on the market is Quallofil. It is similar to Hollofil, but Quallofil has four tubes inside every fiber to increase the amount of insulating air even more. The material is also reported to regain its full loft quickly after compression. Hollofil is used, in addition, for weaving the new warm and quick-drying pile materials such as Evervel and Borglite.

continuous filaments

Developed by Celanese and produced by Reliance Products in Oakland, CA, Fortrel Polar-Guard has earned a loyal following as the polyester fiberfill that has continuous filaments. This means that PolarGuard clothes, sleeping bags, and even insulating curtains can be made without any need for quilting, and the siliconized PolarGuard has an even softer feel.

And from the Eastman Chemical Products Div. of Kodak come three types of Kodel polyester fibers. They are KodOfill, tubular filaments crimped for extra loft; new KodOsoff that has additional softness, loft and resilience; and KodOlite, with microfine fibers for light and trim insulation.

New outdoor gear

INJECTION-MOLDED WADER

The traditional fishing and hunting waders that were famous for their bulky weight, clumsiness and, eventually, leaks, may be outmoded by new models from Red Ball, Box 3200, Manchester, NH 03105. High-pressure molding of the Master Waders (about $80 with insulation) are light, flexible and said to be virtually impervious to leaks except by puncture.

RESISTING RECOIL

Any high-powered gun is going to kick. PAST Recoil Shields, however, have reduced the impact up to 85 percent in measured tests. The pads, in magnum rifle or trap/skeet thicknesses, are made by PAST Corp., 210 Park Ave., Columbia, MO 65201. They are said to spread the impact rather than causing a sharp bounce. The shields are available for approximately $30.

CAMP STOVE SYSTEM WITH EVERYTHING

Campfires were fine when firewood was abundant and the scars of a camp would be trampled out by herds of buffalo. However, open fires really are inefficient and they're certainly hard to keep going in wind and rain.

Consequently, Pyromid Environmental Systems, Box 3138, Saratoga, CA 95070, is producing an all-purpose, fold-out model that's claimed to provide for a multitude of camping needs.

It is, the makers report, an all-weather campfire, stove, heater, rotary grill, broiler, barbecue, baking oven, smoker, dehydrator, steamer, hot-water wash basin and emergency reflector. In addition, the stove, side serving tables, pots and pans drawer, grills, firebox enclosure and chimney all fold neatly into a compact carrying case.

A smaller unit called a Pyropacker stores in a 12x12x4-inch package and costs about $200. The larger Pyrocamper packs down to 18x18x4 inches, is 51 inches high when set up and holds four gallons of water below the fire for heating. This bigger unit, as set up above, costs approximately $300. Both stoves are made of stainless-steel components.

Either model can be stowed in a car trunk, under the seat of a camper or aboard a boat, ready for campground or beach cooking that won't bother the ecology.

DECOY GEESE WITH PLASTIC

So light that a hunter can carry 75 decoys in a 30-pound backpack, these waterproof cones set up quickly to resemble snow and Canada geese sentinels and feeders. Heads and bodies of the Canada and snow decoys are about $40 a dozen from Farm Form, Box 748, Galveston, TX 77563.

HIGH-HUNTING HARNESS

An independent support or a safety harness for hunters and photographers on a fixed platform, the approximately $42 Treesling from Anderson Designs, Box 287, Gladstone, NJ 07934, can hold a heavy hunter without damaging the tree and even allow shots straight down. The device can also double as a game drag.

Create your own circus music

Bring back those nostalgic sounds with a mini-calliope built of at-hand materials. It's tuned and played just like the real thing

By GEORGE CAMPBELL

■ IF THE HAUNTING sounds of the circus bring back happy childhood memories, or if you have a budding musician in the family, a miniature calliope could be the perfect shop project for you. This little pipe organ, made from readily available materials, whistles with air from hair dryers built into the cabinet. Building the calliope should take about 40 hours.

To begin, cut the cabinet and wind-chest components—parts A through Q, T and U (see the materials list at the end of this story). Bore pilot holes for all screws connecting the cabinet parts with a No. 6 bit. Counterbore all pilot holes with a ⅜-in. bit to receive the plugs (V). Then lay out and bore guide holes in the keyboard base (E) and the rocker support (I).

A drill press or drill guide for your portable drill is a must for accuracy. Clamp together the top and bottom pieces of the wind chest (parts L and N) and bore them simultaneously so the holes will align. Use a depth stop to prevent boring through the bottom board. If you don't have a radial drill press or one with an adjustable table, bore the angled holes in the rocker support by using shims under the workpiece to establish the correct 5° angle.

Make a trial assembly of the chest. Once everything fits properly, sand and finish the cabinet and the screw hole plugs (V). I applied mahogany stain and finished the piece with varnish. When dry, remove wind chest, keyboard back (G), music rack (J), rocker support (I) and its cover (K).

Next, prepare the keyboard. Rip ⅞-in. strips from the type wood used for the cabinet. Cut white keys (parts X_1, X_2, X_3 and X_4). Cut the black keys (Y) from ½-in. molding stock. Bore pivot holes as accurately as possible through the sides of the keys. Then bore ¼-in. holes on the undersides of the keys for the guide pins (Z). Bore a ⁵⁄₁₆-in. dimple at the back of each key.

Sand all the keys smooth, removing a total of about ¹⁄₃₂ in. from the width of each key to ensure proper clearance between them when they're in place. Install the guide pins and apply several coats of spray paint to the keys.

When the keys have dried, insert them through the keyboard back in order. Insert the pivot rod (BB) through the holes in the sides of the keys, slipping a felt washer onto the rod between each pair of keys. Between keys 12 and 13 (notes B and C), insert the center pivot support (CC). Attach the two end supports (DD2) and secure the assembly with the pivot rod nuts.

Attach a length of foam weatherstripping (EE) to the keyboard base and install the keyboard. Check that all keys move freely and make adjustments to the elongated guide holes where needed.

After the keyboard is set, install the two blowers (WW) in the cabinet. The General Electric hair dryers used in this project are a common item in second-hand stores, but if you can't find that type, similar units or commercial blowers will work.

Disconnect, and remove the heating elements from the hairdryers. Hook up wiring through the switch (YY, see wiring diagram, page 177). Bring power cord wire through the ⁵⁄₁₆-in. hole in the panel (B). Knot the wire on the inside of the hole to prevent strain on the connections.

the rocker assembly

Next, begin work on the rockers. Cut the rockers (S) from ½x⅞-in. molding. It's faster to bore pivot-rod holes and dimples before you cut the individual pieces. Sand the sides of the rockers smooth, then add the screw hooks (HH) and counterweights (II). Insert the pivot rod (BB) through the rockers and attach the support brackets (DD1).

Cut the push rods (AA) and install the rocker support (I) in the cabinet, threading the air hoses through the 1⅜-in. holes. Attach the height adjuster assembly (R), then insert the push rods making sure they seat in the keys' dimples.

Mount the rocker assembly on the support (I). Adjust the height of the keys individually by screws (FF) to level the keyboard in the "up" position. You may have to alter the lengths of some of the push rods, as well. When the keyboard is level, the rockers should rest at approximately 15° from the horizontal plane. Finally, install the angled guide pins (GG). Establish the proper clearance by screwing the hooks (HH) in or out as needed. Check to see that the rockers are moving freely.

The next phase is forming the pipes: Carefully follow the specs in the chart, particularly those concerning the sound-producing (D-shaped) notches. Use a hacksaw to cut the aluminum tubing and remove all burrs with a mill file. Bore the round air hole near the bottom of each pipe with a 5/16-in. bit. Position a flue stopper of the correct size as noted in the chart and insert a cork in the bottom of each pipe as shown in the pipe-assembly detail. Test each pipe by blowing gently through the 5/16-in. hole. Each pipe should make a clear note.

air-release assemblies

Make the 25 air-release assemblies as shown in the detail at the top of page 175. Glue the felt pads (QQ) to the PVC discs (OO) with contact cement or other glue for non-porous surfaces. Fasten the hinge leaves (SS) to the bottom of the dowel (NN) and to the bottom of the wind chest with brads that come in the hinge package. Form the springs (TT) by cutting the heads off 1½-in. safety pins and bending ⅛-in. of each cut end with needle-nose pliers to create "ears." Reas-

WHEN YOU depress calliope keys, air from internal blowers rushes into pipes, producing tones that sound like an orchestra of flutes and whistles.

semble the wind chest, leaving off the top, and caulk all the joints with silicone sealant.

Tie an 18-in. length of braided fishing line (KK) to the screw eye on top of each dowel and thread each through its matching nylon tubing guide (MM). Mount the top of the chest and caulk all the joints.

completing the calliope

Insert the pipes through the holes in the top of the wind chest. Manipulate the air-release assemblies by pulling on the lines until each pipe seats in the base and each felt pad seats over the round air hole. Glue felt strips to the back of the

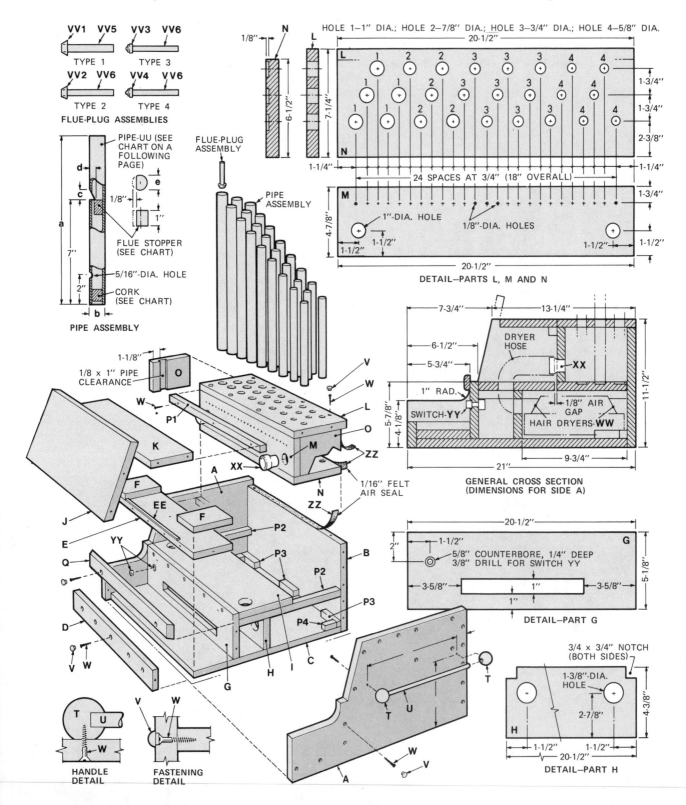

HOLE 1—1″ DIA.; HOLE 2—7/8″ DIA.; HOLE 3—3/4″ DIA.; HOLE 4—5/8″ DIA.

FLUE-PLUG ASSEMBLIES

PIPE ASSEMBLY

DETAIL—PARTS L, M AND N

GENERAL CROSS SECTION
(DIMENSIONS FOR SIDE A)

DETAIL—PART G

DETAIL—PART H

HANDLE DETAIL

FASTENING DETAIL

WHEN YOU CUT the sound holes, cut slightly inside the layout marks, then file to the perfect size.

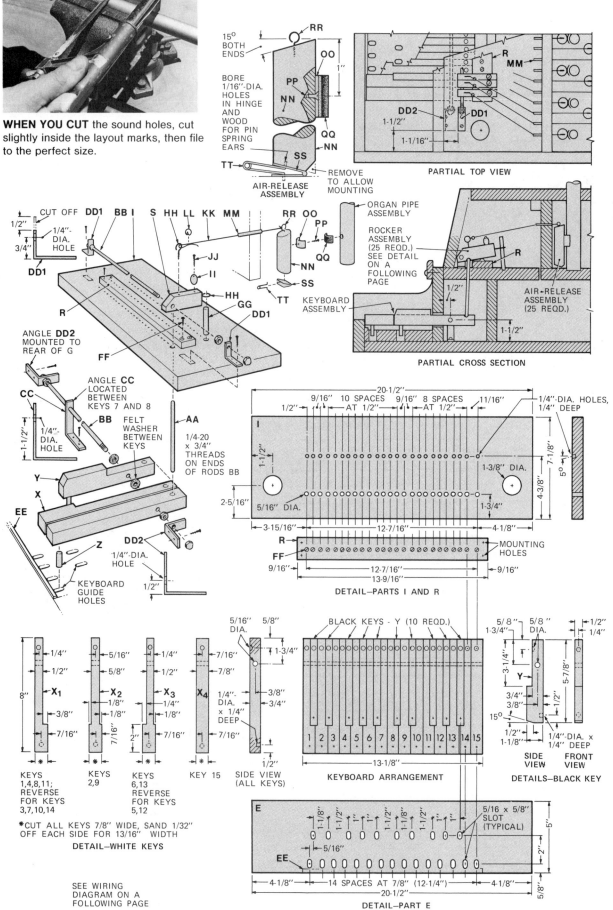

wind chest and install it in the cabinet. Be sure to tighten the screws enough to compress the felt and seal the chest.

Attach the air hoses of the dryers to the copper pipe reducers (XX) mounted to the front of the wind chest. Turn on the dryers. By pulling on the lines, you should be able to make each pipe

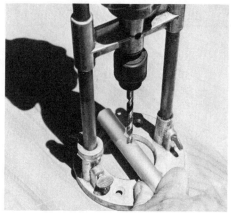

ROUND HOLES bored near the bottom of each pipe let air enter when keys are depressed. The 5/16-in. holes may have to be enlarged if pipe tones are weak.

sound in turn. If any pipe produces a weak tone, enlarge the air hole to ⅜-in. dia.

Work in order, attaching the lines to the hooks on the rockers. Take two turns of the line around each hook, adjusting the line so it's tight, but doesn't lift the air-release assembly enough to let air enter the pipe. Crimp a split shot on the line to secure the adjustment.

Once all 25 lines are attached, test the action of the keyboard. If you find a sticky key (and you probably will at this point), loop a small rubber band around the base of the counterweight (II) and the rocker guide pin (GG).

Install the music rack (J), music stop (Q) and the rocker cover (K), then apply the screw hole buttons (Y). Finally, tune the pipes to a piano or other instrument, using the flue plugs in each pipe.

FLUE PLUG, flue stopper and cork above are shown outside the pipe, parallel to their actual positions when they are installed inside.

Pipe No.	Length (a)	Outside Dia. (b)	NOTCH Height (c)	NOTCH Depth (d)	Flue Stopper Dowel o.d. (e)	Cork Size	Flue-Plug Type
1	21"	1"	⅝"	5/16"	⅞"	10	1
2	20⅜	1	⅝	5/16	⅞	10	1
3	19⅞	1	⅝	5/16	⅞	10	1
4	19⅛	1	⅝	5/16	⅞	10	1
5	18⅝	1	⅝	5/16	⅞	10	1
6	18⅛	⅞	½	5/16	¾	9	2
7	17⅝	⅞	½	5/16	¾	9	2
8	17¼	⅞	½	5/16	¾	9	2
9	16¾	⅞	½	5/16	¾	9	2
10	16⅛	⅞	½	5/16	¾	9	2
11	15⅝	¾	7/16	¼	⅝	5	3
12	15⅛	¾	7/16	¼	⅝	5	3
13	14¾	¾	7/16	¼	⅝	5	3
14	14⅜	¾	7/16	¼	⅝	5	3
15	14	¾	7/16	¼	⅝	5	3
16	13¾	¾	7/16	¼	⅝	5	3
17	13⅜	¾	7/16	¼	⅝	5	3
18	13⅛	¾	7/16	¼	⅝	5	3
19	12⅞	¾	7/16	¼	⅝	5	3
20	12½	⅝	½	3/16	½	3	4
21	12¼	⅝	½	3/16	½	3	4
22	12	⅝	½	3/16	½	3	4
23	11¾	⅝	½	3/16	½	3	4
24	11½	⅝	½	3/16	½	3	4
25	11¼	⅝	½	3/16	½	3	4

SPECIFICATIONS—CALLIOPE PIPES AND INTERNAL PARTS

CUT NO MORE than ⅛ in. from the dowels used for flue stoppers. The flat plane forces air out through the sound hole.

IF YOU DON'T have a band saw, use a table-mounted saber saw to cut keys. Good keyboard action requires accuracy.

WITH KEYBOARD on the pivot rod and the wind chest and blowers in place, the keyboard must be leveled with adjustments to the guide holes.

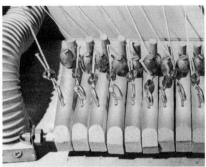

RIG LINES from the air-release assemblies to the rockers, using crimped split shots to maintain correct tension.

THE FLUE PLUGS are used to tune the pipes. Four different sizes are needed to fit the varying pipe diameters.

ASSEMBLED wind chest is shown above with lines for air-release assemblies threaded through nylon tubing guides.

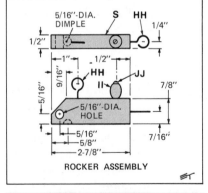

WITH PIPES inserted, the air-release assemblies are shown with the felt pads in place over the air holes. Check for correct alignment of all parts.

MATERIALS LIST—CALLIOPE

Key	No.	Size and description (use)
A	2	¾ × 11½ × 21″ pine (cabinet sides)
B	1	¾ × 10¾ × 20½″ pine (cabinet back)
C	1	¾ × 19½ × 20½″ plywood (cabinet bottom)
D	1	¾ × 2¼ × 20½″ pine (cabinet front)
E	1	¾ × 5 × 20½″ pine (keyboard base)
F	2	¾ × 3⅝ × 4¼″ pine (keyboard borders)
G	1	¾ × 5⅛ × 20½″ (keyboard back)
H	1	¾ × 4⅜ × 20½″ pine (internal baffle)
I	1	¾ × 7⅛ × 20½″ pine (rocker support)
J	1	¾ × 8 × 20½″ pine (music rack)
K	1	¾ × 5⅛ × 20½″ pine (rocker cover)
L	1	¾ × 7¼ × 20½″ pine (windchest top)
M	1	¾ × 4⅞ × 20½″ pine (windchest front)
N	1	¾ × 6½ × 20½″ pine (windchest bottom)
O	2	¾ × 4⅞ × 5¾″ pine (wind-chest sides)
P₁	1	¾ × ¾ × 20½″ pine (top cleat)
P₂	2	¾ × ¾ × 13¾″ pine (cleats)
P₃	3	¾ × ¾ × 3″ pine (cleats)
P₄	2	¾ × ¾ × 2¼″ pine (cleats)
Q	1	½ × 1¼ × 20½″ pine (music stop)
R	1	½ × 1½ × 13½″ pine (key height adjuster) with four 1″ No. 6 rh screws
S	25	½ × ⅞ × 2⅞″ pine (rockers)
T	4	1½″-dia. pine (ball-shape handle supports)
U	2	½″-dia. × 11¼″ hardwood dowels (handles)
V	60	⅜″-dia. screw hole plugs
W	75	1¼″ No. 6 fh screws (cabinet screws
X₁	8	¾ × ⅞ × 8″ (white keys, Nos. 1,3,4,7,8,10,11,14)
X₂	2	¾ × ⅞ × 8″ (white keys, Nos. 2,9)
X₃	4	¾ × ⅞ × 8″ (white keys, Nos. 5,6,12,13)
X₄	1	¾ × ⅞ × 8″ (white keys, No. 15)
Y	10	½ × 1⅛ × 5⅞″ (black keys)
Z	25	¼″-dia. × 1″ dowel (keyboard guide pins)
AA	25	¼″-dia. × 4″ dowel (push rods)
BB	2	¼″-dia. × 15″ steel rod threaded

Key	No.	Size and description (use)
		¾″ on both ends; four ¼-20 acorn nuts; four ¼-20 hex nuts; 24 felt washers (pivot rods)
CC	1	2 × 2″ angle with two ½″ No. 6 fh screws
DD₁	2	1½ × 1½″ angles with four ½″ No. 6 fh screws
DD₂	2	1½ × 1½″ angles with four ½″ No. 6 fh screws
EE	1	⅛ × ¼ × 13″ self-stick foam weatherstrip
FF	25	¾″ No. 6 rh screws (keyboard adjuster screws)
GG	25	¼″-dia. × 2½″ dowel (rocker guide pins)
HH	50	⁷⁄₁₆″-o.d. × 1″ screw hooks
II	25	½-oz. egg-type fishing sinkers
JJ	25	1″ No. 4 rh wood screws
KK		50-lb. test braided fishing line (50′)
LL	25	No. 5 split shot fishing sinkers
MM	25	⅛″-o.d. nylon guide tube (at auto parts store)
NN	25	¾″-dia. × 3″ dowel (air releases)
OO	25	¾ × ¾″ sections of 1″-dia. PVC (for pipes Nos. 1 to 10); ¾ × ¾″ sections of ¾″-dia. PVC (for pipes Nos. 11 to 25)
PP	25	½″ No. 4 fh screws
QQ	25	⅛ × ¾ × ¾″ felt
RR	25	½″-long screw eyes
SS	25	⅝ × ⅝″ butt hinge; ⅝″ brads (100)
TT	25	1½″ safety pins
UU	as reqd.	Anodized aluminum tubing (organ pipes); 9′ of 1″ o.d.; 8′ of ⅞″ o.d.; 8′ of ⅝″ o.d.; 12′ of ¾″ o.d. See Pipe Chart (page 114) for individual pipe sizes
VV₁	5	⅞″-dia. cone washers
VV₂	5	¾″-dia. cone washers
VV₃	9	⅜″-dia. faucet washers with ¾″ No. 6 rh screws
VV₄	6	Size 00 faucet washers with ¾″ No. 6 rh screws
VV₅	5	½″-dia. × 3½″ dowel
VV₆	20	⅜″-dia. × 3½″ dowel
WW	2	General Electric Deluxe cap-type hair dryers or equivalent
XX	2	¾″ × 1″-dia. copper pipe reducers
YY	1	S.p.s.t. pushbutton switch such as Selecta* S.S. 216-11 screw-turn or S.S.215-10 pigtail type; plug; 3 solderless connectors; lamp cord
ZZ		¹⁄₁₆″ × 1-sq.-ft. felt

Misc.: Wood stain; varnish, silicone seal, white spray paint, black spray paint, contact cement, white glue, tape. *Selecta, Box 1585, Covina, Calif. 91722

ROCKER ASSEMBLY

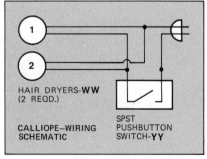

HAIR DRYERS-**WW** (2 REQD.)

SPST PUSHBUTTON SWITCH-**YY**

CALLIOPE—WIRING SCHEMATIC

Those physical fitness machines

Can exercise machines build new and better bodies? If you know how to use them—and you are willing to do the work— the right units can do the job

By ROBIN NELSON

■ WHEN IT COMES to exercise, resistance is everything. Resistance—via friction—forces you along the track as you run, or through the pool, thanks to the viscosity of water, as you swim. So there's nothing new about resistance. But there are plenty of marketable new ways to package and apply it.

In designing machines to provide physical work, mechanical *dis*advantage becomes a desired characteristic. Special linkages to weight, friction, elastic, hydraulic and electromagnetic resistances are being incorporated into equipment sold primarily for home use.

As in any leisure-boom area where competition is keen, each manufacturer claims special benefits and properties for its particular design, including the mode of resistance that is used.

contradictory research

An extensive survey of available scientific literature prompts the conclusion that overstatement is the everyday language of the equipment suppliers. While there has been much research into the essential nature of strength and fitness—the composition of muscle tissues and associated neurological biochemistry, for example—in the past 25 years, it has yielded nearly as many contradictory possibilities as firm conclusions.

Equipment makers pick and choose from among these theoretical pathways, funding the supplemental studies most likely to advance sales of proprietary apparatus. As an example, millions of dollars worth of heavy, expensive weight machines have been sold to institutions on the basis of a variable-resistance feature provided by lever arm (Universal Gym) or cams (Nautilus). By increasing resistance near the full extension phase of exercises, this is supposed to provide better, quicker results. Perhaps so, but there are at least four independent studies in exercise-physiology literature which indicate this has no measurable effect.

Doctors and health researchers know that the key to any rehabilitative program—whether we're talking about serious injury or the generally run-down condition most people pass off as "normal"—is positive reinforcement. If you're like most people, you need to be fed regular, frequent and precise results from an exercise program or you simply won't stay at it. The newer forms of packaged resistance are tailor-made for the job: They are light and compact enough to fit into an appropriate space in the home—accessible—and designed to permit quick, convenient adjustments of resistance to a wide variety of routines.

no guarantees

That's what they are, and here's what they aren't: No device made can guarantee you either added strength or cardiovascular conditioning "for a few effort-free minutes a day." And no machine can guarantee you a set of bulging muscles—no matter how hard you work. Whether or not your muscles hypertrophy—take on the distended appearance characteristic of body-builders' physiques—depends on your genetic makeup.

And finally, no machine can, by itself, add beautiful pounds or remove ugly ones. Yet by deciding in advance exactly what aspects of your physical being *you* want to restructure, you can select a resistance machine that can provide a format for dramatic results.

have a physical exam

It will depend on your age, current physical condition, specific activity interests and even, to some extent, your outlook on life. First of all, if you haven't been exercising regularly, regardless of age, don't start in on a resistance machine of any kind without a physician's examination. If you intend to work to near exhaustion, in order to build cardiovascular endurance or skeletomuscular strength, and you are over 35 years old, a maximal stress test (usually administered on a treadmill) is advisable.

Until recently, fitness enthusiasts have tended to belong to either one of two distinct camps: aerobic conditioners (joggers, swimmers and so on) and strength freaks. The home resistance machines are helping to bring about a synthesis. One-sided exercise programs, whether on the track or in the gym, have one thing in common: They're boring. But lately, statistics have accrued showing that they also may prove counterproductive. Sooner or later, most one-dimensional fitness fanatics overdo their particular routines; joggers pile on the distances, weight lifters add poundage. Fitness, technically, is not a static condition—you're either improving or deteriorating—because the body acclimates rapidly to incremental demands. Too often, the result of onward, upward movement *in one regime* is injury, usually chronic.

versatility is important

Home exercise equipment, therefore, should be assessed on the basis of versatility, as well as the basic parameters of construction, compactness, safety and so on. Can you do exercises easily to train both the upper and lower body? How wide is the range of resistance? If cardiovascular conditioning is your primary goal, does the machine permit rapid adjustment between exercises so that pulse-rate elevation can be maintained?

It should be noted that no multistation resistance machine will offer anyone, except a member of the Chinese national acrobatic troupe, as effective an aerobic routine as a machine designed specifically for aerobics—such as an exercise cycle. Yet by combining a pure aerobic program, such as jogging or swimming, with resistance training, you can progress with multiple benefits.

On the other side of the coin, free weights—the

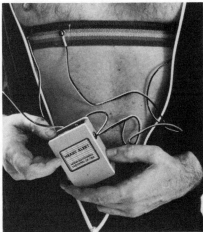

A **SIMPLE** and inexpensive cardiac monitor, like the Heart Alert (above, about $110 from Edmund Scientific, 101 East Gloucester Pike, Barrington, NJ 08007) sounds a beeping tone when set heart rate is reached and a continuous tone at a higher level of effort (usually the maximum desired). A machine like the Soloflex (left), may have an entirely different feel at a nominal weight setting than free weights for a given exercise, but with the heart monitor and stopwatch or metronome, you can get an idea of equivalency. This can also tell you if resistance components, like bungee cords, begin to degrade. But remember: As your fitness improves, it takes more effort to reach the same heart-rate levels.

STEP ONE UNIT uses friction pads that adjust to give resistance for iso-kinetic (speed-controlled), rotational movements. Our evaluation: Can be awkward to use until you've worked with it a while, but versatile, and probably best suited to multirepetition, light-resistance toning and endurance exercises. It's approximately $600.

traditional barbell with graduated plates—are also a desired adjunct to resistance machines. Why do you need a set of weights after you've bought an expensive machine that's supposed to replace them? Because they provide a yardstick. Hydraulic cylinders, friction plates, elastic cords—even fairly simple mechanical linkages—can deteriorate or go out of adjustment in time. A hundred pounds next year, however, weighs the same as 100 pounds did at the time of the Flood.

In addition, exercise with free weights adds factors of balance and what biomechanics people call "ballistic motion." These may be more valuable in training for various sports than similar routines performed on a machine with the same strength-building potential.

The Step One unit seemed better adapted to multiple-repetition, lower resistance routines (usually associated with toning and cardiovascular conditioning). The Soloflex, on the other

THE SOLOFLEX machine is heavily built so bungee-cord resistances of more than 200 pounds can be loaded for different exercises. Our evaluation: Adjustments and operations require considerable caution; the elastic-resistance "feel" takes some getting used to, but gives a definite workout at extreme range of motion. Cords can deteriorate over time, but are replaceable. Unit is about $500.

UNIVERSAL POWER-PAK weight unit sets the standard for home-exercise equipment of its type. Our evaluation: Precise action and overall simplicity of adjustment are strong points; must add extra-cost components to get much versatility. It's rugged and well finished, consistent with price in $600 range (bench extra).

MANUFACTURERS LIST
Soloflex Inc.: Hawthorn Farms Industrial Park, Hillsboro, Ore. 97123.
Reneau, Relyea & Associates (Step One): 8222 Jamestown Dr., Suite C-131, Austin, Tex. 78758.
Universal: Box 1270, Cedar Rapids, Iowa 52406.

hand, is designed more as a high-load system in which 8 to 12 repetitions will bring the user to near exhaustion (also producing added strength and, possibly, cosmetic benefits). Universal's conventional weight-pack system is still as convenient in terms of rapid and precise adjustment as anything on the market, offering both aerobic-type and high-resistance potential. Optional components needed for a full range of upper and lower body training, however, add considerable cost to a home system.

All three machines seem relatively expensive in terms of what components they entail. Our survey of the market, however, suggests that quality and utility tend to drop off drastically in lower priced equipment claiming to do the same thing. And there are far more expensive machines—stationary cycles, rowers, treadmills and so on—with far fewer capabilities in terms of overall, balanced fitness.

Make music in your shop

Tuned like a dulcimer and played like a banjo, a banjimer combines the sound qualities of both instruments. It's a joy to play and a great source of pride to the maker

By SAM ALLEN

■ HERE IS A PROJECT for the beginner or intermediate woodworker that is both challenging and fun to build. No two musical instruments are ever exactly alike. The drawing and materials list provide dimensions for an instrument of ideal construction in a technical sense. To make your instrument fit together well, you will have to adjust and fine-trim some of the dimensions.

Start construction by making the fret board. Choose a piece of clear, straight hardwood for the board. Lay out the positions of the frets and the nut by carefully following the measurements given in the drawing. This is one of the most crucial steps in the construction of the instrument. If any of the frets are in the wrong location, the notes will be off pitch.

Use guitar tuning pegs (called tuning machines by instrument builders). Buy the tuning ma-

chines (available in pairs) from an instrument repair shop. The dimensions of the peg box depend on the type of tuning machine you get, so buy a pair before doing more work on the fret board.

Use the machine to position ⅝-in.-dia. pilot holes for the slot and then bore them. Next, bore three holes in the edge of the peg box to accept the tuning machine. The holes in the edge are blind; they don't go all the way through the board. Use a coping saw to cut out the slot. Then cut the notch for the nut. The nut is a piece of hard plastic about ¼ in. thick. Use a piece of scrap sheet acrylic or buy a guitar nut.

The frets are made of commercial fret wire. Fret wire has a T-shaped cross section with small barbs on the tail that extend into the wood. It requires no gluing, but the slot cut for it must be very thin. Use a coping saw or a very thin hacksaw blade to make the kerf.

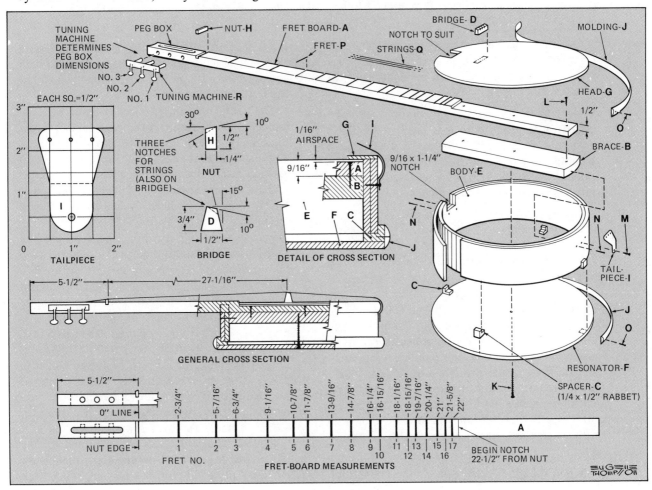

MARK POSITIONS of the frets and nut carefully, using a combination square. This is a most critical step.

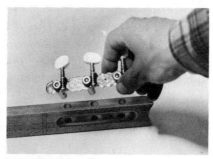

TUNING MACHINES like one shown here have a rigid metallic construction. They must fit firmly into peg box.

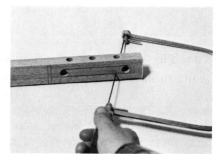

CUT THE SLOT in the peg box with a coping saw after you have finished boring the peg holes.

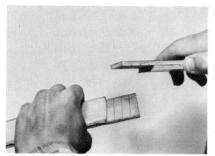

JOIN BODY PARTS as shown with half-lap joints and glue. Be sure that parts are cut to produce a fine fit before applying glue. Stagger the kerfs.

AFTER GLUE is applied to inner sides of body pieces, wrap body unit around a circular mold, such as a 10-in. pot. Secure with a web clamp or rope.

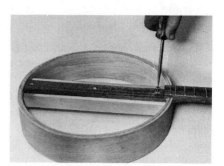

SCREW FRET BOARD to the brace. Nail the brace and glue it in place immediately after you have removed the body unit from its gluing mold.

Use a file and sandpaper to round over the rear edges of the fret board. Stop the rounded edge where the fret board will join the body, and just below the peg box.

Once all the woodworking operations are completed on the fret board, put the frets in place. Tap each fret in with a block of wood and a hammer. File the ends of the frets flush with the sides of the fret board and round them slightly so no rough edges catch your fingers.

Cut two ¼-in.-thick strips of plywood or prefinished paneling to form the cylindrical body. The two strips will be laminated together to form a ½-in.-thick piece. Make saw kerfs across the width of the strips ½ in. apart and ⅛ in. deep to allow the body pieces to bend. Use a cylindrical object like a large pot with a 10-in. outside diameter as a mold and wrap the strips around it. Cut the strips to the exact length necessary to fit around the form and make a tight lap joint. Stagger the kerfs in the two strips to achieve maximum strength. Spread carpenter's glue evenly on the kerfed side of each strip and place the glued sides together; clamp the strips around the form with a web clamp or a rope twisted like a tourniquet.

When the glue is dry, remove the body from the mold and cut the notch for the fret board. Make the brace and install it inside the body with glue and four 1½-in. finishing nails; then, screw the fret board to the brace.

The head, or sound board, is made of ⅛-in. tempered hardboard. Cut the head slightly larger than the outside diameter of the body and cut a notch to fit over the section of the fret board that extends inside the body ring. Glue the head in place and clamp it securely. When the glue is dry, file the edges of the head flush with the sides of the body.

Prefinished vinyl molding (the type used in wall paneling) is used to cover the joint between body and head. Use contact cement to secure it in place. Put a small, prefinished paneling nail at each end of the molding for additional strength.

The resonator, or back of the instrument, is made of ¼-in. plywood or prefinished paneling. Cut it ½ in. larger in diameter than the diameter of the body and glue the four L-shaped blocks in place, as shown in the drawing. The rim around the resonator is also made of prefinished vinyl molding. Use contact cement and ½-in. brads to attach the molding to the resonator.

A penetrating oil finish is well suited for the fret board. If you used prefinished paneling for the body, no further finish is needed. If you used

CLAMP A WOOD STOP to your miter saw for a ⅛-in.-deep kerf. Then use miterbox to make kerf cuts ½-in. apart.

USE PREFINISHED vinyl molding to cover the joint between the body and the head. Vinyl bends easily. Use a contact cement and small nail at each end.

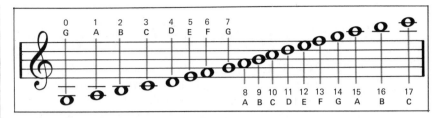

THE NOTES on the musical staff are identified above, along with the number which corresponds to the numbered fret on your banjimer. Use this key to play the melody for a few lines of the traditional folk song, "Red River Valley," below.

FROM	THIS	VAL-LEY	THEY	SAY	YOU	ARE	LEAV-ING.		WE	SHALL	MISS
4	7	9	9	9	9	8	9	8	7	4	7	9

YOUR	BRIGHT	EYES	AND	SWEET	SMILE.		FOR	THEY	SAY	YOU	ARE
7	9	11	10	9	8		11	10	9	9	8

TAK-ING	THE	SUN-SHINE,		THAT	HAS	BRIGHT-ENED	MY	PATH	FOR	A-WHILE.
7	8	9	11	10		5	5	4	7	8	9	8	8	7

unfinished plywood, you can use a penetrating finish or varnish. Once the finish has been applied to the rest of the instrument, mask around the head and spray it with flat white paint.

When the finish has dried, install the strings. Start by installing the tuning machines. Then make the tailpiece from any type of sheet metal. Cut it out, using the pattern in the plans and attach it to the end of the banjimer with a round-head screw.

The bridge is made of a hardwood (maple). Shape it to the cross section shown in the drawing. File notches in the nut and bridge for the strings. Use a triangular file and file the notches at an angle, so that the highest point of contact with the string will be closest to the playing surface of the fret board.

The three strings are No. 3 banjo strings. Run each string through a hole in the tailpiece until the end stops against the metal. If your strings have loop ends, install three small screws in the tailpiece for the loops.

The strings then pass through notches in the nut and the slot in the tuning peg. Turn each tuning peg to wrap each string around it. Once all the strings are installed, but not tightened, install the bridge. The bridge is not glued in place; it is held on by string tension alone.

MATERIALS LIST—BANJIMER

Key	No.	Size and description (use)
A	1	¾ × 1¼ × 38¼" hardwood (fret board)
B	1	¾ × 2½ × 10" pine (brace)
C	4	½ × ½ × ¾" hardwood (spacer)
D	1	½ × ⅜ × 2" hardwood (bridge)
E	2	¼ × 2⅜ × 36" plywood or paneling (body)
F	1	¼ × 11½"-dia. plywood (resonator)
G	1	⅛ × 11"-dia. tempered hardwood (head)
H	1	¼ × ½ × 1¼" plastic (nut)
I	1	1½ × 2⅝" sheet metal (tailpiece)
J		¾" × 6' vinyl molding
K	1	2¼" No. 12 fh screw
L	3	1" No. 10 fh screw
M	1	½" No. 6 rh screw
N	4	1½" finishing nail
O	4	½" brad
P*	1	Fret wire, Constantine No. G36
Q	3	No. 3 banjo string
R*	1	Tuning machine, Constantine No. G31

Misc.: Carpenter's glue, flat white (spray) paint, finish. *Tuning machines are sold in pairs for $6.95 plus shipping. A 20-piece set of nickel silver fret wire is $3.25 plus shipping. Order from Albert Constantine & Son Inc., 2050 Eastchester Rd., Bronx, N.Y. 10461.

The distance from the edge of the nut to the bridge must be exactly 27 1/16 in.

Adjust the height of the nut and bridge by filing them until there is 1/32-in. clearance between the strings and fret No. 1 and ⅛-in. clearance between the strings and fret No. 17.

Tune the melody string (No. 3) to any pleasing note, then fret that string at the fourth fret and match the drone strings (Nos. 1 and 2) to the pitch produced.

Pluck the strings with a guitar pick held in your right hand and fret the third string only.

Build a professional garage workbench

■ THE PROFESSIONAL GARAGE usually has one great advantage over the do-it-yourself garage: adequate space. And because of this, the nonprofessional has to make some compromises when outfitting a shop. But a good sized workbench—like the one shown here—is one place where corners should not be cut. Its top has plenty of room for safe and efficient work, while the drawers and shelves below provide convenient storage where you need it most.

But size is only part of the story. Strength is the other. This bench was built of heavy-duty, construction-grade lumber and was designed to hold a complete V8 engine without a word of complaint.

joining legs and rails

Begin construction by cutting all the legs the same length and ripping the rear middle leg ¾ in. thinner than the other five. Then cut a ¾x¾-in. rabbet in each rear leg to accept the back.

Cut the upper and lower side rails to length and join them to the end legs, using glue and ⅜-in.-dia. dowels, as shown. We bored the dowel holes at 45° angles for added strength. But if you don't have a drill press with a tilting table to perform this task, use two dowels per joint instead of one and install them conventionally. Clamp the assemblies, check for square and allow them to dry overnight.

Next, cut the remaining rails to length and cut

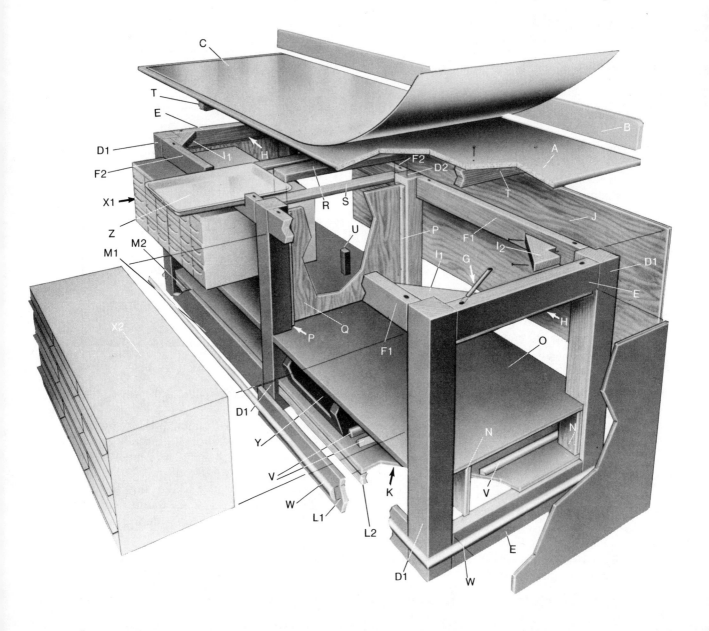

STURDY WORKBENCH was built to withstand the unique rigors of heavy-duty auto work. It includes adequate storage.

the notch in the left front rail (F2) for the metal tray. Join these rails to the legs as explained above. Be especially careful to clamp these assemblies square. Otherwise the metal drawer cabinets will not fit properly later.

Install the four corner blocks with glue and 2½-in., No. 10 flathead screws. Note that the notches in the front and rear blocks are not the same because the workbench back is rabbeted into the rear legs. The front blocks are shown in the detail drawing on page 188. The rear block notch is 1¼x2 in.

installing bottom and shelf

Join the back to the legs using glue and 6d common nails, then cut the bottom to size and shape. Attach the front support cleats (L2, M2) to the underside of the bottom, and glue and nail the bottom into place. Attach the quarter-round tray guides, allowing ⅛-in. clearance on both sides of each tray. Then attach the toe kicks with glue and 6d common nails. Install the shelf cleats

(N), making sure to recess them ¾ in. from the outside of the end legs.

Cut and install the shelf. Attach the rail cleats (H) and install the plywood side panels.

Cut the middle partition and cleats and install. Toenail the top support (R) into the front and rear legs and set the nailheads to prevent the top from rocking once it's in place.

Next, install the tray supports (S) by nailing them into the small cleats shown in the front view detail drawing. Or, because they carry little weight, these can be nailed directly in place, using 8d finishing nails driven through the front and rear bench rails.

top and drawers

Cut and join the top and back splash using glue and 2½-in. No. 10 fh screws. Then position the stiffening cleats (T) on the underside of the top by measuring 18 in. in from both ends and 3 in. in from the front.

Next, attach the cleats with glue and counter-

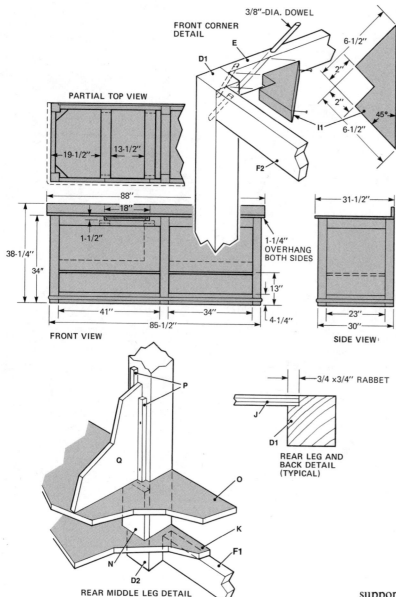

FRONT CORNER DETAIL

3/8"-DIA. DOWEL

6-1/2"

2"

2"

45°

6-1/2"

PARTIAL TOP VIEW

19-1/2"   13-1/2"

88"

18"

1-1/2"

38-1/4"

34"

1-1/4" OVERHANG BOTH SIDES

13"

41"   34"

85-1/2"

4-1/4"

FRONT VIEW

31-1/2"

23"

30"

SIDE VIEW

3/4 x 3/4" RABBET

REAR LEG AND BACK DETAIL (TYPICAL)

REAR MIDDLE LEG DETAIL

MATERIALS LIST— GARAGE WORKBENCH

Key	No.	Size and description (use)
A	1	3/4 × 31 1/2 × 88" particleboard (top)
B	1	3/4 × 3 1/2 × 88" particleboard (back splash)
C	1	1/16 × 30 × 86 1/2" sheet aluminum
D1	5	3 1/2 × 3 1/2 × 34" fir (leg)
D2	1	2 3/4 × 3 1/2 × 34" fir (leg)
E	4	1 1/2 × 3 1/2 × 23" fir (rail)
F1	3	1 1/2 × 3 1/2 × 34" fir (rail)
F2	3	1 1/2 × 3 1/2 × 41" fir (rail)
G	20	3/8"-dia. × 6" dowel
H	2	3/4 × 3/4 × 23" fir (cleat)
I1	2	1 1/2 × 6 1/2 × 6 1/2" fir (front corner block)
I2	2	1 1/2 × 6 1/2 × 6 1/2" fir (back corner block)
J	1	3/4 × 34 × 80" plywood (back)
K	1	3/4 × 28 1/2 × 84" plywood (bottom)
L1	1	3/4 × 4 1/4 × 34" plywood (toe kick)
L2	1	3/4 × 1 1/2 × 34" plywood (cleat)
M1	1	3/4 × 4 1/4 × 41" plywood (toe kick)
M2	1	3/4 × 1 1/2 × 41" plywood (cleat)
N	6	3/4 × 2 3/4 × 8" plywood (cleat)
O	1	3/4 × 29 1/4 × 84" plywood (shelf)
P	4	3/4 × 3/4 × 19 1/2" plywood (cleat)
Q	1	3/4 × 19 1/2 × 23" plywood (partition)
R	1	1 1/2 × 3 1/2 × 23" fir (top support)
S	2	3/4 × 4 1/2 × 26 1/4" fir (tray support)
T	2	1 1/2 × 3 × 26 1/4" fir (stiffening cleat)
U	1	1 1/2 × 1 1/2 × 4" fir (support leg)
V	†	Quarter-round pine molding (tray guide)
W	150"	Half-round pine molding (trim)
X1*	1	18-drawer metal cabinet
X2*	1	9-drawer metal cabinet
Y**	†	Plastic tray
Z***	1	Metal tray

Misc.: 6d common nails, 1 1/2" and 2 1/2" No. 10 fh screws, glue, sandpaper, primer, paint.

†As required.

*Available from: Equipto, 225 South Highland St., Aurora, Ill. 60507.

**Available from: Akro-Mils, Box 989, Akron, Ohio 44309.

***Available from: Any restaurant supply outlet.

Air hose reel available from C & H Distributors Inc., 400 South Fifth St., Milwaukee, Wis. 53204.

NOTE THAT back is rabbeted into rear corner legs, but runs behind middle leg. Rip middle leg 3/4 in. thinner.

supported only by the upper rail and one leg, it is wise to cut and fit a small wood leg (U) underneath the back right corner. Toenail this block into the shelf, then screw down from the inside rear corner of the cabinet into the top of the block.

finishing touches

Insert the plastic storage trays, then cut the sheet aluminum to size and place it on the top. To add the multi-outlet fixture shown in the photo, just screw it to the front rail and wire a 12-2 cable with ground, extension-cord pigtail to the back of the fixture. Run the cable above the drawer cabinet and through a hole bored in the workbench back. Plug it into an existing outlet. The air hose reel shown is available from C & H Distributors of Milwaukee (see materials list) and merely hangs from the bottom of the front rail.

sink 1 1/2-in., No. 10 fh screws driven down through the top. Because the top is not fastened to the bench, these cleats keep it from moving during heavy use. If you prefer to attach the top, just screw it to the corner blocks from above.

Next, glue and nail the half-round trim pieces to the bench sides and front. Miter the corners. Then sand the entire bench with 100-grit sandpaper; prime and paint.

Now, remove the drawers from the metal cabinets and hang the shelves from the legs and upper front rails. Use wood screws driven from inside the metal shelf. Because the left cabinet is

VERSATILE AND practically indestructible, hanging wall bins are capable of doing a job that shelves just cannot match. They resist oil, gasoline and a variety of mild acids.

How to increase your garage storage space

By TONY ASSENZA

■ NEXT TO MONEY and cheap gasoline, the commodity most people never seem to have enough of is storage space. Even if you're not a pack rat and try to keep your inventory of accumulated material to a minimum, you almost always end up looking for more places to put things.

We've just about run out of wall space in our garage, so hanging anything else on the walls was out of the question. Luckily, our garage has a high ceiling; as a result, a loft appeared to be the ideal way to maximize the total volume of the garage.

You can build a loft out of just about anything, but we decided to use slotted angle iron rather than wood for the main support beams. The virtue of using slotted angle iron is that you can assemble it with nuts and bolts and easily disassemble it if you need to modify the design or expand on it later. Wood just doesn't give you that ease of flexibility.

The first thing you have to decide is how high the loft should be. That may sound like an obvious bit of logic, but keep in mind that it not only has to be high enough to allow you to work un-

A STORAGE LOFT is an ideal way to store items that you need to use only occasionally.

THE METAL BRACKET for the storage bins can be installed right to the wall with screws or lagbolts.

ONCE BRACKET is installed, bins attach by press-fitting lips at back of bins into channels.

STEEL CHEST of drawers will literally hold a ton of fasteners and other small parts and wire.

derneath, but must also be high enough to clear your car's raised hood with the front end of the car jacked up. Overhead clearance is especially important if you own a pickup truck.

Once you've established the height, you can assemble the four uprights. We attached "feet" to the uprights and anchored the feet into the cement floor. Ideally, you should tuck the loft into a corner of the garage. That way, you will be able to anchor three of the uprights to the walls and ensure adequate vertical rigidity.

Since we planned to use sheets of 4x8 plywood for the platform, we placed the uprights 8 ft. apart. Once the three uprights were anchored to the walls, the free-standing upright was anchored to the floor and the lateral platform pieces were bolted in.

After the perimeter of the platform was installed, we bolted in two stiffening ribs in the middle of the platform to support the plywood sheets.

In using angle iron, we've discovered that nuts tend to get loose and back off the bolts. We cured that problem by using Loctite on the bolts before screwing on the nuts and torquing them down. You can paint the underside of the loft white and install a light fixture. It gave us quite a large light-reflecting surface and kept the loft from looking like a cave.

One of the neatest ways we found of storing odd, but frequently needed, bits and pieces, was to use hanging storage bins. These heavy plastic bins can be stacked on top of each other if you want them to be mobile, or they can be hung on a wall with a metal bracket.

The bins attach to the bracket by press-fitting the lips at the back of the bins into the slots on the bracket. No other fasteners are used, which makes the whole setup very versatile if you need to use the bins elsewhere. The only source we know of for these bins is Akro-Mils, Box 989, Akron, OH 44309.

The last piece of storage equipment we've found invaluable for holding nuts, bolts, solderless connectors, wire, clamps, and the like is a steel chest of drawers. Although our philosophy is to build, rather than buy, we couldn't find an efficient, cost-effective alternative to this Equipto unit (225 South Highland St., Aurora, IL 60507). This piece will hold just about everything you'll probably ever need. If you outgrow it, you'll probably be ready to open your own hardware store.

Index

The page number refers to the first page on which specific information can be found.

METRIC CONVERSION

Conversion factors can be carried so far they become impractical. In cases below where an entry is exact it is followed by an asterisk (*). Where considerable rounding off has taken place, the entry is followed by a + or a – sign.

CUSTOMARY TO METRIC

Linear Measure

inches	millimeters
1/16	1.5875*
1/8	3.2
3/16	4.8
1/4	6.35*
5/16	7.9
3/8	9.5
7/16	11.1
1/2	12.7*
9/16	14.3
5/8	15.9
11/16	17.5
3/4	19.05*
13/16	20.6
7/8	22.2
15/16	23.8
1	25.4*

inches	centimeters
1	2.54*
2	5.1
3	7.6
4	10.2
5	12.7*
6	15.2
7	17.8
8	20.3
9	22.9
10	25.4*
11	27.9
12	30.5

feet	centimeters	meters
1	30.48*	.3048*
2	61	.61
3	91	.91
4	122	1.22
5	152	1.52
6	183	1.83
7	213	2.13
8	244	2.44
9	274	2.74
10	305	3.05
50	1524*	15.24*
100	3048*	30.48*

1 yard =
  .9144* meters
1 rod =
  5.0292* meters
1 mile =
  1.6 kilometers
1 nautical mile =
  1.852* kilometers

Fluid Measure

(Milliliters [ml] and cubic centimeters [cc or cu cm] are equivalent, but it is customary to use milliliters for liquids.)

1 cu in = 16.39 ml
1 fl oz = 29.6 ml
1 cup = 237 ml
1 pint = 473 ml
1 quart = 946 ml
  = .946 liters
1 gallon = 3785 ml
  = 3.785 liters
Formula (exact):
fluid ounces × 29.573 529 562 5*
  = milliliters

Weights

ounces	grams
1	28.3
2	56.7
3	85
4	113
5	142
6	170
7	198
8	227
9	255
10	283
11	312
12	340
13	369
14	397
15	425
16	454

Formula (exact):
  ounces × 28.349 523 125* = grams

pounds	kilograms
1	.45
2	.9
3	1.4
4	1.8
5	2.3
6	2.7
7	3.2
8	3.6
9	4.1
10	4.5

1 short ton (2000 lbs) =
  907 kilograms (kg)
Formula (exact):
  pounds × .453 592 37* = kilograms

Volume

1 cu in = 16.39 cubic
  centimeters (cc)
1 cu ft = 28 316.7 cc
1 bushel = 35 239.1 cc
1 peck = 8 809.8 cc

Area

1 sq in = 6.45 sq cm
1 sq ft = 929 sq cm
  = .093 sq meters
1 sq yd = .84 sq meters
1 acre = 4 046.9 sq meters
  = .404 7 hectares
1 sq mile = 2 589 988 sq meters
  = 259 hectares
  = 2.589 9 sq
    kilometers

Kitchen Measure

1 teaspoon = 4.93 milliliters (ml)
1 Tablespoon = 14.79
  milliliters (ml)

Miscellaneous

1 British thermal unit (Btu) (mean)
  = 1 055.9 joules
1 calorie (mean) = 4.19 joules
1 horsepower = 745.7 watts
  = .75 kilowatts
caliber (diameter of a firearm's
  bore in hundredths of an inch)
  = .254 millimeters (mm)
1 atmosphere pressure = 101 325*
  pascals (newtons per sq meter)
1 pound per square inch (psi) =
  6 895 pascals
1 pound per square foot =
  47.9 pascals
1 knot = 1.85 kilometers per hour
25 miles per hour = 40.2
  kilometers per hour
50 miles per hour = 80.5
  kilometers per hour
75 miles per hour = 120.7
  kilometers per hour